fly = hae

W
hat is
a "fly-ku?"
That is obvious:
haiku about "flies."
Why *flies?* Because
(<u>Do not skip the Foreword</u>!),
flies create *fly-swatters* and
that re/presents a dilemma:
To kill, or not to kill

This evokes zen
(and zaniness) turning
all the old-time haiku poets
into im/moral philosophers.
True, great poems about ***hae***
are few and far between, but
that only makes it easier
for me to translate,
as the pressure
is less!

Fly-ku
also has a nice ring
to it, right? Believe it or not,
the pun works better yet in Japanese
where "haiku" becomes "***hae****ku*,"
"*haijin,*" (haiku poets) "***hae****jin,*"
"*haikai,*" (haiku world)
"***hae****kai,*" etcetera. [1]

---

1. ***Haikai*** = 俳諧, the term for haiku, prior to Shiki, who made "haiku" 俳句 *the* word for it. The above *haikai,* 俳界, however, refers to the world 界 of haiku, i.e. the people and organizations comprising it; but it could also have been 俳会, where 会 means "society" or "club" (See why Japanese *needs* Chinese characters?) ! The author hopes that the separation of the *ku* = 句 from the *hai* = 俳 in "fly-ku" can help English speakers come to feel at ease with the use of *ku* by itself to signify individual haiku poems, as it does in Japanese, where they are counted *ikku, niku, sanku hyakku senku,* or one-*ku*, two-*ku*, three-*ku*, a hundred-*ku* and a thousand-*ku*, and, outstanding *ku* are called *shûku* 秀句, good ones *kaku* 佳句, foolish ones *guku* 愚句 and poor ones, such as mine, *daku* 駄句. Someone who does haiku is a *haijin,* lit.: "haiku person," but *haikuman* or *haikuwoman* are awkward, so "haiku poet" is the usual translation.

all
translations,
unless otherwise indicated,
are by the
author

F*l*y-ku*!*

a theme from

In Praise of Olde Haiku

with many more poems and fine elaboration

by

robin d. gill

道可道
非常道
paraverse press

蠅　　　蠅

This is the fourth book published by paraverse press,
home of truly creative nonfiction, which is to say,
nonfiction that is neither journalism, nor history,
nor how-I-overcame-this-or-that, nor narrative.
Our books will not help you get rich, healthy
or up-to-date. Whatever their subject,
they offer one thing always the same
yet different; and that is ideas,
"food for thought,
all you can eat!"

but, please do not let that trouble you
for you may quote whatever you want, so long as
you cite this book and take care to check the ***Errata*** at
our web site:
http://www.paraverse.org/

We hope the Library of Congress will help us catalog
someday, for as you can see below, we need help! Meanwhile
our Publisher's Cataloging-in-Publication:

Fly-ku!
a theme from
IN PRAISE OF OLDE HAIKU
with many more poems and fine elaboration
(compiled, translated, introduced and essayed) by robin d. gill
with the original japanese for all poems
and an essay in japanese.

p. cm = IPOOH

ISBN# 0-9742618-4-X (pbk)

1. Haiku – Translation from Japanese to English
2. Japanese Poetry – 17th - 21st c. – haiku and senryu
3. Natural History – flies (housefly: *musca maledicta*)
4. Literary Criticism – translation and interpretation
5. Anthropomorphism in poetry
6. Kobayashi Issa (1763-1827)

1st edition (9/04), corrected & revised
slightly (1/05), printed by Lightning Source
in the United States and United Kingdom. Distributed
by Ingram, at least. Amazon, Barnes & Noble and other
mail-order stores should have it listed. If not, give 'em hell!
To learn more, please visit our website, or send a stamped envelope to:
Paraverse Press / pmb #399 / 260 Crandon blvd, suite 32 / Key Biscayne, FL 33149-1540

h o u s e   f l y

家 蝿

蝿の子の止まりっぷりも物馴れて 高澤良一

fairy familiars

– "house or window flies" of john clare[1] –

These little indoor dwellers, in cottages and halls, were always entertaining to me; after dancing in the window all day from sunrise to sunset they would sip of the tea, drink of the beer, and eat of the sugar, and be welcome all summer long. They look like things of the mind or fairies, and seem pleased or dull as the weather permits. In many clean cottages and genteel houses, they are allowed every liberty to creep, fly, or do as they like; and seldom or ever do wrong. In fact they are the small or dwarfish portion of our own family, and so many fairy familiars that we know and treat as one of ourselves.

..

1. John Clare (1793-1864) Today, this English poet, who was driven insane by poverty, hopeless love and regret for nature lost to development is no longer as well known as the top Japanese haiku poets. While many of his nature poems have an overly precious "I love this, I love that" style, they are deeply ecological at heart and many are seasonally oriented. *Little Trotty Wagtail* may be the best bird poem for children, ever, and one long poem, the name of which I can not recall, is a remarkable indictment of land "development" and a lament *from* the perspective of a once wild place. In a letter, old Clare wrote "If life had a second edition, how I would correct the proofs." *Amen.*

Table of dis/Contents

preface WHAT HAIKU IS (try 7-beat!) & IS NOT = **7** ACKNOWLEDGMENTS = **8**

foreword THE PARADOX OF FLY-SWATTING IN JAPAN ("to kill or not to kill" a bug) = **9**

ch.1 ____ISSA'S FAMOUS *FLY-KU* ENGLISHED (why language, not the translator, betrays us) = **13**

ch.2 ____THE WARRIOR-PRIEST BEHIND THE FLY (a senryû about benkei, also called musashi) = **21**

ch.3 ____THE FRIGHTENED YOUNG BRACKEN (anthropomorphic haiku, or, "hands in nature") = **29**

ch.4 ____A SUPPLICATION OF FLIES (what rubbing hands means in japanese and olde haiku) = **39**

ch.5 ____SWAT THEM AND PRAY (*namuamidabutsu*, or, what does a buddhist who takes life do?) = **45**

ch.6 ____THE CRIME & THE PUNISHMENT (morality and how it is expressed in fly-ku) = **55**

ch.7 ____THE ZEN OF SWATTING (perhaps there is nothing to it) = **65**

ch.8 ____THE FLY THAT WAS NOT THERE (missing them is half the fun) = **77**

ch.9 ____SHOO FLY (have you ever tried to get rid of one without killing it?) = **85**

ch.10____DON'T BOTHER ME! (why are flies synonymous with annoyance in Japan?) = **91**

ch.11____A TRANSPORT OF FLIES– (how they hitch-hike, get under your hat and ride piggyback) = **109**

ch.12____LIVING WITH FLIES (or, *musca benedicta,* mostly by issa,) = **115**

ch.13____WEAK & DYING FLIES (pity grows in the fall but winter flies are unpopular seniors?) = **127**

ch.14____SUNDRY FLIES (including some original english language fly-ku. Check: maybe yours was caught!) = **137**

ch.15____100 MODERN FLIES (there are 500 or so old haiku in the book; here is some balance) = **173**

afterword FLIES & I, A CONFESSION = **209** REVIEWS = **228** OTHER BOOKS = **229**

日本語初公開！ 一茶名句＜やれ打つな＞の背後に＜やれたつな＞の川柳あり = **213**

Calling All Fly Experts!

Glosses from entomologists are wanted for facts about flies in or not in this book. Longer essays are also welcome, if, after reading this book, you feel they will contribute something. They will be added to the second edition.

Haiku and Haibun on flies in English are also welcome.

I see no reason not to add the best 100 haiku on flies *in English* and encourage people to send me their own haiku or haiku by others. Short interesting prose such as Aubrey's, Beirce's and Clare's are also welcome.

前置

What HAIKU is & is not

A caveat to start with: haiku is not quite what most who know *something* about it think it is.

All readers, I would guess, know that Japanese haiku generally include a seasonal reference (thus, fly-ku belong to the summer, unless otherwise indicated), but how many know they can be crude and personal, as well as fine and untainted by subjectivity? I often see *bona fide* haiku mislabeled, or worse, *put down* as senryû by non-Japanese editors who know the boundaries of neither field very well. So saying, I cannot get upset at these editors, for their views reflect those of Japanese who make the very same judgment. I can also appreciate the desire of the professional poet to identify "haiku" with *the best of haiku* and to breed a thoroughbred line of poetry; but, in my opinion, such a monocultural approach risks losing more than it gains (For a greater grasp of the breadth of the haikai and, haiku culture in Japan, see my huge book of holothurian haiku, *Rise, Ye Sea Slugs!* and for a better understanding of senryu, a forthcoming book of salacious marine metaphor *The Mullet in the Maid*).

Style requires less qualification. Titles (not usual in Japanese) help keep the poems short and ensure the original wit is not lost in translation. So does multiple translation, though in some cases it reflects my inability to choose. Lengthwise, I do not apologize: it is just plain *wrong* to insist upon 5-7-5 in English, because our syllables tend to be far longer than Japanese *syllabets* (my word for the uniformly short, elemental parts or letters of the Japanese syllabary). Blyth, not long before his death, finally got it right when he settled on 2-3-2 [accented] beats. If you go for that, you cannot go wrong. But don't get me wrong: it is fine to be wrong sometimes, too.

In Praise of Olde Haiku & new

While there is much in modern haiku to praise, it was old haiku that first captured my heart. Perhaps this is because haiku was young when it was old and, as such, not a few poems are disarmingly blunt and easy for the foreigner to appreciate. Later, I discovered that, in seeming contradiction to this, olde haiku often boasted enough layers of meaning to qualify as codices (if codex in this usage can be so pluralized), the 17 syllabets holding enough condensed information to fill a page of prose (although, haibun prose, for its part could be denser than Joyce). A 1,400 year-old monolingual history of written poetry – that started off with long poems and ended up with tiny ones – can do that to you.

Ideally, a haiku both strikes you naturally *and* contains an allusive bonus that makes a second reading even better than the first. While this is more likely with old haiku than with new (20th and 21st c.) haiku, I have belatedly come to appreciate other good points in modern haiku. This was entirely due to my attempt to find *all* sea cucumber (*namako*) haiku for *Rise, Ye Sea Slugs* (I selected about 900 and will add 100 more for the 2nd edition) because it forced me to spend time with modern haiku. The one point I find most attractive is the variety and subtlety of the *associations* (as opposed to the *allusions* of old haiku). Some are humdrum or even petty, but a surprising number are surreal, mysterious, subtle or seemingly accidental. With Dhugal J. Lindsay, a native speaker of English who writes good haiku in Japanese, I marvel at the ability of the Japanese poets to come up with incredible yet, in retrospect, perfectly natural associations or, in some cases, disassociations. At the same time, I must confess that I am often frustrated at not being able to make the connection. With the allusions of old haiku, research (for which the *Kokugodaijiten* is most valuable) could often solve the problem, but with associations, the only certain way to know is to ask the poet, and this is not always possible. Yes, I know it is not necessarily best to know when reading the poem in its original language. But translation between tongues lacking parallel grammar and vocabulary requires all the help it can get.

Acknowledgments, up front

The on-line haiku pub Ukimidô = 浮御堂 was, again, invaluable. The host, Saibara Tenki = 天気, communicated my desire to find good modern fly-ku, set up a fly-ku collection bottle, a Q & A place for me to question others, assembled a tentative best 80 modern Fly-ku and answered many Q's himself. I am grateful for the help of Akyû = ∀Q = 痾窮 (top *ku*-finder), Furiko = 振り子, Hagizuki = 萩月, Tetsurô = なむ♪, Tôjin = 東人, Kikko = きっこ, Tokki = とっき, Miyoko = 美代子 Zankuro = ざんくろー, Shigeno = 紫野, Suiseijin = 水星人, Ako = 亜子, who also participated in an Ukimidô *hae*kukai, or Fly-ku Fest, & Mihoko = 美保子。

Professor Kikuchi Shinichi of Konan Women's University, (to whom I owe much for help with the collection and interpretation of sea cucumber haiku for *Rise, Ye Sea Slugs!*) was a tremendous help with my essay in Japanese (appended in full) on the relationship of a certain senryû and Issa's famous haiku, although he continues to hold strong doubt about whether I *proved* there was a relationship. (I hope to publish it in Japan and have more opinions for the second edition). The first three chapters benefit from this. Hoshino Takashi = CZ helped too.

The editor and everyone connected with *Simply Haiku* magazine were so enthusiastic about my *Zen of Fly-swatting* article, that I decided not to wait for next summer to finish this book, but squeeze it in before getting on with finishing my next large work, the first half of the New Year section of the IPOOH *saijiki* (haiku almanac).

foreword
序文

the paradox of fly-swatting in japan

Do not kill the fly!
See how it wrings its hands,[1]
Its feet!

Kobayashi Issa (trans: Blyth 1952)

***To swat or not to swat*:** that is the question posed by many if not most of the thousands of haiku written about flies over the past four or five hundred years. The answer, if there is an answer, is not simple. Most Japanese poets did not share John Muir's sense of kinship for "our horizontal brothers," who "make all dead flesh fly," much less John Clare's gushy affection for "our fairy familiars." Even the haiku of the most merciful poet of all, Kobayashi Issa (d.1827), whose feeling for flies comes closest to that of the American naturalist and English nature poet, did not really condemn swatting as most of his Western and, for that matter, Japanese readers, usually imagine.

Not only were the pre-modern Japanese (including Issa) less *precious* than we would have it today, but they reveled in poems about killing the little beasties. *Hae-uchi* – "fly-swatting" or "fly-swatter" – has long been a *bona fide* seasonal term in haiku. While house-flies lack the aesthetic appeal of fire-flies (the latter boasting over 6x more old haiku), are less powerful than the strident cicada (over 4x more), and less troublesome than mosquitoes (2x), they enjoy a respectable presence (150 haiku in Shiki's *Categorical,* [2] the source of the above figures). I believe the heart of that respectable presence is this: *flies present poets with a personal dilemma.* On the one hand, the Japanese poets feel a strong compulsion to swat; on the other hand, they believe, or once professed to believe, that the wanton taking of animal life is sinful and would endanger their own soul's future.

..

I exaggerate, for the samurai class from which most haiku poets came was not deeply religious but what Captain Golownin (a

Russian imprisoned in Japan from 1812-14) described as "free-thinkers." But, even then, as poets of a tradition centered on seasonal phenomena, their questionable Buddhism [3] was shored up by their special connection with and affection for nature. So it is doubtful that any Japanese poet felt *entirely* good about taking *any* life. If I may be pardoned a somewhat tasteless analogy, *hae-uchi,* or fly-swatting, did and still does for haiku what *cheating songs* – by pitching emotion against morals – does for country music and *enka* (the Japanese equivalent to country): it provides stimulating tension.

That does not entirely explain the undying popularity of Issa's poem, which is by far the most famous *fly-ku*; and ranks within the most well-known dozen or so haiku of all time. But, I think it is a start.

Musca maledicta is not a universal concept. There are many cultures where flies are not maligned. We see photographs of people, alive and healthy, yet utterly unconcerned with the flies upon them. They stand there smiling. The flies make as much of an impression on them as the movement of the corpuscles through our blood vessels makes on us. *Why in the world do so many Westerners and Japanese dislike them so much?* In the West, it goes without saying that living things not servant to man, and therefore indirectly under God's rule, were all too often relegated to the side of the Devil. Not surprisingly, we swatted flies – known to serve witches as imps – long before hygiene based on germ theory gave us a scientific excuse to do so. In the East, where wild creatures were not demonized by religion, the justification for fly-swatting is not so simple, but this we know: *if anything, the Japanese revulsion for flies may be more deeply seated than ours.* Japanese not only killed flies, but, as Luis Frois, a Jesuit with a reputation for accurate detail noted in 1585, "princes and lords" pulled off their wings! [4]

How could *this* come to pass in a Buddhist country?

..

According to a line of reasoning the Japanese call *fudoron* (climatic cultural determinism), it is because the muggy summers (unlike the dry heat of the European summer) made Japanese hate stickiness and remove it with daily baths. This is echoed on the metaphysical level, *ablution* being the prototypical Shinto ritual, and reified by the clean, sharp-edged design sense known to the world as Japanese aesthetics. One might even argue this *anti-stickiness mindset* is reflected in the Japanese word-sense, for what we English speakers feel to be "softening" a sound ("k" → "g," "t" → "d," etc.), Japanese call "dirtying" it! [5] Consciously or unconsciously, the fly, then, flies in the face of a deep-seated desire to escape from what we might call "yuckiness." This is something more basic than the Shinto taboo on blood as unclean. It brings to mind *sukkiri-shita,* or "[feeling] refreshed," a Japanese phrase including untranslatable connotations of the clean-cut and streamlined. Most Japanese want to feel *sukkiri-shita,* and *that* the flies will not allow. Buddhist monks were only supposed to *shoo* flies, not *swat* them. Religious men and women may have tried to do likewise, but it might be argued that, given the perversity of our species, the presence of this *peccadillo,* far from protecting the fly, only served to increase the desirability of swatting the damn thing.

To be sure, Japanese might not joke about killing flies if their Buddhism were closer to, say, the Tibetan variety.

In Tibet, *a soul was a soul was a soul.* All souls were equal, even if incarnated differently. All sects of Japanese Buddhism hold the same tenet. But, a look at respective eating habits of the two people shows a subtle difference. The Tibetans ate *oxen*, for one beast= soul would support a village for a week. They offered up candles and prayed for its soul, then offset the loss by freeing a small animal. I might add that this is even true for the high priests of Tibetan Buddhism. They are presented with platters of roasted ox. In Japan, on the other hand, it would appear that there are *souls* and there are *souls*. Japanese, who would not dream of eating a large farm animal, ate multitudes of tiny fish, in the case of the smaller-than-minnow *shirasu*, dozens of souls are consumed with every mouthful, hundreds or even thousands with a meal. A Tibetan Buddhist would turn pale at such spiritual carnage. Japanese think nothing of it. If they were forced to justify themselves, they might say the fish is further down the chain of reincarnation and liable to be reborn into a better position. Be that as it may, my point is that, Zen catechism aside, the Japanese did not show much concern for the souls of most animals. If myriad minnows could be eaten without qualm, the lives of flies were, likewise, no big thing.[6]

I wanted to use a Zig-Zag "wave" suitable for flies but this so-called "border" failed to PDF. Unfortunately, WYSInotWYG! Damn.

1. *Flies wringing their hands.* We shall soon enough see why this *apparent* anthropomorphism is *not found in the original*, but derives from insurmountable problems in translation between mutually exotic tongues. In other words, laugh if you will, but please, forbear judgment about both the translations and the original poem!

2. *Shiki's Categorical.* The 12-volume haiku almanac (saijiki) properly called *bunrui-betsu haiku-zenshû*, or the complete categorical anthology of haiku. See the annotated bibliography.

3. *Questionable Buddhism.* There are exceptions. Issa, who was the son of a fairly well-off farmer (no samurai) in a poor country town was a serious Buddhist. (See David G. Lanoue's *Pure Land Haiku: The Art of Priest Issa.*)

4. *Pulling wings off flies.* Frois was less concerned with cruelty – elsewhere, he shows Japanese are less quick to kill non-human animals than Europeans – than with the *dirtiness* of the act. The entire distich:

> *Among us, killing a fly by hand is [considered to be] a filthy thing; in Japan, princes and nobles do it, and rip off the wings, toss them out.* (item 14-23 in my *TOPSY-TURVY 1585*)

I guess the bodies can be thrown further without the wings to slow them down! Be that as it may, Frois inadvertently teaches us that flies were thought filthy by the Luso-Iberians, at least, long before germ theory proved them so. As for the behavior of these Japanese, is it callousness born of the situation in 1585, when centuries of warring ended and these men (biting the bullet under the newly consolidated state) were extra-ordinarily full of pent-up aggression? Or, were they simply, as TK guesses, "spoiled lords?" Or, were they religiously *putting the flies out of commission* rather than *taking life?* Or, was it a habit started to feed pet sparrows?

5. *Dirty Sounds* The eighteenth century nationalist Moto-ori Norinaga even conflated so-called "dirty" sounds and mimetic expressions, claiming both were foreign (Chinese) and beastly aberrations unworthy of the divine purity of Japanese. More rational contemporaries, such as Ueda Akinari, putdown such ideas as ethnocentric error, but there is *some* psychological validity in Norinaga's claim.

6. *Tibetan souls.* For more on Tibetan culture, see Rin Chem (Rinchem) Lha-Mo's utterly charming classic *We Tibetans* , in whatever edition you can find.

I

Issa's famous *fly-ku* englished

what there is to be learned from even the worst translation

Shall I break God's commandment?
Little fly
Rubbing its back legs

– Jack Kerouac[1] –

The reader will be delighted or disappointed to learn that I am *not* going to print a 100 different versions of Issa's *fly-ku,* as Hiroaki Sato has done with the most famous haiku of all time, Bashô's pond-plopping frog/s.[2] I forbear not only because of the slimmer pickings – unless we are to include possible paraverses [3] such as Kerouac's, above – but because the *fly-ku* presents insurmountable problems of translation which leave less room for creativity. This is a blessing in disguise for it provides us with more insight into the problems of translating an exotic tongue than would otherwise be the case.

..

やれ打な蝿が手をする足をする 一茶
Yare utsu na hae ga te wo suru ashi wo suru
(hey hit not[!] fly-the [its] hands rub, feet rub)

Do not kill the fly!
See how it wrings its hands,
its feet!

– trans. Blyth: [4] 1952

I used this translation at the head of the *Foreword*, not because it was my favorite, but because it best conveyed the meaning without supplementary explanation outside the poem. With "wring" substituted for the original "rub," English readers can notice the fly's distress without having to learn that hand-rubbing in the Sinosphere is a form of supplication or prayer. The downside is that the wringing cannot help but introduce something Issa avoids: *pathetic fallacy.* In the original, the fly is practicing the perfectly natural behavior of rubbing its hands/feet. At the same time, rubbing has a connotation in Japanese that suggests we may interpret the fly's behavior as prayer *if we so wish.* The extra "See how" in Blyth's translation not only gives a bit of the colloquial exuberance of the *yare*, or "hey!" – which might have been too much to fit into the five-syllable first line – but, lessens the artificiality of "wrings" by moving the fly into our mind's eye. Wringing hands were not invented by Blyth. An earlier translation published in the *Osaka Asahi* in 1929:

Wait! don't strike that fly!
he's wringing his hands there
and wringing his feet.

– trans. Glenn Shaw

This translation comes from an article by Earle Joshua Stone called "That Lovable Old Issa" (google it!). Stone comments that "this humorous action of the fly rubbing its forefeet together, and then the hind feet, . . . indeed appears to be a wringing of the hands in expectation of a blow." In his classic *Haiku Poems Ancient and Modern* (1932/1940), Miyamori Asataro prints the Shaw translation without the exclamation marks and with three commas added. The influence is seen in his own version.

Don't beat the fly!
He wrings his hands,
He wrings his feet

– trans. Miyamori Asataro

All of Miyamori's translations extend in steps, something I find very logical, for it shows indirectly the fact that Japanese haiku are usually printed in a single line. Needless to say, Miyamori could have used a strong-minded English editor to beat the "beat" out of his head (It only works if we assume the fly stands for a person, but since people do not use their feet to pray for mercy . . .).

Ah, do not kill the fly!
It rubs its feet,
It rubs its hands!

– trans. Blyth (1960)

Anyone with one good eye cannot help but immediately notice a fly rubbing its hands (fore-feet) together, but noticing the feet *behind* that fly calls for the sharp perception which comes from interest. Blyth apparently failed to register this difference and, hence, the importance of saving the feet for last, as a sort of *ochi* or "punch-word" (The English "punch-*line*" does not work when the entire work is a line long.), and used his poetic license to move the fly and its feet closer together for the sake of alliteration. Blyth's concern was more with the broader interpretation of the poem. The explanation following his 1952 translation is classic Blyth:

..

> "Issa was of course perfectly aware that the fly was not rubbing its hands together in supplication for its life. But this is not fancy, . . . It is humorous pretence. Issa hides and thus reveals his insight into the living nature of the fly. Blake's "Am not I / A fly like thee?/ Or art not thou/ A man like me?" [my space-saving] comes near it, but lacks the poetry of Issa's humor." The fly is alive. And, whether conscious of the fact or not, wants to be.

yare utsu na	oh, don't swat!
hae ga te o suru	the fly rubs hands
ashi o suru	rubs feet

– trans. William Higginson + Sakurai Emiko (*The Haiku Handbook*)

As English, this sounds strange, for we demand our feet and hands to be articled, pronouned, or otherwise modified. Lacking "his," "hers," or "its," we cannot help feeling something comically *primitive* or *oriental,* which, of course, is not felt in reading the natural Japanese of the original. The rub with directly translating "rubs" is that a reader unfamiliar with the body-language of the Sinosphere doesn't get it. Higginson immediately follows his translation with a fine one-line explanation: *"The fly prays twice as much as most humans."* (my italics) But, can readers guess from this alone that hand-rubbing connotes supplication? To his credit, Higginson is the only translator I know to notice the obvious – and, as I will later explain, *crucial* implications of rubbing the hands *and* feet *twice as much.* If his minimalist translation seems a bit too much, or should we say, too *little,* it has an incontestably valid *raison d'etre.* His comments on the opposite style of translation of Issa *in general* are well-taken:

> " . . . his [Issa's] relative calm in accepting his difficult life is often obscured by excessively melodramatic and wordy translations of the poems. [deletion] We have . . . translated them [Issa's poems] in ways that parallel the originals' lean, un-self-pitying language as nearly as possible." (Ibid)

It is a fact that Issa's *fly-ku* has not a few cloying translations. I would only qualify Higginson's criticism by adding that *all* translations – even the worst – have *something* positive to offer. Let us next dissect a couple of *real doozies.*

Don't kill that poor fly!
He cowers, wringing
his hands for mercy

– anon. trans. (www.geocities.com/Tokyo/Island/5022/issa.html)

This *cowering* fly is a good example of the "excessively melodramatic" style of translation Higginson decries. *"Poor," "cowers," "wringing," "for mercy"* – talk about overkill! Granted that "poor" is a ploy to gain sympathy for the subject, and that as ridiculous as a "cowering" bug might seem, there is a point to describing it that way because Japanese traditionally begged for money or for their lives (or whatever), bent over close to the ground, or even flat upon it.

But Issa's fly is hardly *that* abject and, lacking the feet – none of Issa's versions lacked the "feet" (*ashi*) – might as well be a human in this translation. I can't help thinking of a new line to follow "Don't kill that poor fly!" . . . *Kill the poor translator!*

..

OH DO NOT SWAT THEM . . .
UNHAPPY FLIES
FOREVER
WRINGING THEIR THIN HANDS

– Issa (anon. trans. JAPANESE HAIKU 1955 The Peter Pauper Press)

If the last translation was melodramatic, this is *hideously* sentimental. I wish I knew who to *blame* for it, but Peter Pauper doesn't say. You might think that many American presses are trapped by a Cyclops, for they habitually attribute translations to *no man* in particular. Here, *no man* is exceptionally creative, for he adds two adjectives and an adverb, while removing the *fly-ku's* single real innovation, the praying feet! "Unhappy" would have been "poor" had the translator not been desperate to achieve the allegedly proper syllable count, mindless of the excessive length (at least 10 beats, where 7 or 8 would do!) of his poem. The "thin" is useless, for who thinks a fly ham-handed? Moreover, it makes the "unhappy" redundant, for, until strange 20th century American ideas changed the concept of beauty, thin was, by definition, *sad.* As we shall see, Issa once wrote a "crazy-verse" (*kyôka*) about rubbing one's hands together in supplication and running about to make ends meet with the result that his limbs turned to pestles. The chance that so poor a translator read this little-known complaint is close to nil, but the "thin" in his translation does jive with it. While Issa's poem doesn't say so, it may well be true that a fly at rest *is always* moving its hands/feet and we can excuse the "forever" as rhetoric (hyperbole) and even turn the poem into a just-so story: an explanation for why it is cruel to swat flies: *those poor skinny limbs!* That would save Peter Pauper from hideous sentimentality, but I am afraid it would not make the translation *Issa.*

Oh, don't mistreat
the fly! He wrings his hands!
He wrings his feet!

– Henderson

In the Tokugawa era even the peasantry produced a great haiku poet, Issa (1763-1827). He wrote of insects birds and animals [sic], manifesting a strong compassion for all living things. For instance, seeing a fly about to be swatted, Issa felt that it was praying for mercy and cried out:

Oh, don't swat
the fly! He wrings his hands!
He wrings his feet!

– Hane

Mikiso Hane included the Issa *fly-ku* (as the last of five haiku) in his *JAPAN – a historical survey* (1972), with a footnote to the effect that "the author has substituted "swat" for "mistreat" in Henderson's translation." Henderson's "mistreat" is a wonderful/horrid example of the smarmy that rhyme can bring to an otherwise fine translation. Hane's view of Issa's mindset expressed in the above passage is probably the most common Japanese view of the birth of Issa's poem. Such a reading is, I believe, far too naïve, for Issa was well-versed in poetic tradition and there was, as we shall soon see, ample precedent for flies praying for mercy.

> Look, don't kill that fly! It is making a prayer to you by rubbing its hands and feet.
>
> – Yoshi Mikami: *Issa's Haiku Home Page*

Japanese haiku may typically be written in one line, but that line is vertical, and therefore resembles an object (in the French sense of an *object de arte*), whereas ours is but a horizon or, worse yet, a straight road. Be that as it may, Mikami demonstrates a Japanese literary practice we might call "explanatory translation" that is often used to translate Chinese poems and ancient Japanese poems into modern Japanese. Rather than using a gloss to *explain* that "rubbing" means supplication, Mikami explains *within* the poem: "It is making a prayer to you." I am the first to admit that when an exotic tongue is translated, understanding demands explanation. The question is *where to put it*. I prefer it *outside* of and *immediately after the poem*, for putting it inside of the poem, like Mikami does, kills the poetry, and hiding it at the end of the book as if it were a mere technicality, a footnote for the sake of bibliography or further reference, is inconsiderate, for readers cannot appreciate the poems without that information.

> "Do Not Ever Strike!"
>
> Do not ever strike!
> The fly moves as if to pray
> With his hands and feet
>
> Yoshinobu Hautani and Robert L Tener trans.

Here, the haiku has not only been explained (in a vague and creative manner, to be sure) but, with the *ever,* has been turned into an injunctive maxim! All of that, mind you, concocted as part of a note to Richard Wright's "a fly crawls slowly / over a sticky paper, – / How chilly the dawn!" (*Haiku*: This Other World 1998)

> Hey! Don't swat:
> the fly wrings his hands
> on bended knees
>
> Faubium Bowers (1996)

One must give Faubium Bowers a red star for courage for those bended knees – a new way to get the legs in and translate the apparent desire of the fly to beg/pray for its life – but it is a fact that fly "knees" bend up rather than down and, for that matter, are always bent when it alights. While the "his" is far from unique – of 14 translations, 7 he/his/him's the fly, 5 it/its' it, 1 them/theirs' it and 1 avoids all pronouns – but, *together with those knees*, in this translation it turns the hint of anthropomorphism in the original into a cartoon. Indeed, it made me think, what if it were *"her hands and knees?"* To his credit (and Dover's), Bowers' *"The Classical Tradition of HAIKU An Anthology"* offers fine footnotes for almost all the haiku (kudos to him and to Dover for that!); but the fact this poem had none suggests he, like others before, did not realize the seriousness of the pathetic translation problem.

KOAN

What if a housefly on the swatter stands
In perfect faith, and wipes its feet and hands?
– Zen paradox

KANNON'S ANSWER

Oh, do not kill that fly! It would entreat!
See how it wrings its little hands and feet.
– Issa

(trans. Harold Stewart)

Kannon is the Buddhist God/dess of mercy. The ever-considerate Stewart not only added a title to his couplet, as he always does, but found or made up a *koan*-like haiku to contextualize Issa's *fly-ku.* I cannot find proof such a *koan* exists, but *ben trovado!* If it does not, it well *might.* I like the "little" before the hands, because – unlike Peter Pauper's "thin" – it is a subtle term of endearment that indirectly increases our affection for the fly, rather than directly appealing to our pity.

A word on Stewart's couplets. On the whole, they read better than the generally boring English syllable-based translation published before him. His 10-beat is also a bit long (compared to Japanese) but the rhyme helps save the original wit often lost in translation and he is the pioneer of the witty use of titles in haiku. Stewart teaches us that there is more than one way to flesh a haiku.

Don't hit me!
the fly wrings its hands
and wrings its feet

(trans. Stephen Addiss with Fumiko and Akira Yamamoto)

Note the "me!" Hitherto we have seen "the fly," "that fly," and the more generalized "them" serving as the direct object of the potential violence. Higginson+Sakurai's simple "Don't swat!" is like the Japanese, for it does not specify whether the "don't" is directed from the fly to the poet, the poet to all men, to his readers, or, say another person in the vicinity of the poet. I think the original's exclamation, *yare,* best fits a somewhat sarcastic third-person, but this does not rule out the implicit first-person (i.e., *as if to say* "Don't hit me!"). Addiss and Yamamoto's "me," like all other choices, betrays the original's ambiguity while improving its readability in English. In combination with the wringing, it increases the anthropomorphism to a ludicrously high level, yet is simple enough to still be touching. The repeated "wrings," like Stewart's "little," endear. This may partly be because repetition is a mark of baby-talk, but it is also because "wring" has an emotional connotation. The double "rub" found in Blyth's later translation (1960) and Higginson+Sakurai does not do this, for "rub," in English, means only *rub*.

tabulating the verbs

I have saved an explanation of the first verb in the *fly-ku* for last. Of the fourteen translations, we find 5 *kills,* 4 *swats,* 2 *strikes,* 1 *hit,* 1 *beat* and 1 *mistreat.* The original *utsu* has an exceptionally broad range of connotations. *Batting* (a ball), *typing* (a typewriter), *shooting* (a gun), *stamping* (a stamp), *beating* (a drum) and, like in contemporary English, *hitting* (the road). It is always used for *swatting.* Strangely enough, it is not used by itself – as opposed to being part of a compound verb – to mean *kill.* Nevertheless, I feel "kill" is not only acceptable but a good translation, for it is not a whack on the behind, but obliteration facing the fly.

my translation

My first inclination was to refrain from translating this poem that cannot be Englished so as to retain both the naturalness and significance of the fly's behavior. But since I critique the attempts of others, it behooves me to at least try. If we know that flies rub their hands/feet together and that this implies praying for mercy, is it not possible to go completely with the connotation (praying) and forget the denotation (rubbing) altogether?

lord, don't swat!
the fly prays with his hands
and with his feet!

Yes, "lord" is not Japanese rhetoric. I use it for two reasons. First, to show my dissatisfaction with the Englishing of the emphatic *yare*. Of the fourteen translations, we find 5 *Oh*s, 1 each *wait!, ah, look* and *hey!*, and 5 nothing-whatsoevers. I like the *hey!* most, but it seems a bit rude. Hence my culturally misplaced "lord." Second, the "lord" reflects what I believe to be the origins of Issa's fly-ku, which will be discussed next.

Notes? Unlike my other books which have more notes than text, F*ly*-ku*!* will, after this chapter, be noteless.

1. ***Kerouac's Haiku***. Kerouac is almost certainly making an indirect comment on Issa's fly-ku as he knew it, in translation, by creating this paraverse (see 3. below). It reads naturally and, unlike the other translations does not make the fly seem suspiciously human. Yet he keeps us thinking about the moral relationship of deity, humanity and flies, by switching the nature and the location of the *killing* problem: the 6th Commandment is generally thought to apply only to us.

2. ***Hiroaki Sato.*** Japanese names in this book generally follow the Japanese order: family first, but Hiroaki Sato writes in English in the United States and choses to have his name given in the Occidental (excluding Hungary) order.

3. ***Paraverse.*** A word found in science fiction in opposition to "universe." I use it to mean an alternative poem that may range from a loose reading, i.e., *version* to a creative reading, i.e., *take-off* of another. Paraverse may also be used as a verb. More information on paraversing may be found at my website Paraverse. org.

4. ***Reginald H. Blyth.*** Readers who are new to haiku should note that Blyth was not only the foremost translator of haiku out of Japanese in the 20th century but a very witty writer with extensive knowledge of English literature and the history of Zen Buddhism.

<u>IF THE PROBLEM OF TRANSLATION BETWEEN (MUTUALLY) EXOTIC TONGUES ITSELF INTERESTS YOU, PLEASE READ *ORIENTALISM & OCCIDENTALISM: IS THE MISTRANSLATION OF CULTURE INEVITABLE?*</u> (Please see the summary at the end of this book.). BECAUSE THE SYNTAX OF ENGLISH AND JAPANESE ARE CONTRARY TO ONE ANOTHER, EQUIVALENCE IN FLOW OF THOUGHT DEMANDS THE WORD ORDER BE REVERSED, BUT THE ORDER IN WHICH ELEMENTS OF A POEM ARE REVEALED IS OFTEN IMPORTANT AND DEMANDS THE WORD ORDER BE MAINTAINED. BECAUSE OF THIS, IN MOST CASES, PRECISE WORD-FOR-WORD TRANSLATION IS IMPOSSIBLE AND A CONSCIENTIOUS TRANSLATOR MUST USE HIS OR HER IMAGINATION TO COMPROMISE AND RE-CREATE THE POEM. THERE IS GREAT AGONY AND ECSTASY IN THIS ENDEAVOR.

蝿蝿蝿蝿蝿蝿蝿蝿蝿蝿蝿蝿蝿蝿蝿蝿蝿蝿蝿蝿蝿蝿蝿蝿蝿蝿蝿蝿蝿蝿蝿蝿蝿蝿蝿蝿

Yare! Yayo! Sore! Suri, Suru

Readers who don't know Japanese might best skip this box. Serious students should note that Issa's famous *fly-ku* appeared in many slightly different versions of which each has aspects closer to and farther from the original.

1. *yare utsuna hae ga te o suri ashi o suru*
   – baijin-hachiban (bunsei printing & two more)
2. *yayo utsuna* " " "
   – hachiban-nikki (his basic notebook)
3. *yare utsuna hae wa* " "
   – sekiseisui?-shohen (1st book & 2nd)
4. *sore utsuna hae wa te mo suru ashi mo suru*
   – kacho-bunko

The first of these is now the standard version. The second apparently is the first Issa wrote down. The *yo* is less pushy, or should I say more pleasant than *yare* with its *re*. It is almost like "Hi, there!" Issa may have hoped to get away from the harder, biting *re*. Semantically milder or not, the second syllabet in *yayo,* unlike *yare*, is strongly enough accented to beat. This slows the transition to the *utsuna,* or, "hit-not," and hurts the rhythm of the total haiku. Issa had the best sound-sense of all the major haiku poets. So, I doubt that he would have written *yayo utsuna* in the first place if the senryû was not in the back of his mind – *I think he sought to increase the difference.* The *wa* after the fly in the third version is a particle English lacks which is sometimes translated as "as for." Here, it might call attention to flies in general, what they do – in senryû, *wa* is quite common for this reason – rather than a particular fly's behavior, which is more suitable to the concrete haiku style. Sound-wise, it is also is a bit much and comes close to adding an extra beat. The fourth version also has the *wa,* and exchanges the objective case post-position *o* to *mo,* meaning "too." That is to say, *it makes emphatic* the fact that *flies* rub *both* their hands *and* their feet. It brings out the idea in the haiku far better than the standard version. The *sore* is in between *yare* and *yayo* in that it is less caustic than the former and more pointed than the latter. There are three problems with this version. *Sore* lacks *yare*'s perfect vowel-rhyme with *hae;* the *wa* and two *mo* slow down the poem; the idea is made too explicit for Issa's taste.

I found Blyth's version (below) in the Kaizôsha Saijiki alone. It may be a typo, for hand-written "(w)o" を and "mo" も are similar enough to cause trouble.

yare utsu na hae ga te wo suru ashi wo suru.

蝿蝿蝿蝿蝿蝿蝿蝿蝿蝿蝿蝿蝿蝿蝿蝿蝿蝿蝿蝿蝿蝿蝿蝿蝿蝿蝿蝿蝿蝿蝿蝿蝿蝿蝿蝿

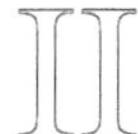

the *Warrior-priest* behind the fly

the neglected senryû behind the celebrated haiku

やれ打つな蝿が手をすり足をする　一茶（文政四）
やれたつな " " で武蔵数珠をすり Y 24-30 玉柳追善 (寛政 3)

yare utsuna hae ga te o suri[1] *ashi o suru* – Issa (1821)
yare tatsuna tatsuna de musashi juzu o suri – *Yanagidaru* (1791)

(hey, hit not! / fly/flies hands rub/s / feet rub)
(hey, stand/rise not! / " " " " –as, musashi / prayer-beads rub)

1. ***Suri* vs. *Suru*** The hyper-attentive reader may have noticed the *"suri"* here, rather than the *"suru"* found in the version used by Blyth (and Higginson) used in chapter I. Issa's versions are all given at the end of this chapter. I, like Blyth and Higginson *like* the *"suru,"* but 3 of 4 versions are *suri* and that brings the haiku closer to the senryû.

Haiku scholarship, whether it be Japanese or international, has a weak point. It is too highbrow. Just as we find few sonnet and blank-verse writers well-versed in limericks and country music, we find few haikuists well-read in *senryû,* the oft-maligned and misunderstood sibling of haiku.. That, I believe, has hindered the full appreciation of Issa's *fly-ku.*

The word *senryû* is no longer under probation. It is well enough known in English today that I feel I can justify dropping the italics. Its meaning, however, is a different matter entirely. I shall not attempt to define senryû outright, but will instead offer examples which will show how some senryû can be completely different from haiku, while others are only distinguishable by their sources. Here, again, there is a resemblance to the loose boundaries between country and pop in American music. Dolly Parton sang *"I Will Always Love You"* and it was country's top hit-song two years in a row. When Whitney Houston redid it with little change other than dropping Dolly's tear-jerking recitation two decades later, it was pop. Or, as a certain country star put it when questioned as to the nature of the song he was doing: "If I do it, it's country." Japanese *enka* singers have said the same about *their* songs.

It is well known that *senryû* parody famous haiku and haiku poets. Bashô's famous verse "Old pond: / a frog leaps in / water's sound" (William J. Higginson trans.) spawned dozens of senryû including "the old pond: / the sound of water scares / old master" (misplaced original), his death-verse: "Ill on a journey, my dreams roam o'er the winter moor" becomes "Grounded, my dreams roam o'er the pleasure quarters," (*zashiki-rô yume wa kuruwa o kakemeguri*), and so forth. Issa is little parodied, for he was not nearly as well known, but one very pleasant senryû might refer to our *fly-ku.*

蝿のいる國だからこそ一茶の句　　久夫

hae no iru kuni dakara koso issa no ku – hisao [Tanroku?]
(flies-are/exist-country: therefore especially issa's haiku/s)

It's because
This is a country of flies
That Issa could make haiku.

(trans. Blyth)

I found this senryû in Blyth's *Japanese Life and Character in Senryû* (1960). The name for the author in English, usually matches the Japanese, but here he gives Tanroku. Perhaps it is a typo. That does not matter, but the date does; for if the senryû is post-WW II, "country" would mean all-of-Japan as opposed to abroad (we will see the fly-country consciousness in the supplement to the next chapter = pg.27-8). If, however, the senryû is older, "country" might not mean Japan but Issa's Shinano, one of the most insulted places in Japan. There are dozens of senryû joking about the gluttony, naïvite and moronity of Shinano bumpkins, who flood into Edo in the agricultural off-season ostensibly for work but really for food. I cannot help but recall a riddle of my youth in Miami: Q – *Why do flies have wings?* A – *To beat the Cubans to the garbage cans!"* (Now, as we all know these "flies" run Miami, but that is another story). In other words, there may be more here.

issa's *fly-ku*	**issa's *fly-ku***
the masterpiece: only because shinano's a country of flies	he owes it to his country a country of flies

The identity of the country is not the only ambiguity in the original. It does not say let us know whether the reference is to 1) Issa's haiku in general (as Blyth translates), 2) the type of animal-loving haiku Issa became identified with, 3) his various fly (and, by extension, mosquito and flea) *ku* or 4) that most famous *fly-ku* alone. Blyth's translation of the senryû favors 1), while his explanation ↓ appears to favor 3).
..

> This is terribly and universally true. If there is no murder there is no Christianity, no *Hamlet,* no *Faust.* . . . What would even doctors, let alone poets, do without flies and mosquitoes and microbes. (Ibid)

It would seem that Blyth has come to the aid of the God insulted in Ogden Nash's famous couplet:

> God in his wisdom made the fly
> And then forgot to tell us why.

But I prefer to save this type of metaphysics for a book on haiku'ed *mosquitoes*, a subject dear to my heart and easy in Japanese but pursued to great disadvantage in English because of the tiny bug's absurdly long name – an expanded fly – owing to the Latin tendency to create the diminutive by adding syllables and the failure of English to word itself. Be that as it may, the senryû may be saying this:

peasant poets

because our land
can feed its flies, issas
can poeticise

Flies were identified with beggars and metaphorical parasites, such as poets. Issa himself felt terribly guilty about not being out in the field working, or at least professed to be time and time again. The senryû poet would probably not feel that guilt, but he might have thought his nation was comparatively soft on human as well as non-human flies. If so, the senryû means:

flies Яus

because our land
is full of flies, we love
issa's bugginess

flies Яus

because our land
is full of flies, don't hit!
it might be me!

But only a scholar of the national mindset of the time the senryû was written could say for sure whether Japanese thought of themselves in that way, as flies.

研究者諸君へ

＜蝿のいる國だからこそ一茶の句＞という久夫（？）の川柳の作句時点、出典などご存知なら、教えて頂けませんか。たぶん、國＝日本だが、古きものなら國＝信濃の可能性もある。「一茶の句」も、かの＜やれ打つな＞句のことか、一茶の百姓っぽい句か、などの細かい解説＝欄外注を求めております。

The reverse vector that runs from senryû to haiku is not so well known. My impression is that haiku scholars do not particularly like to admit that their high art has been influenced, or rather, sullied by a lower one. Because a large portion of senryû are as obscene as the worst in the *Epigrams* of Martial, one can understand their aversion. Most modern scholars also do not care much for parody and borrowing, though there is a fine word for it: *honka-tori,* "original-poem-taking." This last term covers a practice which I call *paraversing*. Long ancient poems, *waka,* are paraversed in 31 syllabet *tanka* 500 years after they were first written and then 500 years later are again reduced to 17 syllabets, i.e. haiku. Sometimes, the first 12 syllabets are copied exactly from the ancient verse, but the last 5 usually contain some surprise to justify the haiku as a creative work. (Western readers should not raise their eyebrows too high, for our top poets redid classic verse for centuries and were not even creative enough to shorten it.)

Issa, because of his tendency to write humorous poems – putting an old text into a new circumstance tends to make those who recognize it chuckle – was a notorious borrower, though he was so careful not to borrow from his employer/teacher/patron/colleague Seibi that he asked permission to use a term simply because it had been used to good effect in Seibi's poem first. Supposedly, the haiku world was quite strict about such things, but I find Issa borrowed *much* more than even the most borrow-conscious scholars have noticed. And this was true with respect to the haiku of earlier poets as well as classic poetry and senryû.

Today, the most well known – at least in Japan – of Issa's debts to senryû is the oft-translated *daikon[2ft-long-radish]-puller-points-the-way-with-a-daikon* (*daiko-hiki daikon de michi o oshiekeri*) haiku. Until the late 1980's, no one that I know of mentioned that debt in Japan. This was very strange considering the fact the poem they now say he copied can be found (Indeed, I found it myself before knowing others knew) in the very first chapter of the most famous senryû collection, the *Yanagidaru* (*hin nuita daikon de michi o oshierare*). But I doubt *that* senryu was what Issa read, because the senryû is *better* than his haiku and, no joking, *more Issa-like* – I refer to the mimetic feeling of the lead (*hin-nuita*), which brings the great root into the mind's eye of any Japanese reader – than Issa's plain poem. In every other instance where Issa borrows, I find he does good. As someone once put it, an aphorism belongs to whoever improves it. The same goes for 17 syllabet poems. So I think Issa, rather, read and built upon the shorter (7-7) version found in the 4th book of the older MUTAMAGAWA collection: *nuita daiko de michi o oshieru.* The fact the better *hin nuita* senryû is not mentioned in any Japanese book I know of suggests that people who care for haiku rarely get past the first book of a senryû collection.
..
Why do I write so long an aside? I do so to explain why it would seem that I am the first person to discover the senryû from which Issa borrowed the structure of his *fly-ku.* In 1996 or 1997, I stumbled across that senryû in book 24, which is to say about 19,000 poems into the YANAGIDARU. This particular book was published when Issa was a young poet in Edo. See the senryû attributed to Hôcho (fragrant-butterfly) next to Issa's famous haiku and compare for yourself!

the senryû = *yare tatsuna tatsuna de musashi juzu o suri*
issa's haiku = *yare utsuna hae ga te o suri ashi o suru*

senryû = hey, stand/rise not! (X2) musashi rubs [his] rosaries
haiku = hey, hit not! [the] fly rubs [its] hands, rubs [its] feet

Musashi is nickname of the great and faithful warrior-priest Benkei – not to be confused for Miyamoto Musashi, the greatest lone sword-fighter in history – who only knew woman once, before he died with more arrows in him than spines on a porcupine. Most readers, at first glance, might think Benkei is trying to control his unruly member. Popular songs and senryû often have deceptively dirty words that have a perfectly clean explanation; in this case, the senryû *really* describes a scene in a play called Boat-Benkei (*Funabenkei*) where he is praying for the sea to calm down! If proof is needed, another senryû states baldly:

へどをふみふみ弁慶はいのるなり　柳樽
hedo o fumi-fumi Benkei wa inoru nari – yanagidaru 2-251, 31-29
(puke treading-treading, benkei-as-for, praying is/becomes)

treading puke
treading away, benkei
starts to pray

Returning to the senryû retroactively important because of Issa's famous fly-ku. The risque double entendre depends on the same verb being used to get a rise out of waves and the male member. While "rise" does work in English, it does not work as well as *tatsu,* the basic denotation of which is "stand," and the common connotations of which include rise, go-up and get-rough. The only way I can think of saving this in English is by a freer translation, which drops the *up* side entirely:

hey, down!
get down! musashi strokes
his rosary

In Japanese, the verb *suru,* not only means "rub", but "stroke," so there is a secondary allusion to the double entendre as well. Issa, who was himself quite the lover in his old age – or at least leaves some incredible statistics in his diary: 5x in one evening in his mid-fifties (which led one amateur scholar to hypothesize that *thin sperm* explained the weak constitution and early death of all but the last of Issa's children) – may well, like most of us, have misinterpreted the senryû at first glance. Perhaps that is how it caught his eye. Regardless, I hypothesize he borrowed the senryû's structure and general concept for his fly haiku. The lightly caustic *yare* ("hey") is very rare in haiku. Add to that the similar negative-conjugation of the first verb, the common second verb *suru/suri* ("rubs/rubbing"), the parallel content and circumstantial evidence (eg. the timing of Issa's first prayer-bead-rubbing fly-ku), and the haiku's relation to the older senryû is, to my mind, obvious, though I must admit I have not yet convinced enough Japanese to dare claim it is "undeniable."

蠅蠅蠅蠅蠅蠅蠅蠅蠅蠅蠅蠅蠅蠅蠅蠅蠅蠅蠅蠅蠅蠅蠅蠅蠅蠅蠅蠅蠅蠅蠅蠅蠅蠅蠅蠅

Roasting Benkei

The warrior-priest and other greats treated sacrilegiously

弁慶に二夕夜と持たぬ紙帳かな　素丸俳句聚？
benkei-ni futa-yo to motanu shichou kana – somaru?
(benkei's two-nights last-not mosquito-net 'tis)

a mosquito net
that would not see a second
night with benkei

If the gun-fighter slept with his boots on, Benkei slept sitting with a full complement of weapons on his back. Some had blades and stuck out. The poem was in an old anthology of haikai, not senryû. So it is a haiku. Note that the mosquito net (a summer theme) is *the* subject of the poem as it should be for a haiku.

むさし坊水車程しょって出る（よいかげんなり）
musashibô mizuguruma hodo shôte deru – senryû
(benkei: waterwheel as-much carries[on back] appears)

the well-armed warrior

it's benkei!
shouldering the likes
of a windmill

Waterwheels were common in Japan, but not windmills. I just thought the windmill image would work better and maybe even conjure up the image of an opponent, a certain woeful knight.

弁慶いゝが小町はおしいもの Y 142-28
benkei wa ii ga komachi wa oshiimono – yanagidaru
(benkei-as-for fine but komachi-as-for, regretful thing)

benkei is fine
but it hurts to see komachi
go to waste!

The male senryû writer is not troubled to know Benkei was celibate, but feels that the female poetess who reputably was "hole-less" virgin to her death – a matter disputed by other senryû, for her forte was poems about love! – was a hell of a waste. With the population of Edo 70 or 80% male, his view is understandable.

弁慶いじかり指で数珠をもみ Y 143-23
benkei wa ijikari yubi de juzu o momi – yanagidaru
"Benkei / with curved fingers strokes / his rosaries"

The first 12 syllabets hint at something single men do. But, actually, it is the perpetual halberd in his hand that curves the fingers.

武蔵坊小便してもかき廻す槍
musashibô shôben shite mo kakimawasu yari ??
benkei urinating-does-even whirls around spear

benkei
urinating, whirls
his spear

I don't know which senryû collection I copied that from, but let's hope Benkei was not in a WC or it will follow the mosquito net.

But, seriously, Benkei gets off easy. Senryû give Urashima Tarô (Japan's equivalent of our Rip Van Winkle) hexagons on his buttocks (he rode a turtle to the underwater palace), they give piles to a boy serving the fat Chinese god of harvest (Hotei), because said God's belly is so round he cannot reach down far enough to rub his own rosaries, if you get the drift. Why, even the sacred Japanese archipelago that was supposed to have formed from the drips off a god's halberd is not sacrosanct. It is depicted as clusters of poop growing in a cesspool beneath a crapper! Had senryû, rather than haiku, became famous internationally, the stereotype of the super-polite Oriental would already be long gone!

蠅蠅蠅蠅蠅蠅蠅蠅蠅蠅蠅蠅蠅蠅蠅蠅蠅蠅蠅蠅蠅蠅蠅蠅蠅蠅蠅蠅蠅蠅蠅蠅蠅蠅蠅蠅

While borrowing was no crime, when a favorite poet does it, we cannot help wonder about his intent. In the case of the *daikon* poem, I'd guess that Issa read the MUTAMAGAWA 7-7 senryû when he was young and later redid it for the hell of it, or that it just popped out of his mind as a haiku without his being aware of it. The situation with the *fly-ku* is more complex and I see two distinct possibilities.

The first scenario has Issa starting with an idea in search of a vehicle. As we will soon see, both fly-swatting and flies praying/begging/pleading (as flies or as metaphor) was nothing new; but, the way both hands *and* feet were worked in to the haiku *was*. Once Issa made that fine observation, he may have looked about, or, rather, thought of a way to develop it into a poem. Then he read, or remembered reading the Musashi senryû and *shimatta!* or, in English, *voila!*

The second scenario, has it the other way around. Issa remembers the pleading fly trope while reading the senryû, or when, soon after, he observes a fly up close, at which time the "and legs" idea is born by this coupling of memes. "Well, flies might not have rosaries, but they do rub=pray with more body parts than we do!" he may have chuckled as he reworked the seasonless senryû into a summer haiku (fly-swatting being a *bona fide* summer theme).

Either way, we will never *know* whether Issa borrowed the senryû's good phrasing merely to give his idea the powerful form he wanted for it or whether there was more to it. Was Issa perhaps implying that men – even great priest-warriors with pure hearts like Benkei – praying to the larger elements, rubbing on their rosaries – are but flies? If so, perhaps we should not find too much cheer in the famous fly-ku: how can we expect our prayers to be successful, when most of Issa's flies are, as we shall see, swatted:

a-mu-na-mi-da-bu-tsu!

When Issa wrote his *fly-ku,* the *Yanagidaru* senryû series had over half a century of history and was still going strong. He had to know that his contemporaries would know where he found the *yare~na ~suri* structure. He also knew that they would not fault him for it. Rather, if my understanding of the contemporary Japanese intellectual culture is correct, the existence of a *honka,* or original poem, even if a senryû, would increase the worth of his haiku, not simply because it was a respected way of creating a poem, but because it provided another layer of meaning, more food for thought than would a poem created *ab nihilo.* With the allusion to a human's rosary-rubbing, the significance of the fly's feet – praying twice as much – becomes so much clearer and, I think, *more interesting.*

If Issa's contemporaries knew about the senryû, the question that remains is why nothing was written about it. Was it unnecessary to write what everyone knew? A decade after his death, Issa's already weak star (charts of haiku poets resembling those used for Sumo wrestlers put him in the middle ranking – under dozens if not scores of poets) faded until the early 20th century when he enjoyed unprecedented popularity as a sort of *proto-proletariat* poet. But those who read haiku no longer read senryû. The rift between the two forms had finally grown too far to jump. What had been too transparent to write was now too opaque to read.

This book is my first time to publish my discovery of the senryû and hypothesis concerning the birth of Issa's poem. It remains to be seen how many Japanese scholars will find my evidence sufficient and logic plausible.

蝿蝿

Japan as Fly Paradise:
(1946, 1947 & 1950, 1953)

"The voice of god in the popular tongue" pronounces upon fly eradication in the Far East.

In the *Foreword,* I discussed the traditional attitude toward flies in Japan and in the West. My iconoclasm led me to play up fly-love in the West and fly-hate in Japan. The following excerpts from the most famous editorial voice in post-War Japan, the liberal newspaper *Asahi Shibun*'s "Tenseijingo," (*Vox Populi Vox Dei*) provide needed balance. First, from the July 15, 1946 editorial titled "Mosquitoes, Flies and the Occupation Army."

With every nook and cranny a vegetable garden, the flies and mosquitoes this year should have been awful. It was feared our scant meals would be blackened with flies. But, as it happens, here we are and flies are few and far between. The effectiveness of scientific eradication by spreading DDT from low-flying planes is amazing.

In haiku, the mosquito and fly even became seasonal themes and gained a share in the sphere of human activity as quasi-family members. Who could ever think of total extermination? One-bug-one-kill was about as far as it ever went. But now, in the neighborhood of the Occupation troop's living quarters, one may pass the summer without a mosquito net. Of course, the insects that carry pollen

> disappear as well, so human assistance is needed to pollinate the pumpkin. . . (*Tenseijingo* 1946/7/15)

The ecological qualms began and ended with the pumpkin. The article continued to decry the manner in which Japanese required warnings to clean up their act "or else the Occupation army will fine you!" rather than draining ditches and whatnot of their own volition, as people with an independent spirit ought to do.

~~~~~~

The flies are back on June 11, 1947. The title, taken from the last editorial is: *"One-Bug-One-Killism."* After a philosophical paragraph on how Japanese do things *ad hoc*, rather than really fixing them, and another paragraph with anecdotal evidence, i.e., an American laughing to see Japanese students bring stepping stones to use in a flooded restroom, where "an American would install a pipe," we get to our subject:

> Flies swarm our dinner tables. We energetically hang up fly-paper and even invent contraptions to capture them, but we usually end up chasing them to make one-bug-one-kill by hand. We don't even think to annihilate them in the egg or larva stage, or to remove the source of the outbreak. For generation after generation, we have raised great hordes of mosquitoes in ditches and reservoirs, while burning smudge against them. Meanwhile, we have gone about blithely turning out haiku about mosquito larva! (*Tenseijingo* 1947/6/11)

Indeed, Issa wrote quite a number of haiku about "dancing" larvae, but I save that for another book on mosquito haiku. The editorial continued to explain how Japanese let mosquitoes grow out of old tin cans, while the GI's always took care to squash cans under foot. And, not only that. Most Japanese only wash their hands *after* eating, not before, where even middle class Americans . . .

~~~~~~

The next of the series dates May 15, 1950 (note: each year, the article moves up a month. This time it is almost early enough to aid in prevention.) The title is *"This Paradise for Flies, Mosquitoes and Parasites."*

> It has grown hot quickly and the fly population is burgeoning. In houses and eating establishments, these filthy little carriers are buzzing up a storm. . . . Fly subjugation is, as always, one-bug-one-killism. A big man runs about with a fly-swatter, a merciful maiden works her fan, the area occupied by a dish alone is kept out of bounds [little screen boxes are used to cover individual dishes]. The kitchen garbage isn't picked up for days, even if ditches are cleaned, the gunk lies about . . . . The household garden cultivates flies and parasites along with vegetables. The reason so many Japanese sleep in the trains [something often pointed out by foreigners and generally attributed to the high carb = rice diet today] is said to be because of their chronic vitamin deficiency and the zoos of parasites in their bellies. Be that as it may, Japan is a fly paradise, a mosquito paradise and parasite paradise. Thanks to our benevolent protection policies, the prosperity of the fly and mosquito tribes has been assured, and parasites as our *mi-uchi* ("in-laws:" a pun, for literally it reads "body-inside!") are treated to the best portion of our victuals.
>
> If there is a party that will put the eradication of parasites from the archipelago on its political agenda, I will be the first to vote. . . . (*Tenseijingo* 1950, 5/15)

The editorialist goes on to admit that to create a brave new world that would put the makers of mosquito nets and fly-swatters out of business, would require an underground sewage system for the entire nation, completely changing to chemical fertilizer, bug-killer in all stagnant water that can't be drained, and perfect garbage collection.

~~~~~~

The last of the series was published on April 4, 1953, and was titled "Flies of the North-Capital [Beijing]." Relating an old joke about how various nationalities would react to a fly in their beer, we learn that the stereotypically dirty Chinese (here Japanese and Occidentals were of a mind) might drink it down without even thinking about it.

> But in the new China, flies, mosquitoes and fleas are gone and the extermination of rats is well along. . . . . . In Beijing, cement underground sewers have been completed, ... water puddles filled in, . . . even pigs are no longer allowed to scavenge . . . One person caught 12,000 rats. It is said that two tons of flies were caught last year in Chokei [手元にない和文からの和風発音。正しくは?] . . .
>
> That a people who used to say a black coating of flies is proof that food is good have managed to make their environment that clean, attests to the strength of the spirit of new-China-building [any better translation?]. . . . The reactionary conservative government of Japan can at least try to eradicate flies.

Thanks to the *red scare*, the American occupation reversed its popular democratic policies for a crooked vote-buying conservative farce that naturally forced all self-respecting intellectuals to move further left. The pendulum went too far and *Asahi Shinbun* became infamous for its biased reporting on China over the following two decades. The paper swallowed up anything the Communist officials fed them. I doubt the newspaper's fly-phobia played much of a role in pushing it so far left. But I think it is certain that editorials such as these helped create the stereotype of coldly rational Western people living *against* nature, including flies, in opposition to the gentle Japanese, living *with* nature, including flies.
~~~~~~

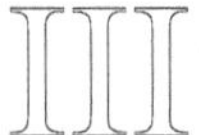

the frightened young *Bracken*

or, why Japanese flies have "hands," where ours do not

If the *structure* of the *fly-ku* comes from a specific senryû, the *idea* comes from a long tradition of anthropomorphic hands going back at least as far as the proto-haiku of Matsunaga Teitoku.

おられじと手をつくねたる蕨哉　長頭丸 崑山集
orareji to te o tsukunetaru warabi kana – teitoku (1651)
(broken-not so, hand/s kneading/clutching/clenching bracken 'tis)

spring

the wee bracken:
lest she be nigh broken
clutches her hand

I first thought *tsukuneru* (*tsukunetaru* is a fancy conjugation) meant something similar to the "rubs" (*suru*) in Issa's fly-ku. My (mis)translations:

if plants could talk

don't pluck me!
the little bracken, she
wrings her hands

the plant's plea

"eat me not!"
the bracken she wrings
her dainty hands

Unfortunately, *kneading* and *wringing* require two hands clasping and moving against or upon each other. A close check of the dictionary, confirmed by Japanese experts, suggest what common sense should have told me. The bracken is clenching its individual "hands" into fists. I must confess to a bad case of cognitive dissonance: the desire to see this poem as a close model for Issa's fly-ku made me write something ridiculous. It also read better than the "correct" translation.

Brackens put out shoots that looks like fingers curled up into a tightly clenched fist, called a "fiddle-head" in English (Ridiculous, isn't it? We should call the upper ends of our musical instruments "fern-heads" – no need to call them "fern-*hands*" after the Japanese – rather than the vice versa! *After all, who was here first, the fern or the fiddle?*). The poem above is inherently weak because the fist is not *made* but there from the start and because the clenching reality must be pushed to active clutching.

In early Spring before the leaves unfurl, the first wee fists breaking through the ground or snow are all that is visible of the plant. The naturally suggested parallel with man is enhanced by the Japanese name for this fern, *warabi,* which is close to *warabe,* meaning a "little child (*kid*, *tot*)." In parts of Japan where the *i* and *e* sounds are conflated, they are even perfect homonyms. Folk etymology – of which Japanese is particularly rich – guesses the name derives from *warawa-te-furi,* literally "tot's-hand-quivering." I admit to anthropomorphizing with my "she" and "her" in the translations – the "breaking" suggests women, for reasons soon to be explained, so "he" also would not do – but if I had not done so, I would have had to use "it," for English needs *something.* Grammatically speaking, *it/s* is neuter, acceptable but for the unspoken message, namely, "do not attach emotion to me." The hand/s of an *it* just do not appeal as successfully as those of a *she* or *he.* So, by using *it,* I would have weakened the pathos, be it humorous pretense or not, in the original. If the reader would enjoy emotion without specified gender, I suggest he or she *learn Japanese*, for, in Japanese, one is not forced to make this horrid choice. Obviously, the same thing goes for the fly/ies in *fly-ku.*

Bracken is broken off and carried home to be prepared and eaten. Since breaking (*oru* /*orareji*) – particularly the branches of flowering trees – often alluded to sexual conquest, Teitoku's poem has a faintly erotic quality. Westerners sometimes find it surprising that Japanese eat bracken, for livestock can poison themselves over-eating it (Those little bracken fists pack a punch!). Even the edible "ostrich bracken" is caustic unless carefully prepared and serves as antibiotic vermifuge (like many foods, it is mildly carcinogenic and best eaten in moderation). I think of *warabi* as tonic: together with *seri* (*Oenanthe javanica*) and *udo* (*Aralia cordata*) shoots, *warabi* smells like the essence of new plant-life. Indeed, (another) folk etymology claims *warabi* comes from *haru-mi*, or "spring-taste" (*w* and *h,* and *m* and b are closely related in Japanese).

..

Although the author, Teitoku, is often credited with the invention of what later came to be called "haiku," few of his haiku are introduced to modern readers, for his word-play – especially that revolving on the names of things – is *despised* for being shallow and bearing no relation to the objective (?) world of nature. I happen to *like* his much-maligned *slobbering icicle*, or Year of the Ox *ku* (see IN PRAISE OF OLDE HAIKU, *New Year* Volume, Annual *Animals* chapter). This bracken poem, however, I will admit is a bit too much. Blyth, in an aside on the logic of vegetarianism, once wrote that it may be true that vegetables have as much feeling as animals, killing them is easier for "cabbages don't scream so loud." (Thanks to Blyth's heightening my awareness of cabbages, I have seen a patch of decimated cabbage as so many beheaded men: the remaining leaves resemble the collars which framed 16th century European heads. Were I the owner of the patch and had washable paint on hand, I would have turned the cut cabbages into bloody necks and painted faces on the remaining cabbages and turned it all into an Installation (I dare say more interesting than 99% of those by "artists.") Still, the "hands" are not so anthropomorphic as they sound. To be fair to Teitoku, the original Japanese allows for a natural interpretation. Scrolled-up, delicate new stems will be less liable to wind damage or being eaten by small animals. Brackens keep their baby "fingers" tightly clenched as long as possible so as to protect them from the natural elements before they have hardened.

~~~~~~
~~~~~~

Here are a dozen bracken poems mostly by Teitoku or other Teimon, which is to say Teitoku school, poets. While none of these bracken beg or pray for mercy, for reasons that will be obvious later, they add to our understanding of Issa's *fly-ku.*

やせたるは折かひもなし蕨の手　長頭　崑山集
yasetaru wa oru mo kai nashi warabi no te – teitoku (1651)
(skinny-as-for, break=take-value-even not: bracken-hand/s)

Skinny ones
are not worth plucking:
bracken hands

Here, "plucking" is not quite so exciting (or mysogenist) as *oru* (break/fuck). Teitoku almost certainly alludes to his taste in women (or, boys?).

..

喰よりは折手嬉しきわらび哉　嘯山 葎亭句集
kuu yori wa oru te ureshiki warabi kana – shôzan (1801)
(eat-more-than break-hand delighted bracken tis/!/?)

eating them is
less thrilling than breaking
bracken hands

..

Or, to drop the "hand," reverse the syntax, and play a bit: *bracken: the plucker is higher / than the eater.*

山姫の手をしめて折わらびかな　失名　塵塚俳諧集より
yamahime no te o shimete oru warabi kana – name lost (1670)
(mountain-princess's hand grab/squeezing-break bracken 'tis/!/?)

catching the hand
of the mountain maiden it
breaks: bracken.

Please pardon my parsing. The original's punning transfer from girl to bracken, or maiden to maiden-hair fern beats the translation.

盗人といはぬに手出す蕨哉　重明　ゆめみ草
nusubito to iwanu ni te dasu warabi kana – chômei (1656)
(thief-as say-not-though, hand stick-out bracken!/ 'tis)

though no thief
its little hand darts out
– the bracken

No comment needed.

蕨手の雪かきわくる山路哉　正綱 ゆめみ草
warabi-te no yuki kakiwakuru yamaji kana – seigô (1656)
(bracken hands' snow stir-separate mountain-path!/'tis)

bracken hands
break through the snow
a mountain path

The original allows both the bracken and the poet to break the snow on the road.

猿候が露の月とる蕨の手　成利 ゆめみ草
enkô ga tsuyu no tsuki toru warabi no te – seiri (1656)
(monkey's dew-moon [obj.] takes bracken's hand [subj.])

simian dew?
they, too would scoop the moon
bracken hands

if monkeys were
to reach for the moon in dew
bracken hands

Thinking of the Chinese poetic trope of monkeys trying to capture the moon's reflection in a river, the poet asks *How about the dew holding the moon the bracken grasps?* I had to re-create "the-monkey-dew-moon-grasping bracken hands."
..

百足より蕨手多しくらま山　長頭丸崑山集
mukade yori warabi-te ôshi kurama-yama – teitoku (1651)
(centipede more than bracken hands many, kurama mountain)

bracken hands
outnumber centipedes
on mt kurama

The name for centipede in Japanese is *written* in Chinese characters identically to English, "hundred-feet," but all of the etymologies of the word itself make the "feet" hands: *te.* If it were a modern haiku, we could assume that mountain was particularly overgrown with bracken, but here, there is probably something else. But, what?

手占せよ遅き桜の下わらび　貞徳？崑山集
te-uraseyo osoki-sakura no shita-warabi – teitoku? 1651
(hand=palm-reading late-cherry[blossoms]-below bracken)

read its hands!
beneath the late cherry
a maiden-fern

So the late-blooming cherry has a long life-line as revealed by reading the fortune of the bracken hand? The fern is the usual, but I could not resist making up the word "maiden-fern" – there is a maiden-hair fern, but it is Adiantum (also called *kujaku-shida,* or "peacock fern"), a different species if not genus.

雪消て手に汗にぎる蕨哉　魔さ（地方名？）政辰 崑山集
yuki kiete te ni ase nigiru warabi kana – seishin (1651)
(snow melting hand-in sweat-grip bracken 'tis/!)

the snow melts
and the bracken is bathed
in cold sweat

The original says "clenches sweat in the hand," a Japanese idiom meaning "to be terrified." Terrified of people coming to pick and eat her?

手鏡と見るや蕨の露の玉　玄才十雹？ゆめみ草
takagami to miru ya warabi no tsuyu no tama – genpi[?](1656)
(hand-mirror-as see!/: bracken's dew-drop)

looks like bracken
holds a hand-mirror:
a large dewdrop

The poem does not specify the size of the dew drop/s. I imagine a large one in the curl of a sideways-held "hand."

築山は人の手つたふわらびかな　千代
chikusan wa hito no te tsut[d]au warabi kana – chiyô (d.1775)
(chiku-mountan-as-for, people's hands transmit/pass-along bracken 'tis/!/?)

bracken pass
from hand to hand
mt. chikusan

mt chikusan:
the bracken lend a hand
to people

mt. chikusan
we climb hand over hand:
like bracken

mt chikusan
hand to hand men
and bracken

This poem by the nun Chiyo makes us think about the literal meaning of the idiom for help, *tetsudau* = hand-relay. I do not know which reading is correct. (専門家は？)

~~~~~~

To this dozen bracken, we shall add *one* to make a baker's bouquet. It is by Shiki, the father of modern haiku and is unique for showing the plant at a later stage in its life cycle. Because Shiki was well-versed in the haikai play with bracken hands, I suspect we have bracken=*warabi* suggesting children=*warabe* trying to catch hold of the skirt of the departing goddess of spring (Saho-hime), but since Shiki was also an advocate of objectivity, I realize such an interpretation is anathema to some. One of
~~~~~~

the readings does not, however, rule out the other. A haiku can always have 2-sides.

行春に手をひろげたる蕨哉　子規 明治27
yuku haru ni te o hirogetaru warabe kana – shiki (d.1902)
(leaving-spring-to/with hands[obj] expand bracken 'tis/!)

Opening their hands to the departing Spring: bracken.

(*for a picture of saho-hime, departing*)

bracken hands
open to clutch the skirt
of spring's train

The common factor in all these poems is the "hand." Though it may do anthropomorphic things, take note: the *te* (hand) itself is not anthropomorphic. I say this not so much because the bracken shoot has some resemblance to a hand – from the point of view of the English speaker, the resemblance is minimal – but because the Japanese "hand" (*te,* sometimes *de, ta* or *shu*) has a far broader range of meaning than the English one. It not only refers to the five-fingered appendage found on primates but to what we would call a front paw of a cat or the tips of the front feet of a fly. Moreover, it is occasionally used to refer to the arm and even feelers are called "touch-hands!" (*shokushu*). English-speakers have less difficulty with a fly rubbing its *feet*, for they tend to think of all six of its limbs as legs. Until we become used to the idea of front legs being called hands, the "hands" of *fly-ku* seem unnaturally human. But that has nothing to do with Issa or his poem. It is only because of the way English has named things.

蝿蝿蝿蝿蝿蝿蝿蝿蝿蝿蝿蝿蝿蝿蝿蝿蝿蝿蝿蝿蝿蝿蝿蝿蝿蝿蝿蝿蝿蝿蝿蝿蝿蝿蝿蝿

Japanese bracken reinvented within Contemporary Usanian Culture

If an early-21st century Usanian were to play with the early bracken's "fists," the result might be the following haiku:

spring triumphant

winter's back
broken, the wee bracken
pumps its fist

fuyu ni kachi gattsu-pohzu no warabi kana
(winter-over wins, guts-pose-bracken 'tis)

spring high

here and there
early bracken pumping
tiny fists

achi kochi ni gattsu-pohzu no warabi-chan

I know of two origins for fist-pumping. In 1968, I was seated in that stadium in Mexico when two black-Americans wearing black gloves rose their fists as a political protest. They did not, however, do any noticeable pumping. In Japan, where I have also lived, a famous Japanese *puro uresura* "Gattsu (guts) Takahashi" was said to have held his fists high and shook them long before anyone else did. Sports papers called it his "Gattsu-pohzu" or "guts-pose" (a term many Japanese now assume came from abroad and which is used to describe all fist-pumping.). But such antics remained for decades in the realm of the ridiculous world of pro-wrestling. I do not know how this mannerism suitable to protest and posturing spread like an epidemic throughout the world of athletics to grew into the ubiquitous fist-pumping we see today. *Someone, write a book about it, please!*

Personally, I *hate* fist-pumping. To me this tensely performed fucking of the air incarnates the hard and selfish body-culture of late-20th century Usania. I love the gentle culture of the waving palm, soft body language which applauds for others but not for oneself. Sure it's fun and natural to jump up and down in glee or wave to acknowledge the applause of a crowd, or even to use the occasion when one is the focus of attention to entertain others with interesting antics (here, I strongly disagree with football regulations discouraging such creativity – so long as it is gentle and not violent, why not?); but, mark my word, fisting the air is an obnoxious if not unnatural behavior for celebration. I will grant that it looks perfectly innocent coming from little children, but if body language has any influence on our heart, it is teaching them something far worse than any so-called "bad words" could. On a purely psychological level, our spreading the fisting virus around the world is every bit as much a disaster as AIDS. Moreover, unlike AIDS, we even propagate this insanity backwards into time. I cannot count the number of television programs and movies which have characters pumping their clenched fists (often to the accompaniment of the strange new exclamation: "Yes!") long before anyone would have dreamed of doing it in reality. I ask, if we harden the human spirit *everywhere* and *everytime* how will it ever recover its peaceful nature? At least hip-hop, with its aggressive vocal tone (the words are secondary to the testy, damn-you/up-yours!) is not being foisted on on our parents and grandparents in the way that *fists* and *yeses* are.

蝿蝿蝿蝿蝿蝿蝿蝿蝿蝿蝿蝿蝿蝿蝿蝿蝿蝿蝿蝿蝿蝿蝿蝿蝿蝿蝿蝿蝿蝿蝿蝿蝿蝿

Envoi

Issa has no *haiku* about bracken "hands;" but he does use them as a metaphor in such a manner to suggest he may have read and remembered Teitoku's poems. Here he is describing his year-and-a-half old daughter Sato:

> I believe this child lives in a special state of grace . . . when the evening comes when once a year we hold memorial service for the dead, and I have lit the candles on the family altar and rung the bell for prayer, she crawls out swiftly, wherever she may be, and softly folds her hands, like little bracken sprouts[*sawarabi no chiisaki te*], and says her prayers in such a sweet, small voice – in such a lovely way . . . I am ashamed to think my child, who is only two years old is closer to the truth than I. And yet no sooner do I leave the altar than I sow the seeds of future torments, hating the flies that crawl across my knee . . .
> (transl. Nobuyuki Yuasa in Robert Hass: *The Essential Haiku*, brackets, mine.)

This is found in *Ora-ga Haru*, a book Issa made shortly after his daughter's death, a couple years before the famous fly-ku. The praying bracken hands did not work.

蝿蝿

Little *pathetic* in this!

types of *anthropomorphic pretence* in japanese poetry

Much we tend to read and denigrate as anthropomorphism, or smugly believe liable to "the pathetic fallacy" is, on closer reading, not so. This is especially true when the text in question has been translated between tongues as remote to one another as English and Japanese. Since this type of misunderstanding seems to be particularly rife in *fly-ku,* I thought this supplement might be useful.

Blyth gives a senryû which he translates "the fly comes up, / Bowing / And rubbing his head" (*tonde-kita hae ogande-wa kubi-o nade* 飛んで来た蝿拝んでは首を撫で), after which he writes:

> this is a satire on the servility of human beings, who in Japan bow to express embarrassed respect. Issa's haiku is entirely different . . .

As we have seen already, for better or worse, it is not clear that Issa's *fly-ku* is *entirely* different, as Blyth assumes. Moreover, the senryû does *not* mention "bowing" but uses a general term for worshipping (*ogande*) which suggests hand-rubbing. Combine it with the head-rubbing – to me it looks more like they are sleepily rubbing their eyes – and the details are also on a similar high level with Issa's poem. Who can say if it is really *just* satire.

~~~~~~~~~~

We tend to exaggerate the blurry line between senryû and haiku. Even Blyth, who has defended what others mistakenly label as a pathetic fallacy more often and far better than anyone I know of, sometimes is too hard on senryû when he compares it with his favorite genre, haiku.

> The tendril of the pea / Is thinking / "Where shall I go now?" – trans. Blyth (*kono saki-o kangaete-iru mame no tsuru* – kijiro = this ahead/future thinking bean-vine), or, in my translation –

the tendril
of the pea is thinking
where to now?

"It is odd," writes Blyth, "that senryû should be so much more mystical and animistic and personificating (if the word is in the dictionary) than haiku." Well, actually, Blyth's "where shall I go?" is *much* more anthropomorphic than the original, which is, as Charles Darwin, who carefully studied the phenomeon, would surely agree, *about right.* "The reason is no doubt that haiku has set its face resolutely against all intellection [sic], whether obvious or concealed, and mysticism or animism is always consciously anti-intellectual. But anti-intellectual is also intellectual." The same thing could be said about Zen and its best explainer Suzuki Daisetsu, but all I want to say is that *had the pea "senryû" been within a collection of haiku, I doubt that even Blyth would have challenged it as "intellection" or any other supposedly unhaiku thing.*

~~~~~~~~~~

> The moon told her / To get up and shut / The skylight – trans. Blyth (*hikimado o tsuki-ga oshiete okite-tate* = sky-light, moon-the teach / taught awaken-shut)

"The odd thing is that in Japanese poetry, it is senryû only which personifies, which looks animistically upon the things of the outer world," writes Blyth. Of course, this senryû personifies the moon, but, I think, joking rhetoric should not be confused with animism. Many Japanese will disagree with me on principle for Japanese like to call themselves animists, but I do not feel they are *that* religious. They are agnostic animists or romantic animists, but little real animism in Edo.

~~~~~~~~~~

> The responsibility for remaining unsold / Rests on the apples, / Twenty yen a heap. – trans. Blyth (*urenakatta sekinin-ga hito-mori niju-en-no ringo-ni aru* – shomenshi)

Blyth's translation is fine. This is a sarcastic picture of human nature where the unstated subject, the shop-keeper treats the apples as humans in that he holds them responsible. But does the poem itself anthropomorphize? Of course not. How about this?

> The toad's / Is the right posture / To look at a hanging picture – trans. Blyth (*hikigaeru kakemono-o miru sugata nari*)

This just states a fact. No one is saying that frogs appreciate art. The poem is rare if not original, because the usual tropes were frog-as-politely-seated-underling or practitioner of meditation. While it has no "like ~" in it, we take it as playful simile.

~~~~~~~~~~

> The morning sun / Shakes and wakes the bamboos / Sent to sleep by the snow – trans. Blyth (*yuki-ni neta take-o asahi-ga yuri-okoshi* (snow-in/by slept bamboo morning-sun/sunlight shook awake)

the morning sun
shakes awake the bamboo
snow put to bed

The sun's personification is rarer in Japanese than in English; but note that this "sun" is also "sunlight" and the sunlight *does* melt the snow so the bamboo can spring back up from the horizontal "sleep." It is factual.

> The stone image of Jizo / Kissed on the mouth / By a slug – trans. Blyth (*namekuji-ni kuchi-o suwareta ishi-jizo* = slug-by mouth sucked/kissed stone-jizo)

"This senryû" writes Blyth, "makes Jizo a teacher of Zen. This is 'being all things to all men' and all slugs." I love these comments. The quoted line is the Jesuit motto. Blyth's Japanese are being more catholic for including all life. In Japanese, to "kiss" is to *suck.* The "kiss" is there but, as always, it is not so unnatural=anthropomorphic as in English translation because the *ku* is literally true.

> The cicada sings / With an unyielding spirit / To the thunder – trans. Blyth (*kaminari ni makenu ki de naku semi no koe* (thunder-by not lose feeling-with cicada's/s' voice)

"This I suppose might be called the 'Zen of cicada,' writes Blyth. It is magnanimous of him to grant Zen status to something in a senryû. I would just say *it could be a haiku.* The cicada seem to be acting competitively like the woman who, "tit for tat" farted at the thunder. I recall thinking I heard cicada raising their voices, not only for thunder but for passing trains. I thought it might only be an acoustic effect. (This could be scientifically tested! If anyone does so, I would like to know.)

> A short-sighted centipede / Is making love / To a millipede – trans. Blyth (*kingan-no mukade gejigeji-o kudoiteru*)

This is ridiculous, but could be true. Animals in the natural world often misplace their affection, or act unnaturally, as the Christians put it. In the original, the disgusting sound of the names *mukade* and *geji-geji,* not to mention the fact that the latter, the millipede is synonymous with ugly eyebrows, made this a visceral senryû, where our Latinate *centi-milli-* sounds intellectual.

To the late riser / The morning glory / makes a wry face – trans. Blyth (*asagao-wa asane-no hito-ni shigami tsura* (morning-glory morning-sleeping-person-to puckered-up/wry countenance)

Morning glory is called a "morning-face" in Japanese, so the senryû puns on the name rather than just personifying the flower for the hell of it. Moreover, the adjective translated as "wry," *in Japanese*, also denotes *a puckered-up surface*, such as the shriveled up blossom in question. Like Issa's *fly-ku,* the senryû is both facetious anthropomorphicism *and* an "objective" description written in a natural way. I would even accept it as a haiku and, indeed, there is such a haiku expressed that ambiguity in a more abstract way by haiku's first woman, Chiyo: "Morning glory / the truth is / the flower hates people" (transl. by Donegan and Ishibashi. あさがほや誠は花の人きらひ *asagao ya makoto wa hana no hitogirai*).

蝿蝿蝿蝿蝿蝿蝿蝿蝿蝿蝿蝿蝿蝿蝿蝿蝿蝿蝿蝿蝿蝿蝿蝿蝿蝿蝿蝿蝿蝿蝿蝿蝿蝿蝿蝿

○ ○

a *Supplication* of flies

a whole lot of rubbing/praying going on!

As flies to wanton boys are we to the gods – Shakespeare (*King Lear*)

Now that we have the Japanese *te* firmly in *hand*, let us see all the rubbing, i.e. pleading, it did *before* Issa's poem appeared. While there is occasional hand-rubbing outside of flies (and prayer beads) in old haiku – "The cuckoo rubs, rubs, and is passed down the check-point road" (*suru-suru to tôse sekiji no hototogisu* するするととをせ関路の郭公) = Chiri (?), where the cuckoo stands for a lover on the move – the fact that hand-rubbing, and hence pleading, is not attributed to other animals but strictly confined to flies, who really do put their "hands" together, proves that whatever figurative fancy is pretended, the poets demand at least a semblance of reality.

つまれて手をする蝿の命かな　嘯山？ 葎亭。。
tsumamarete te o suru hae-no inochi kana – shôzan ? (d. 1801)
(pinched[between fingers], hand-rubbing fly's life 'tis)

where there is life . .
a fly already pinched
rubbing his hands

the pitiful bug

the fly
i pinch, wrings its hands:
dear life!

the pitiful thief

pinched, he rubs
his hands for life is life
even for a fly

Whether read as metaphor or description, this poem, antedating Issa and his *fly-ku* by almost a hundred years (Shôzan had a very long life), contains much in common with it. The *inochi kana* is a fine phrase which can be translated in many ways: "life 'tis!" "oh, life!" "it means my/its life" "it'll be the death of me/it." I think Shôzan means it is a matter of life or death to the fly, which it is. As I cannot imagine a fly pinched between fingers would rub its legs together, I also suspect my first translation is correct, though it is wrong for not maintaining the "*fly's* life." As usual, it is hard for English to keep the ambiguity of a life that is the fly's *and* the poet's. The entire poem is a modification of the "life" which cannot be kept properly linked together (i.e., *the life of a fly rubbing its hands while pinched!*) without reversing the life-comes-last syntax, except by strange re-constructions.

手を摺て拝むやのりにたかり蝿　貞房
te o surite agamu ya nori ni takari-hae – teibo (1651)
(hand/s rub, praying:/! glue-on/to, swarming flies

the faithful

they rub their hands
and pray, flies gathering
on fly-paper

religious gathering

wearing down
their hands with prayer
flies on fly-paper

The verb *suru* or "rub" also has connotations of wearing-down, so I let one translation pick up on it. Another verb *agamu* means "pray" or "worship." This poem directly followed the last:

蝿が手をするは菩薩の御台哉　正次
hae ga te o suru wa bosatsu no odai kana – seiji (1651)
(the fly/ies-hand/s rub/s/pray/s-as-for, bodhisattva's base!/?/'tis)

the place the fly rubs its hands?
the base of the bodhisattva

所得た

on the base
of the bodhisattva
a fly prays

Next, two lines from a *renga* , or "linked verse" sequence (in *Danrin Hyakku* 17c), where different poets write a line at a time on the basis of loose association.

蝿にならひて君に手をする　正友
hae ni naraete kimi ni te o suru – Seiyu

Learning from the fly, he/she/I rub/s hands to the lord/lover/you

はげあたま甲をぬいで旗を巻　卜尺
hage-atama kabuto o nuide hata o maki – Toshaku

Baldy removes his helmet and furls his flag

In linked verse, the wit is in the link. Here, the man who gives up and begs for his life fly-style becomes bald because bald heads are sometimes called "fly-sliders" (*haesuberi*) in Japanese! Something kinder, but less witty:

悼＝蝿迄も手をする夏の流哉　兎柳
hae made mo te o suru natsu no nagare kana – Uryû (d.1805)

Funeral　Even the flies rub their hands: a summer miscarriage.

This haiku seems terribly folk. Looked at critically, it is maudlin, affected, false, anthropomorphic and many other bad things; but if you instead imagine the poet grieving for what may be his own long desired child as he zooms in (grief has a way of focusing the eyes on the very close and very far) on the movement of the flies' hands, feeling, if for only a moment that they too prayed for the departed soul, there is something real and even precious in the poem, which, like all we have seen in this chapter so far, predates famous Issa's fly-ku. So does the next, far less famous work of Issa's:

蝿寺や神の下らせ給ふとて　一茶
haedera ya kami no kudarase tamau tote – issa (d.1827)
(fly-temple:/! god/s confer please give [as if praying that] = The *tote* at the end of the original is a Japanese word indicating that what preceeds is something said by words or indicated by gesture.)

a church of flies
please confer this!
confer that!

the fly temple
gods, give us this!
give us that!

The poem does not insult *flies* because Issa knew damn well flies are not praying for favors when they rub their hands together. It does, I think, poke fun at people who think religion is solely for the purpose of supplicating gods for favors. Unfortunately, it is never found in collections of senryû, for Issa is not a senryû poet, yet it is too senryû for the taste of haiku anthologists. Until an anthology of "hidden senryû by haiku poets" is published in Japan, I fear such poems will continue to be ignored.

~~~~~~

The same year Issa wrote his famous *fly-ku,* he wrote another farcical haiku about fly hand-rubbing without actually mentioning the same. I think of it as a just-so story in reverse, for people usually learn from other animals rather than the vice versa:

堂の蝿数珠する人の手をまねる　一茶
dô no hae juzu suru hito no te o maneru – issa (d.1827)
(prayer-hall flies: prayer-bead-rubbing-peoples' hands[obj] copies)

temple flies
copy the hands of people
rubbing rosaries

I use the word "rosaries" instead of "prayer beads" in my loose translation because, despite the unwanted Catholic baggage, description (as opposed to single-word terms) weakens poems and because "rosaries" has but 1 strong-beat (on the *ro*) while "prayer beads" has 2, which would make the haiku too long. Personally, the Japanese rosaries, or *juzu,* remind me not of the fly but of another bug, the cicada. A room full of faithful Buddhists can make a hell of a racket when they rub those beads. Be that as it may, the fact these prayer beads (*juzu*) appear together with flies for the first time in Issa's poems the same year he wrote the famous *fly-ku* may be added to the obvious structural similarities as collateral evidence of Issa's debt to the Benkei senryû introduced in chapter I. The idea of flies learning their behavior from "us" indirectly casts doubt on the efficacy of our own supplication, as do the double-
~~~~~~

prayer (hands *and* feet) in the famous poem. Here is another rubbing/praying poem by a long-lived contemporary of Issa:

涅槃会に出て手をするや去年の蝿　梅室
nehan-e ni dete te o suru ya kozo no hae – baishitsu (d.1852)
(buddha's-anniversary-meeting-at appear/s, hands rub/s: last year's fly/ies)

survivors

they rub their hands
at buddha's anniversary
last year's flies

life-in-death

merciful buddha!
on your day, the old flies
come out to pray

nehan-kai

appearing the day
buddha died, last year's flies
join us in prayer

Having no such holy day, we must use words too long to haiku. Anniversaries for the famous – be they religious, political or cultural figures – in the Far East are always celebrated on *death*-days rather than *birth*-days (Though Buddha's birthday was also celebrated, as described in *Topsy-turvy 1585*). According to the Japanese, Buddha died when the cherry was in bloom: mid-spring, the equinox. Since flies are a summer phenomenon, I guess any flies appearing at a Nehan-e (Buddha [Death]Day, or Enlightenment Day meeting) – unless they were weak old men metaphored as flies who managed to survive the winter. Another old haiku suggests that flies may have been thought to live longer than they really do:

背にとまる蝿覚えけり更衣　太無
se ni tomaru hae oboekeri koromogae – taimu
(back-on stop/sitting-fly remembers[emphatic/perfect] change-robe/dress)

the fly on my back
remembers the change
summer clothes

~~~~~~

足摺や蝿も流罪の鉢の海　調加
ashi suru (*ashizuri*) *ya hae mo ruzai no hachi no umi* – chôka
(foot-rub/bing/scuffing/pawing! fly-too exile/cast-away's bowl's sea)

those woeful feet!
the fly, an exile, looks out
upon the soup

This is an impossible poem to translate. I include it because it is the only other foot-rubbing haiku I know of besides Issa's fly-ku. KZ and KS saved me by pointing out
~~~~~~

that this fly alludes to Shunkan 俊寛, who was exiled to Kikaigashima "devil-world island" 鬼界島 (Kagoshima, with its constant volcanic ash) with some others on the losing side of the Heikei coup de etat in 1177, a merchant ship hove to for a while and rescued the others when he was up on a high peak from which he saw it depart, at which time, according to dramatizations, he scuffed and stamped his feet in chagrin. The poor man had been exiled internally by being enrolled in the priesthood – an alternative to death for ruling family members otherwise killed for fear of a future power challenge – and this pitiful scene of his bad luck in his external exile is etched into the Japanese consciousness. After that, he is said to have quickly pined away and died. In classic Japanese, *ashizuri* (leg-rubbing) had a specific idiomatic meaning which I would put somewhere between scuffing the ground and stamping it in the manner of a kid having a tantrum. At the time the haiku was written, it had dropped such connotation and meant only "rubbing" the feet (perhaps with some of the same connotations as rubbing the hands), but the educated reader would probably think of the older meaning of the body language. Food served in a *hachi* (a large serving bowl/plate as opposed to a small *chawan,* or tea-bowl) suggests a mound of condiments (*gu*) surrounded by hot soup. A fly has alighted on the cooling tip of the mound of *gu* and the poet . . . let's just say he has a hell of an imagination!

~~~~~~

こっちから蝿に手をする昼寝哉　文右衛門 古選

kocchi kara hae ni te o suru hirune kana – bunemon? (1763)

(here/me-from, fly/flies-to [my] hands rub-do: afternoon-sleeep 'tis)

fly noon

i rub my hands
for mercy from the flies
at nap-time

flies, and more flies!

i am the one
doing the hand-rubbing
my poor nap!

role reversal

nap-time
i do the hand-rubbing
to flies

topsy-turvy

noon naps
when we pray
to flies

My favorite rubbing/praying *fly-ku* are the ones that reverse the situation so that we humans are the supplicants. That such a reversal already occurred in 1763 (the date of the anthology with the poem) or earlier proves just how well-known the conceit of pleading flies was before Issa wrote his first haiku. Almost certainly not knowing the above poem, but starting with Issa's famous fly-ku, an American woman from MI came up with a splendid way to describe her situation while joining fly and poet in a novel manner:
~~~~~~

Fly swatter broken
the fly and I
wring our hands

– Kaye Laird (in William J. Higginson: *Haiku World* – an international poetry almanac:1996)

Higginson labels this poem "S" for *senryû*. In my opinion, this is wrong for three reasons. First, fly-swatting is a traditional haiku theme. Second, humor like this was, as you can see from my examples, once clearly part of, if not the very pink of haiku. Even in this boring age, wit need not be shunted aside as *senryû*. And, third, the first-person is extremely rare in *senryû*, which, as a genre, specializes in describing character *types*. So, hats off to Kaye Laird for having written a traditional haiku, all the more traditional for alluding to an older haiku, Issa's *fly-ku!*

Note: *I'd guess Higginson might argue that* today, *such a poem would be a senryû. I think that would indeed be the judgment of* many *in Japan, too, but not that of most fans of old haiku. The fact Higginson includes many "S" poems in his classic book shows that, whatever the label may be, he appreciates the wit they contribute to the* haiku world *we share.*

蠅蠅蠅蠅蠅蠅蠅蠅蠅蠅蠅蠅蠅蠅蠅蠅蠅蠅蠅蠅蠅蠅蠅蠅蠅蠅蠅蠅蠅蠅蠅蠅蠅蠅蠅蠅蠅

俊寛の鬼界島と一茶の此方が鬼なり俊寛の鬼界島と一茶の此方が鬼なり俊寛の鬼界島と一茶の此方が鬼なり

On the *Relativity* of *Cultures & Species.*

I had not planned to pursue the exiled Shunkan any further, for, aside from that one haiku, he has nothing to do with flies! But when I googled him, I found a fascinating article, *"Devil-world Island and Ryukyu (Okinawa) Within Literary Space,"* by Rikkyo University professor Takahashi Hiroaki(?), the gist of which is worth recounting.

Devil-world Island was a common name for un-named islands beyond the purview of the central power=culture. It was by definition a place of enormous deprivation and hardship for cultured people. The list of characteristics was equivalent to the medieval European idea of a desert, which is to say a horrid wilderness with horrid features and horrid sub-humans, if, that is, they could be called human. The exiled hero was said to have died within two years of being exiled to this god-forsaken place.

Professor Takahashi points out that so-called "devil-world islands" were usually populated by perfectly healthy and happy people who might have quite a different idea about who and where they were. The real accounts of exiled Japanese show they did not necessarily do so badly. This discrepancy of historical interpretation was expanded into a bold historical novel by Akutagawa Ryunosuke (d.1927), where the "devil" islanders did not subscribe to the aesthetic values of the Japanese (Miyako, or "capital" people). There is even a clear statement of contradictory ideals of personal beauty in Akutagawa's novel.

What I think the best short statement about cultural relativity ever penned, was not noted in the article. It is a haiku by Issa about Ezo island (Hokkaido and other areas inhabited by Ainu):

来て見ればこちらが鬼也蝦夷が島　一茶
kite mireba kochira ga oni nari ezogashima – issa
(come-see-if/when this-side[we] devil/demon-become: ezo's island)

ezo isle

we came
and found the demons
were us!

In his middle age, Issa wrote many haiku celebrating the advances of Buddhism (some popular Buddhism in Japan was almost as evangelistic as the worst forms of Christianity) into the Ainu's world. I am not certain if he changed his outlook on life or heard too much bad news about cheating merchants and the spread of influenza – both of which he puts in haiku – but the difference is remarkable. (Issa's last three "good" haiku on this subject are found in *Zenshû* 1, and the good and "bad" are found together in Aoki Michio: *Issa-no Jidai* : 1988)

Reading Issa's total work, I felt the relationship of sympathy for other cultures and for other species. Issa wrote many poems about animals fearing people as "devils," and even birds warning their young not to trust the poet.

Swat them and B*less* them?

namuamidabutsu & the justification of killing

> Let me come right out with it. I am repulsed by the standard interpretation of this [Issa's famous *fly-ku*] as a "merciful poem" (*jihi-no-ku*). "Oh, it's rubbing its hands and legs and pleading for mercy, the poor thing! Stop, don't hit it!" I think such a reading is wrong and doesn't fit Issa. So, how should it be read? First, we admit that rubbing hands and legs is perfectly normal fly behavior and Issa is simply observing this (the idea that it is praying is made up by the reader). The "hey, don't hit it!" is admittedly an injunction, but a very light one meaning "C'mon don't hit it! Can't you see how the fly rubs its hands and feet together, so contentedly?" (Kaneko Tôta: *Issa Kushû*)

Paradoxically, because all Japanese are taught about the merciful small-creature-loving Issa when they are children, the cynic in the intelligent grown-up is tempted to question that stereotype. Missing the layers of humor in Issa's "Hey, don't swat the fly" poem, they come to think it betrays the supposedly objective art of haiku and, worse yet, is disgustingly precious. Kaneko is a leading figure in modern haiku, and I admire him for his boldness (uncommon in authorities in Japan), yet I cannot help pointing out that in his admirable desire to acquit Issa of the crime of maudlinity, he seems to have applied a modern sensibility (translation from European languages has brought to Japanese the idea of "rubbing ones hands in glee") and retroactively applied it to Issa. Since Issa recorded a story about the supernatural punishment (impotence) given to a man who kills snakes making love, I can further see how Kaneko may have felt the *ku* represented an extension of the idea that it is wrong to disturb animals feeling pleasure, but, there is *nothing whatsoever* in anything old I have read that suggests *hand(or leg)-rubbing* could have been construed as *something pleasurable*. So, I wrote, **THEN**, *the day before* I finish the book, a friend alerts me to a Chinese poem 冷蠅 by Yang Wan-li 楊萬里(1124-1206). To be fair, I must squeeze in the 28-character, 4-line (AABA rhymed) poem, though I have been warned by well-wishers not to undermine my own authority so often:

> *The Cold Fly*
>
> I see a fly
> warming himself on the window sill,
> rubbing his legs, enjoying the morning sun.
> He seems to know when the light will shift:
> a sudden buzz
> and he's at another window.
>
> trans. Jonathan Chaves (in *Sunflower Splendor* ed. Liu & Lo)

If there is one exception, there may be more, but the evidence for the opposite reading is overwhelming. Take the following crazy-verse (*kyôka*) by Issa, himself:

狂歌狂歌狂歌狂歌狂歌狂歌狂歌狂歌狂歌狂歌狂歌狂歌狂歌狂歌狂歌狂歌狂歌狂歌

Crazy-verse: *Issa the Pestle*

世に住ば手をすり足をすりこ木にしてかけ廻る年の暮哉　一茶　（風間八・文政 2.5）
yo ni sumaba te o suri ashi o suri=kogi ni shite kakemawaru toshinokure kana – issa (d.1827)
(world-in live-if, hands rub/wear, legs rub/wear/grind-down=pestle-into/as make=use, stir=move-around year's end!)

grinding out the end of the year

if you would live
in this world, you rub your hands
you rub your feet;
worn to a pestle, you go around
while you, yourself are ground!

connotative translation

if you would live
on earth, you wear your hands
you wear your feet
down to a pestle while debts
come round the year complete

Beside shopping for holiday goods, the end of the year was *the* time for closing accounts. Issa fit both the running around and the begging to creditors (who might come to visit *you*) into his metaphor. Punning and other word-play aside, the original crazy-verse is hard to translate because the entire poem is a run-on modification of the year's end (*toshinokure*). The poem-as-a-single-modified-subject may be found in the oldest anthologies of Japanese poetry (*Manyôshû, Kôkinshû*, etc.) and, to my mind, is the single most peculiar – at least, not found in Occidental poetry as far as I know – feature in Japanese poetry, so I point it out in all of my books and will only stop doing so when I observe another pointing it out! Now that the significance of the poem has been safely taken care of, some paraverses of the broader meaning, which has nothing to do with the subject of this book:

deadbeat deadline

the end of the year
would be just fine
if only it left us
with a bit more time
and money!

poet run ragged

thank god
it does not last!
the year's end
is a royal, yes, royal
pain in the ass!

the year's end

when human
hamsters must run
faster to keep
turning the wheel of
time and money

But the poem does matter with respect to the meaning of hand and foot rubbing for flies. It came right after a haiku where Issa rubs his hands in order to beg a corner of the mosquito net (*te o surite kaya no ko-sumi o karinikeri*). My guess is that this was at his wife Kiku's home where there was a funeral for her older sister. Funerals cost a lot and doubtless did not help things. It was the 5th month (June-July), which is to say, prime time for flies, whose hand-rubbing, I think we may be certain, reflected not pleasure but the hard lives they shared with Issa and Kiku.

狂歌狂歌狂歌狂歌狂歌狂歌狂歌狂歌狂歌狂歌狂歌狂歌狂歌狂歌狂歌狂歌狂歌狂歌

Kaneko is the only person I know who has tried a radically new reading of Issa's poem. More commonly, sweetness-hating readers are satisfied to note that Issa could have been joking, or discover – and, in some essays I remember, but do not have at hand – dwell upon, if not gloat over Issa's other "hard-boiled haiku" where said fly ends up *dead*. Let us read some of these in a more or less chronological order.

蝿一つ打ては山を見たりけり　一茶
hae hitotsu uchite wa yama o mitarikeri – issa (d.1827)
(fly one strike-as-for, mountain[obj] look[done/continue/emphatic)

i swat a fly
and look upon
the mountain

I am not confident about the grammar, but a timeless present tense seems to work best. "Look *up at*" is also possible, for the next poem in his notebook is: "summer mountain / one step at a time / the sea appears." But, I imagine it from the vantage point of a lodge or temple. This was young Issa's finest *ku* and may well be one of the purest ever written. I didn't dare sully it with a title or stupid explanation. I find it amazing that it is not included in the standard Iwanami anthology of his best 2000 poems (even Maruyama nods) except in a note to a later *ku* that began the same way but ended in a sutra. This, written years later, is not included, period:

蝿打や友となりぬる峰の松　一茶
hae utsu ya tomo to narinuru mine no matsu – issa (d.1827)
(fly strike/-ing]: [my] friend [it] becomes[: the] ridge's pine)

i kill a fly
and the pine on the ridge
becomes my friend

swatting flies
the pine on the ridge
and i grow close

Is the pine the same as the mountain? Or, is it different? Which of my interpretations is correct? I love haiku that inexplicably feel right. Again, I won't try to explain, other than pointing out that pines and mountains have associations to Japanese poets that we miss. Paradoxically, this makes it easier for us to read their haiku in the manner recommended by the Zen-crazed modern (objectively, straight from the heart, etc.) and find them *pure*. This is the poetic equivalent of the alabaster classic sculpture we fail to appreciate as painted, even though we know they were!

蝿打てけふも聞也山の鐘　一茶
hae uchite kyô mo kikunari yama no kane – issa (d.1827)
(fly/flies strike, today too hear it: mountain bell)

swatting flies
today, too, the bell
on the mountain

i kill a fly
and today, too, i hear
the temple bell

In the Sinosphere, mountains were synonymous with two things: *wilderness* and *temples*. It is possible the mountain Issa gazed at was just a mountain and nothing more, but I don't think it true here. This is a Buddhist temple's bell. And, thanks to the dead fly, or dead flies, it left an impression on the poet.

蝿打にけふもひつぢの歩哉　一茶
haeuchi ni kyô mo hitsuji no ayumi kana – issa (d.1827)
(fly-swatting-to/with, today too lamb-walk 'tis)

swatting flies
today, too, a lamb-walk
to slaughter

Most Japanese never even saw, much less ate or wore lamb; but the Chinese expression "a lamb-walk" was known to all educated Japanese. It meant going to the slaughter house. As it walks, its tail swats flies. The poem almost surely alludes to Issa's life (though it is possible he refers to a dying friend, or people in general) and means: "stupidly, i swat flies, knowing each is a tick-tock, in my final count-down."

蝿打に敲かれ玉ふ仏哉　一茶
hae-uchi ni tatakare tamau hotoke kana – issa (d.1827)
(fly-swatting-by, stricken deign to: buddha/corpse 'tis/!)

killing flies
verily i strike
the buddha!

struck by
my fly-swatter
the departed

Perhaps this poem was conceived in the presence of a dead man. A corpse in Japanese is called *hotoke.* But so is a statue of Buddha. Since Issa has many poems about Buddha statues – including: "swatting a fly / on the venerable head of / a tathagatha" (*hae utsu ya amida nyorai no on-atama* 蝿打やあみだ如来の御天窓.) – it is hard to tell when he means a corpse. In this case, Issa used a special helping verb (*tamau*) associated with gods – I hope the Biblical "verily" is not too strange! – which suggests the Buddha; but, as it so happens, the recently dead are considered Buddhas and/or gods of a sort, so there is no way to escape the ambiguity other than finding the day the poem was written (which I have not done). A much later haiku of Issa's is equally ambiguous on the nature of the *hotoke.*

人有れば蝿あり仏ありにけり　一茶
hito areba hae mo ari hotoke ari-ni-keri – issa (d.1827)
(people are-if, flies are, corpse/s=buddha/god/s is/are[emphatic/finality)

things that come together

people
mean flies and
corpses

rule of the universe

you can't have
men without flies
and gods

This poem was written the month Issa's wife Kiku died. That month, he also wrote "an earlobe / with three flies / on it" (*mimitabo ni hae ga sanjô tomarikeri* 耳たぼに蝿が三疋とまりけり), the first part of which he amended (or clarified) at the year's end: "a lucky ear / ~ " *fuku-mimi-ni~*福耳に). Issa had large earlobes, which were thought to guarantee a prosperous and happy life to its owner. Maybe Kiku did too. Such a large ear-lobe, Issa points out, only supplies more space for flies to alight. It is hard to say whether the flies are on his ear or his dead wife's. Either way, it is fine irony if read properly:

lucky earlobes
the better to hold two
or three flies

When Kiku died, she died in the 5th month, i.e. today's July, which was associated with abundant flies. That may be why Issa wrote a large number of *fly-ku* then. Or, it may simply be that she and flies were associated in Issa's mind. I say this because the year Issa married her, his fly-swatting haiku begin to flourish. My guess is that Issa had not pursued flies as a bachelor, but the spunky Kiku was a vigorous exterminator. I could be wrong. At any rate, that is when we get this:

縁の蝿手をする所を打たれけり 一茶
en no hae te o suru tokoro o utare-keri – issa (d.1827)
(veranda's fly: hand-rubbing-while [done] hit-is/was[emphatic+perf.])

A fly on the verandah,
Killed,
While rubbing its hands.

– trans. Blyth

Is this just a description of what *is*? No. It cannot be. No Japanese reader can avoid thinking of the figurative significance of hand-rubbing, i.e.:

a fly on the porch
swatted while begging
for mercy

Does it matter if a figurative crime has been committed? *Perhaps*. On some level of existence. Blyth's "killed" is excellent, for the swatting was given a *keri,* i.e., a conjugation that is emphatic. His passive is right, too, for it preserves the ambiguity of the killer. But I can't help wondering about who was doing the swatting – Issa, his wife, Kiku, or someone else? – and adding two active paraverses.

mercy me!

on the porch
i swat a fly while it
rubs its hands

mercy she!

on the porch
she swats another fly
rubbing its hands

The "my" before the fly-swatter in the next poem, likewise, could as well be "her."

蝿打に花さく草も打れけり 一茶
hae uchi[utsu?] ni hana saku kusa mo utarekeri – issa (d.1827)
(fly-swatter/swatting-by, flower-blooming plant/grass/weed, too/even, stricken[+emphatic])

Striking the fly,
I hit also
A flowering plant.

– trans. Blyth

no bounds

even the plant
in bloom is not safe from
my fly-swatter

Blyth guessed the pronunciation was *utsu* rather than *uchi* which is less likely, hence the verb rather than the swatter. My translation is closer to the original in that it centers on the plant's victimization but otherwise far looser.

The following may well be the most entertaining of all *fly-gets-swatted* haiku.

蝿一つ打てはなむあみだ仏哉　一茶
hae hitotsu utte wa [utteba?] namuamidabutsu kana – issa (d.1827)
(fly one, hit [it]-if/when *"namuamidabutsu"* 'tis)

na-mu-a-mi-da-bu-tsu

each fly
we swat gets
a blessing

the good death

each fly
swatted earns
a sutra

expendable

for each fly
we kill, another *na-mu-*
a-mi-da-bu-tsu

hit-man priest

each fly
that i kill
i bless

When the protagonist is unclear the general rule in haiku is *assume the first-person.* In that case, we have Issa swatting and Issa blessing, as per the last reading. But a general rule is not a law; it does not rule out other possibilities.

namuamidabutsu!

each fly
she swats receives
my blessing

namuamidabutsu

each fly
i swat enjoys
her blessing

namuamidabutsu

a benediction
for every *musca maledicta*
we swat

When someone sneezes, we offer them a *gesundheit,* whatever that is. We stick with this phrase we cannot spell, much less understand, because a concrete blessing for so trite a tragedy – if the loss of a bit of breath and snot can be so called – would seem overblown. *Better to use a foreign phrase.* This *na-mu-a-mi-da-bu-tsu* is based on Sanskrit and is written in Chinese characters beginning with "south-not" (*namu*) and ending in "buddha" (*butsu*). The in-between part is not so easy. We shall skip it. Suffice it to say that it is chanted syllabet by syllabet and the whole phrase can be translated in so many ways it doesn't matter. From my Kenkyusha dictionary:

> "I sincerely believe in Amitabha.
> "Save us, merciful Buddha!
> "May he [his soul] rest in peace!
> "Glory to [whatever sutra name is inserted]

My first six translations of Issa's poem all assume the *third* of these meanings, where the nebulous phrase blesses the dead fly. *Many Japanese I have asked think the second as likely:*

old testament buddhism

each fly hit
is chased by a prayer, god
don't hit me!

sinners

with each fly
we swat, we cry
god save us!

mea culpa

for each fly
i swat, a prayer:
may god have mercy!

a killer's prayer

for each fly
swatted, a plea: heaven
have mercy *on me!*

Or, maybe it is better not to think the prayer is for either the fly or the fly-swatter but for both and all in our *killing-field*-of-a-world. As two correspondents point out, since part of Pureland belief is that we and others are ultimately one, *blessing the fly (that its soul speeds over) is good for the karma of the swatter, too.* I leave further interpretation and poetic permutation of "I," "he," "she," or "we," as you like, to the reader. The "God save us!" may be Japanned to "merciful buddha!" or Englished all the way to "Sweet Jesus!" There is no end to the creative paraverse.

引導を渡して呉れと後れ蝿　痾窮
indô o watashite kure to okurebae – ∀Q 2001/08/27
(pull-road[death instructions] give please [says] dying/defeated-fly)

coup de gráce

a benediction
please, says the dying
musca maledicta

finally swatted
a brave *musca maledicta*
gets last rites

An *indô* is "the last words addressed by the priest to a deceased person's soul at a funeral;" this "for guidance in passage to the other world." In my case, it would be hopeless, for I cannot remember directions *alive* and hardly think death would improve my memory! The *indô* can idiomatically mean the *coup de gráce*. The Japanese conjunction *to* serves to indicate something was said without using the anthropomorphic verb "to say." Still, this is a silly *ku.* It's bad enough for a fly to talk, but a dead fly? 痾窮 *aka* ∀Q, , says it is his early-stage work, i.e., *juvenilia.* I suppose it was juvenile of me to have included it in this book, but if ∀Q was brave enough to post it, I could hardly not include it here.

Back to an olde haiku:

数珠くりて蝿打人の片手かな　雨軒
juzu kurite hae utsu hito no kata te kana – ukan (?)
(prayerbeads counting, fly-hits/hitting person's one hand!/'tis)

prayer beads
wrapped around one hand
swatting flies

counting beads
the one hand of a man
swatting flies

Here, there is no supplication of flies or blessing or mercy-on-me *namuamidabutsu.* That would make it more acceptable to the modern school of objective haiku, but it is not quite so clean in Japanese as in my translation because of the strong focus on one hand, suggesting there is some particular meaning in the juxtiposition.

南無阿弥陀仏南無阿弥陀仏南無阿弥陀仏南無阿弥陀仏南無阿弥陀仏南無阿弥陀仏

Before Issa
***Namuamidabutsu* in haiku**

Pre-Issa *namuamidabutsu* haiku not fly-ku:

落花を南無あみだ仏とゆふべ哉　守武
rakka o namuamidabutsu to yûbe kana – moritake d.1549
(falling-flowers-to, *namuamidabutsu* should-say/evening!)

night falls
so do the cherry-blossoms
namuamidabutsu

This early haiku plays on *yûbe,* either "should say," and/or "evening." Written in phonetic syllabary rather than Chinese characters, *yûbe* is both a homograph and a homophone. Strange enough, I only came to like and, perhaps, appreciate this poem after the above translation popped into mind. [The original poem directs the *namu....* to the blossoms, but both the Buddha and Saigyô (1117-90), the ancient poet-monk most beloved by Bashô managed to pop out of this world in a pink blizzard. So this may be an eulogy, rather than just a days-and-seconds=petals-tick away, "there-but-for-the-grace-of-god-go-I" type of poem.

Bashô also combined blossoms with prayer. The only problem with it is that I am not sure what it means.

世に盛る花にも念仏申しけり　芭蕉
yo ni sakaru hana ni mo nenbutsu môshi-keri – bashô
(world-in-bloom/thriving flowers-to also/even prayers raised)

living large
he even has a prayer
for the blossoms

Nenbutsu is a noun referring to mumbling the words *namuamidabutsu,* telling beads and other Buddhist invocations. The above reading follows the idea of a wining sumo wrestler who, in a poem of Issa's, takes care not to step on a single bug. If the unstated subject is an old man, and we choose to read the *sakaru* as referring to his thriving in this world as well as the cherry, the "living large" (black slang for *living high on the hog*) might be changed to "still alive." But the *sakaru* or "thriving" seems to work more smoothly if it is assumed to modify the entire 12 syllabets that follow:

the current rage:
now they even say prayers
for cherry blossoms

This is possible because *yo-ni-sakaru* can mean that something is fashionable or faddish. For something to *sakaru* is for it "to epidemic" (Something, I fear, we have no verb for!). Bashô may well be describing the growing strength of some Buddhist sect, or, less likely, Buddhist corruption, for the prostitutes of Yoshiwara were known as cherry-blossoms. But the humble verb for the prayer *saying* (*môshi*) implies timidity or humility hardly found in such people.

to the beautiful
flowers of the world, too
yes, i do pray

Yoshida Kenkô wrote that it was permissible for men to enjoy the beauty of flowers (generally meaning that of cherry trees) for they did not engender lasting desire or have consequence (children), but even that appreciation for nature was seen as counterproductive in that it drew our attention away from the real world, i.e. that of religion. Did Bashô feel compassion even for the beauty? I like the above reading, though it may be mine alone.

not only for the dead and dying

i have prayed
for flowers in the pink
of life, too.

why wait?

blooming cherries
of the world, to you, too
our prayers.

pity the living!

to blossoms
in full bloom, too
an invocation

The new twist in this interpretation is in Bashô's performing such an invocation, or prayer, for the souls of the voluptuous cherry in full bloom – in Japanese *sakaru* is also used to describe cats in heat – rather than the scattering petals. Buddhist prayer, unlike Shinto prayer, was, after all meant to address the problems of the dead and dying.

gratitude

the old man
even blesses blossoms
on the tree

an old man
i even bless the pride
of blossoms

aging

ah, do i now
chant my prayers even
for blossoms

A Japanese Bashô expert writes the poem is a chuckle at those old people who have a habit of saying their *namuamidabutsu's* whenever they encounter anything beautiful or find some other reason to be thankful for something. (Satô Takenobu: *Bashô Kushû*). So the three above readings are the most likely ones, though the reader is warned that I bent the second a bit out of shape with that "pride."

~~~~~~

Good God, where have all the flies gone?

Another *nenbutsu* poem takes us back to our subject:

念仏や蝿うつ老の口すさみ　秀蘭　（？）
nenbutsu ya hae utsu oi no kuchizusami – shûran
(invocations! fly-swatting elder's mouth-habit)

lord have mercy!

a prayer stuck
in the mouth of an elder
swatting flies.

namuamidabutsu?

habitually
in the fly-swatter's old mouth
a prayer.

In Issa's case, prayers were not reserved for flies. In fact, he wrote a poem about a *flea* years before his fly-swatting prayer: "With the mouth that bit a flea: *namuamidabutsu*" (*nomi kanda kuchi de namuamida [butsu] kana* 蚤噛ンダ口でなむあみだ[仏]哉). What makes Issa's *namuamidabutsu* for flies (pg. 50-51) an especially good haiku despite being only marginally original is the "one fly: one prayer" idea that gives it a crisp and refreshing quality. Issa would have been a superb copy-writer.

Let us close on an esoteric note, with a question posed by Sôin.

再現＝世の中は何に喩へんなむ阿弥陀　宗因
yo-no-naka wa nani ni tatohen namuamida
(the world? to what shall [we] metaphor [it]? *namuamida*)

big question

what oh what
can stand for our world?
namuamida!

what in the world
can stand for our world?
namuamida!

南無阿弥陀仏南無阿弥陀仏南無阿弥陀仏南無阿弥陀仏南無阿弥陀仏南無阿弥陀仏

I have played up the *namuamidabutsu* stuff because of the Buddhist element in Issa's and many other fly-ku, and because it is a good foil to the excessive attention given to Zen alone. But, balancing itself requires balance and here is the perfect poem to even up this chapter.

蝿打つてしばらく安し四畳半　子規 明治28
hae utte shibaraku yasushi yojôhan – shiki (d.1902)
(fly struck, a while peaceful four-and-a-half mats.)

the fly killed
for a while, peace comes
to the small room

This translation follows the original syntax precisely. To match the tense of the verb,
~~~~~~

the order of the fly and the swat/kill would have to be reversed as per Blyth, from whom I borrowed the "small room."

killing the fly
for some time, the small room
is peaceful

(my centering and de-punctuation)

> A perfectly natural state of irritation and desperation is followed by a sense of peace and calm, both these states being illusory, but the portrayal of illusory states may itself be poetry, for
>
> Every error is an image of truth.
>
> – trans. etc. Blyth (HAIKU vol.3)

Even today, most Japanese measure floor-size in standardized tatami mats. The 4 ½ mat size mentioned in Shiki's original became slang for a typical small room lived in by a bachelor, a poor poet, etc.. In the original poem, it works to create a snappy feeling something like the following:

the fly dead
for a while, four mats
are pacified

But, not quite so martial as this senryû-esque paraverse suggests! Blyth translated the heart of the poem perfectly. I would only add that I like it for its emotional honesty, but prefer the less well known *look-upon-the-mountain* poem of Issa's (pg. 46), which leaves us guessing as to the exact nature of his feelings if any.

..

~~~~~~

The Soul of a Fly. In the *Foreword*, I made it clear that Japanese, unlike Tibetan Buddhists, do not take all "souls" seriously. But, this does not mean the souls are ignored. As explained in my book about a creature made of smart material without a brain (*Rise, Ye Sea Slugs!* re: sea cucumber haiku), Japanese like to repeat a proverb to the effect that "every worm has its soul," heart, will-power, or "gumption" (*Tread on a worm and it will turn.*) I became aware I forgot to mention this when I read the following haiku (posted in time for the first revision by AQ) by Kain (?): 魂を入れて蝿這ふやまた打てリ」花因 The word-for-word: soul putting-in (i.e. with)fly crawls!/: again hit (*tamashi o irete hae hau ya mata uteri*).

"That fly puts / its heart into crawling / hit it again," or, "That fly / *will* crawl on, again / i hit."

I think the haiku is pretty modern because it is carefully neutral. We do not know if this means the poet puts the fly out of its mercy or, seeing it has a chance of surviving, gives the *coup de grace.* Just the facts, Ma'am, just the ..
~~~~~~

VI

The *Crime* and the *Punishment*

fly-swatting, morality and how it is expressed

蝿打やおのか報いをなめし革　石水 33
hae-uchi ya onoga mukui o nameshikawa – sekisui (mistake?)
蝿打や報ひをかへす革+享（なめし）皮　言水
hae-uchi ya onoga mukui o kaesu nameshikawa – gensui (d.1722)
(fly-swatter:/! its own reward/retribution bears(?) tanned leather)

the fly-swatter
you reap what you sowed
a tanned hide

The Buddhist sensibility with respect to taking life may be expressed in other ways than by citing prayer. There is reincarnation, upward or downward depending on one's karma. I *think* the above poem means the following, which I shall express without the *mukui* (reward/retribution) in the original:

the fly-flap

the ox swats flies
dies, and tanned, once again
swats flies

That is to say, the original *might* mean the tail of the ox kills flies which results in retribution against its owner. Call it a convoluted form of poetic justice where the fly-swatting animal ends up a fly-swatter rather than a fly, as might be expected. There is no question that the function of tails was on everyone's mind. We have read Issa's lamb-walk to the slaughter where such was implied and we have much clearer poems such as this one that today would only be written by a child:

馬の尾やをのが身につく蝿払　丸石　坂東太郎
uma no o ya onoga mi ni tsuku haebarai – kyûseki (1679)
(*horse's/horses' tail/s:/! own body stuck-to fly-shoo*)

the horse tail:
fixed to your own body
a fly-swatter!

But, how many flies are actually killed (as opposed to merely injured) by tails? Does anyone know? The *hae-barai* in the original means a fly-shoo or a fly-whisk, but try finding such words in the dictionary! Once 'fly-flap' was a common English word for strips of leather or other devices used to shoo-off flies, but today it seems that all we have is *swatters*. So, if these tails were not so deadly, why such retribution? I think there is another, sadder possibility. Ikkyû, the Zen abbot known for his pranks (see ch.7, "The Scatological Sea Slug" in *Rise, Ye Sea Slugs!*) and knowing the opposite sex, wrote Chinese-style poems to the members of each sex. The female one is a pure celebration of the contradictions of this damned yet blessed place. The male one is not so happy, for as we all know, pride comes before fall and fall it does. To be precise, "it" ends up a leather rag (「。。老去革頭巾」). I do not know exactly what such a rag is or was used for, but it was doubtless soft and unsuitable for poking into holes. In English, "tanned" implies a color, but the Japanese *nameshi* evokes something different altogether: the leather, once stiff, has been broken and softened. *Karma* experienced for one's own actions within one's lifetime was no more common in Japan than heavenly rewards on earth in the West, but it was not unheard of and Issa, as already mentioned, told stories about the dire consequences on the member of a man who killed copulating snakes . . . .

years of swatting
the payback in hand: as floppy
as a fly-flap

But I may be thinking too much (The small font reflects my lack of confidence). Maybe the idea is that a person vigorously swatting flies literally tans his own hide. In other words, years of fly swatting explains the dark skin of the old poet. Santôka, one of my favorite 20th century haijin, put it like this:

自省
蠅を打ち蚊を打ち我を打つ　山頭火
[jisei]hae o uchi ka o uchi ware o utsu – santôka (d.1940)
("introspective" fly[obj] hit, mosquito[obj] hit, myself hit)

the hit-man
(an introspective)

swatting flies
mosquitoes and
my self

..

This abbreviated Aesop's fable was first written about 2000 years ago by Phaedras: "A fly bit the bare pate of a bald man, who in endeavoring to crush it gave himself a hard slap. Then said the fly jeeringly, "You wanted to revenge the sting of a tiny insect with death; what will you do to yourself, who have added insult to injury?" (If it was a horse-fly, though, I feel for the bald man! A horse-fly is a hundred times worse than a mosquito. The flies Moses and God plagued the Eygptians with is translated as *abu*=horse-fly.) Aesop and Phaedres wrote a lot, but Santôka only wrote what was needed. Needed for him, perhaps, but in this case, not quite enough for me to understand, for the *ku* seems purely description, yet the caption, *Jisei* (introspection/self-criticism) implies something more. Did Santôka mean that his lack of self-control with respect to bugs demeaned himself? Or did he, rather, mean to criticize his (well-known) self-destructive tendency? Or, was it not at all criticism but merely an observance of his superego at work? Some haiku can be as hard to swat as the wariest fly.

人間の道徳蝿と相容れず 剣花坊
ningen no dôtoku hae to ai-irezu – kenkabô (19-20c senryû)
(humans' morality: fly-with blend/include-not)

Flies / Are excluded /From human morality – trans. Blyth

incompatible

human morality
has no place
for flies

why we need zen

flies make
a mess of human
morality

Here, I un-parse Blyth for he is way off the mark. The senryû is clearly about incompatibility (rather than exclusion) and is a quite sophisticated statement. It is not that flies do things humans cannot countenance, but that *flies*, by annoying people, force them to swat out and *that* is a stain on a moral system where hatred and the taking of life was officially frowned upon. *Flies make us betray ourselves.* They make it almost impossible for a Buddhist to be a *good* Buddhist. Issa, as we have seen, wrote about striking a *hotoke,* a statue of Buddha or a corpse, while swatting a fly. Keigu paraverses in a more purely philosophical vein including Kenkabô's idea:

蝿打てば即ち仏打ちにけり　敬愚
hae-uteba sunawachi hotoke uchi-ni-keri – keigu
(fly-strike-if/when, namely, buddha hit [emphatic/perfect])

when we swat
a fly, we swat the face
of buddha!

Another senryû by Kenkabô, also given by Blyth, helps show what his last poem was really talking about. It is also examples something rare: *a perfect translation.*

死ぬことがきらいな親爺蝿を打ち　剣花坊
shinu koto ga kirai na oyaji hae o uchi – kenkabô (c.19-20c)
(dying-thing hates geezer fly/flies[obj] hits)

The old chap
Who doesn't want to die,
Swats the fly.

trans. blyth (centered)

Blyth calls this "a deep satire on the selfishness, insensitiveness, and lack of fellow – feeling in so many human beings." I see it more as a pitiful portrayal of an angry man, a man unhappy with his fate. Someone at peace with himself would be more lenient. It also shows the dilemma all who live must face: life is not fair. We all would live, yet who among us has never swatted a fly? Whether killing flies was a sin or not, many Japanese did not think it a good thing to do. So reprobation was unavoidable. As one pre-Issa poem puts it,

蝿打てあとにはなかめられにけり　千那
hae uchite ato ni wa nagamerare-ni-keri – senna (d.1723)
(fly hitting/hit afterward-as-for, glared at [emphatic/ with finality])

i swat
a fly and get
an eyeful

reprobation

i swat a fly
and end up with
an eyeful

instant karma

the fly-swatter
is quickly paid back:
a long glare

the fly lies still
and now they glare
at me instead

Senna is known for another subtler (but equally senryûesque) haiku of cause-and-effect, where frogs in the field sold to a neighbor keep him up at night. "*Swatted* a fly" and "*got* an eyeful" might be more exact, but I prefer the story-teller's present. English lacks grammar to make an action irrevocable, or emphasize it by exaggerating its finality. "End up with," and "get" are makeshift ways to do what Japanese does more easily with a variety of suffixes such "*~shimau*" or the elegant "*~ni-keri.*" (Not the same as the plain "*~keri*" emphatic.) English-speaking folk have evolved ways to fill in this lamentable gap. The expression "for good" is one:

the fly-lover

i swat a fly
and get stared at
for good

Another is the "done ~" of hillbilly and black English. The United States Poet Laureate Robert Hass translates a haiku by Issa using the *S* word ("Writing shit about new snow / for the rich / is not art"), but we are more lenient towards bad *words* than bad *grammar*, even when we have no good grammar to substitute. *Done* don't work:

i hit a fly
and done got me
an eyeful

Over a 100 years later, Shiki paraversed with two changes. First, the victim is specifically an *autumn fly.* That is a definite improvement, for me, at least, because it is hard to feel for the summer flies, faceless in their multitude.

秋の蝿叩いて見れば叩かるる　子規 明治28
aki no hae tataite-mireba tatakaruru – shiki (d.1902)
(fall-fly/flies striking-try/if, [I am] struck/criticized myself)

the censure

"it was gonna die
anyway, so why oh why
an autumn fly?"

the table turned

an autumn fly
as i try to whack one
i am whacked

Kikko told me the first (left-side) translation that assumes "struck" is used idiomatically for "criticized" is unlikely because the grammar favors simultaneous over sequential action, and Shiki, who had not been ill long, was taking out his frustration on flies *and probably got bopped on the back of his head by Soseki* (the great novelist found on the 1000-yen bill) because he was staying at his house at the time. Shiki's illness turned out to be permanent and enough of his haiku were explicitly sick-bed poems that when I surveyed 100 Tokyo Imperial University students in 1997-8, the most common description of Shiki was "a sick man." Sure enough, he left us a sick-man's *fly-ku* dealing with the subject of this chapter:

蝿を打ち蚊を焼き病む身罪深し　子規 明治30
hae o uchi ka o yaki yamu mi tsumi bukashi – shiki (d.1902)
(fly/flies[obj] swat, mosquitoes[obj] burn sick-body's sin-heavy)

burning mosquitoes
swatting flies – the weight
of a sick-man's sins

burnt mosquitoes
swatted flies – how sinful
are the sick!

i burn mosquitoes
i swat flies – to be sick
is a sinful thing.

killing houseflies
and mosquitoes, a sickman's
sins are heavy

Sickness is hot and stagnant. Even when it doesn't stink, it draws mosquitoes, fleas and flies as surely as a magnet does iron filings. But unlike filings, and unlike the unfortunate invalid, these pests (even flies, welcome one at a time, but irksome in droves) are free to fly off. I do not know if anyone really gets jealous over the freedom of a bug – unless it is Issa on the open mating of butterflies (that in another book!). Let us just say Shiki was powerless and bored – not mentally, but *physically* bored – and what better medicine for that than swatting flies? Each crisp and successful whack is probably as good for our immune systems as a hearty laugh. Keigu would put it like this:

病床一句　蝿うつや罪積もっても気の薬　敬愚
[byôtoko-ikku] hae-uchi ya tsumi tsumotte mo ki no kusuri – keigu
([sickbed one-poem] fly-swatting! though sins/pinches pile up-even, spirit-medicine)

sick power

swatting flies
oh, sinful medicine
for the soul

sin, sin, sin

swatting flies
what helps my spirit might
damn my soul

dear medicine

swatting flies
my spirit must borrow
from my soul

life's balance

each fly i swat
helps my spirit
hurts my soul

one life at a time

i feel good
with every fly that i swat
in this life

The first line of the last poem jumped into my ear straight from the soul-man's hit-song! While Shiki didn't put his ideas into haiku this obvious, he, too, had a hyperlogical mind and not surprisingly found a way to *rationalize* some of his sick-bed killings:

愛憎は蝿打つて蟻に与（興）へけり　子規 明治 31
aizô-wa hae utte ari ni ataekeri – shiki (d.1902)
(lovehate=partiality-as-for: fly/ies swat, ant/s-to give[emphatic/perfect])

biased me!
feeding ants the flies
that i kill

favoritism

i swat
a fly and give it
to the ants

partiality

swatting
a fly to feed
an ant

alms

life's unfair!
i kill flies and take care
ants get them

Any reader who doesn't care for the liberty I take with the original by cutting off part of the poem and putting it into a title, is free to reparse the first and third translations so that the title becomes the first line and the first line is combined with the second. You may also change the tense as you wish. I favor the present, for its lasting quality, but also like the past for its testimonial style realism. However, if the second reading were, say, "I *swatted* / a fly and *gave* it / to the ants," I would retitle it *"Confession."*

蝿打てば即ち蟻の罷り出づ　川端茅舎
hae uteba sunawachi ari no makari-izu – kawabata bôsha (d.1941)
(fly swatting/swat-when, then/automatically ants come[boldly/grandiously] out)

swat a fly
and out roll
the ants

The life of Bôsha's poem, matter-of-fact in the manner thought best for much of the 20th century, is the verb *makari,* which I tried to match with "roll." But Shiki's last *ku* evokes more memories and is, thus, better *for me*. As a boy, I remember giving live bugs to ants to see whether they could escape and dead ones to see just how much ants could carry. In retrospect, I should have painted one side of a butterfly wing like a flag. And I caught beetles, more than I needed, to feed my turtles, i.e. watch them fight over and pull apart the struggling bugs. This mentality deserves a senryû: *the kind boy / gives his snapping turtles / live beetles.* Enough confessing for now. An older haiku which Shiki probably read – I found it in his categorized haiku anthology – suggests the possibility of such feeding.

蝿打になるる雀の子飼かな　河瓢（猿箕続）
hae-uchi ni naruru suzume no kogai kana – Kahyô (~1700)
(fly-swatting/er-to accustomed sparrow-chick/s-raising!/ 'tis)

(paraversion 1)

their bird-food!
sparrow chicks grow used to
my fly-swatter

(correctranslation)

fly-swatting
the pet sparrow grows
accustomed to it

(paraversion 2)

orphan sparrow
opens its mouth hearing
the fly-swatter

To quote Ivan Morris, "women and children of the leisured class often kept baby sparrows and other little birds as pets." Here is an item from the *"Adorable Things"* list in his translation of Sei Shônagon's *Pillow Book:*

> A baby sparrow that comes hopping up when one imitates the squeak of a mouse; or again, when one has tied it with a thread around its leg and its parents bring insects or worms and pop them in its mouth – delightful.

By the time the above haiku was written, I would think the friendliest sparrows had long since been eaten (Japanese shish-kebabed them) and parents were no longer so quick to come into the house to feed their chicks. If so, then, it would stand to reason that flies were swatted and given to the chicks. It is also the case that the time the bird would be growing up, early summer would be the time for fly-swatting to start.

~~~~~~

But, we have had humans enough in this chapter. There are other fly-killers out there:

蝿取て家路に帰る小蜘哉　木舟　古今句選
hae torite ieji ni kaeru kogumo kana – mokusen? (1777～鑑 1784～集)
(fly-taken, home-road-on returns/ing small-spider!/?/'tis)

fly captured,
a small spider on the path
back home

carrying a fly
a homeward-bound
little spider

a little spider
with its fly heading
back home

I have run into this poem by a haijin not even well enough known to be in my *Haikujinmei-jiten* (dictionary of haiku poets) many times – why I do not know – and I never fail to enjoy it. There are more good fly-hunting spider *ku* (eg. "A clump of grass / between flies, hunting-spiders / groom themselves" 草むらや蝿取蜘の身づくろひ　中村史邦 (I added the "between flies")), but none grab me like the above poem. The word *ieji,* "home[ward]-path" makes us feel warm because we can not help but identify with that spider. We all have our homeward paths and some of them go back to our unclear past and that allows the spider's tiny trail and ours to superimpose. I dare say not one of us think about the fly for we are all so happy to be heading home, with a full pack of provisions.

蝿曳くる夕日の卓を蟻の列　リチャード・ライト
hae hikuru yûhi no taku o ari no retsu – Richard Wright, trans. keigu
(fly[obj] drag evening sun's table ant's line [in Japanese, the *teburu-kurosu* is too long to use])

across the tablecloth
ants are dragging a dead fly
in the evening sun

richard wright
(my decap and centering)

Flies don't need us or spiders to kill them. They are quite capable of dying on their own (Or, so I imagine. Perhaps a fly-expert would be kind enough to supply a gloss about their sicknesses – *do they ever go blind and run into trees?* for example – and what old age is to a fly and so forth for the next edition.). And, as Wright reminds us, there is always someone else happy to carry them off for recycling. Once, that was true for us, too.
~~~~~~

蝿蝿蝿蝿蝿蝿蝿蝿蝿蝿蝿蝿蝿蝿蝿蝿蝿蝿蝿蝿蝿蝿蝿蝿蝿蝿蝿蝿蝿蝿蝿蝿蝿蝿蝿蝿

The V*anishing* F*ly*.

100 feet away from the window of this rented apartment where I live and write, there is a tree like the one by the house I was raised we called simply "the tree." When it was full of tiny purple bloom, the bees were so thick I heard them coming home from school a hundred or two hundred yards away. This spring the bloom was just like Rachel Carson predicted, *silent*. No bees. This island is full of rich people, *money*. But, there is no *honey*. Worse, I have not seen a fly *for months*. Today, as I stood in the rubble of ex-president Nixon's house (a Mexican friend dragged me and my wheels = golf-cart = there to rummage) a plane flew only a few hundred feet overhead and dumped insecticide on me. *Talk about ridiculous.* On Key Biscayne, if you are stuck by a mosquito, you are supposed to call in a plane bomb them. Needless to say, that is *why* there are no flies. I would prefer a plane flew over dumping out flies and bees and butterflies and lightning bugs and bats to eat the mosquitoes . . . .

And, now, even as I write, the fumes of the insecticide bother my nose and eyes. Everyone says it is *my* choice because I insist upon living in real air rather than the cold conditioned stuff made ultimately by destroying the natural environment and killing our descendents (That is what our hogging of fossil fuel and other scarce resources means in the long run. Had we only decided "no AC and no Cars!" 50 years ago, engineers and the architects might have helped make paradise rather than ruin it). In other words, I am the only person on the island perverted enough to keep his windows open in the summer.

蝿もへり蝿虎も減りけるよ　藤田湘子 (contemp.)
hae mo heri haetorigumo mo herikeru yo fujita shôshi

flies grow scarce
and fly-hunting spiders
grow scarce, too

I could not find a place to slip in the colloquial twist, the *yo* at the end suggesting that the haiku may be quoting the words of an expert asked about fly-hunting spiders. Instead, let me play slightly with the poem:

flies grow scarce
likewise the hunting-spiders
who hunt flies

I hope to receive a white paper on the global situation of flies and another on that of the flies of Japan, for the next edition. (さて、再版前に、専門家による世界の蝿の状況、又は、日本の蝿の全貌・見込みの欄外注を、頼みます！)

蝿蝿蝿蝿蝿蝿蝿蝿蝿蝿蝿蝿蝿蝿蝿蝿蝿蝿蝿蝿蝿蝿蝿蝿蝿蝿蝿蝿蝿蝿蝿蝿蝿蝿蝿蝿

ポツクリと往きたし手には蝿叩　痾窮
pokkuri to yukitashi te ni wa hae tataki – akyû (ukimidô fly-kukai)
(instantly going/dying-want/wish-hand-in, fly-swatter)

wanting to go
just like that, he raises
a fly-swatter

wanting to go
just like that, she swats
a fly like that

fly-swatter
in hand, wanting to go
just like that

the 'go-quickly' temple

coming back
from pokkuri, she picks up
a fly-swatter

swatter-as-god

perhaps flies
also pray to go
quickly

The senryû about the "old chap that doesn't want to die," and the whole chapter forgets something important. Death is not always the enemy, so killing is not always sinful. Akyû writes that there are even *pokkuri-dera* temples specializing in prayers to "go" quickly! (Japanese have temples (*tera*) specializing in this or that. Easy child-birth, passing exams . . .). The last two poems are paraverses, not translations. *Pokkuri* (immediately) is a splendid example of psychological mimesis, a word that sounds like what it means.

○ ○

the *Zen* of swatting

putting your heart into your hand

蝿打て共に生死を軽くせん　幻吁
hae uchite tomo ni seishi o karuku sen – genku (d. 1685)
(fly/ies [i/we] swatting, together-with life-death[obj] lightly make-would)

swatting flies
i'd make light of both
life and death

Since *seishi* "lifedeath" is a single word, the *tomo,* or "together/both" draws out the two parts that might otherwise be taken for granted. The *sen* may be taken in a prescriptive way.

let's play with
both life and death
let's swat flies

A less likely, but not impossible reading takes the *tomo* to mean both the flies and the poet. Like Montaigne and his cat, they play with each other, but for more serious stakes:

fly-swatting
the flies and i make
light of life

Stakes? you remonstrate. *The fly may risk his life, but what about the poet?* Well, that depends upon which life, which *world,* is on your mind. The poet was a Zen priest. He probably didn't believe in reincarnation. Then, again, he didn't *not* believe either. Who knows but that the dead fly turns Buddha and the swatter turns fly?

swatting flies
we forget it's a matter
of life and death

Or, is the poet sitting with an ailing, possibly dying, friend – often the scene of fly swatting? In that case, the *tomo* becomes the "we" above, meaning the two men, and takes on deeper significance.

gods-R-us

with each fly
we swat we play with
life and death

This translation expands too much with "each fly" and only my title keeps it fresh. If folk Buddhism taboos killing, Zen would be above it. Blyth relishes relating stories of cats cut in half for catechism. *What could be lighter than that?* Is the story true? *Do you really want to know?* Then, Zen is not for you. While Zen is beyond taboo, Zen priests, like other Buddhists, are more likely to *shoo* than *swat* flies. But, it is a good guess that when a Zen priest *does* swat he *swats*. "There is *swatting* and there is *swatting*" cannot be Japanesed, but Zen comprehends it well enough.

蝿うちや上手になりし我心　大江丸
haeuchi ya jôzu ni narishi waga kokoro – ôemaru (d.1805)
(fly-swatting better/skilled became, my heart/mind)

swatting flies
my art improves
from the heart

The Zen of Archery or Motorcycle Mechanics is not as *bad* as the Zen of Fly-swatting. But, like Kikaku dreaming his flea-bites are wounds in battle, I suspect a martial allusion for that would be more *haikai,* more sacrilegious than evoking a religion that enjoys sacrilege: *i.e.* the Zen of Swordmanship (See William Scott Wilson's introduction to his translation of Yagyû's *The Life-giving Sword*).

swatting flies / i'm better, thanks / to my mind
fly-swatting / some things improve / head-first
getting better / at swatting flies is all / in your mind

..
Evidently, *my* mind has not made much progress, for I just cannot settle on a translation of this poem that, itself, does not specify the relationship between "my mind/heart" and the poet's improved swatting percentage. Some of my takes diverge too far from the haiku to be called *bona-fide* translations. They are what I call *paraverses,* inspired by but not faithful to the original. As long as I'm sinning, one more:

my mind
marks its progress
swatting flies

If Genku was Kikaku's Zen-master and, judging from the above haiku, had some influence on his philosophical style, Ôemaru was important to Issa and flourished slightly earlier than Seibi, a wealthy Edo merchant who was Issa's main employer and teacher. Their views on fly-swatting and shooing seem very similar, and Zen.

蝿はらい心の外にものもなし　成美
haebarai kokoro[gokoro] no hoka ni mono mo nashi – seibi (d. 1816)
(fly-switch/shooing, heart/mind-outside-of thing/s even not)

shooing flies
we think about
nothing else

In Japanese-English translation, the heart/mind problem means something quite different than it does for philosophy. The single character pronounced *kokoro* (or, in combination with other characters, *shin*) – which has been repeatedly voted the most popular character by Japanese – fuses heart and mind, or, rather does not separate them. I am very happy with how I avoided the problem by ditching the mind/heart for a verb in the above translation.

single-minded

shooing flies
nothing else remains
in the heart

..

I am not sure what Seibi's intent is. Is it simply to depict the way men chasing flies lose themselves? Or, should we add to ourselves, and *that* is not a bad thing! Women may go after flies because they feel they are dirty, but that is more a hate thing, or a fetish. Men do not hate flies. They need to lose themselves in aiming at things. Nothing is so relaxing as throwing or shooting at targets, especially if they move. Sighting devices ruin this benefit. Thank God, fly-swatters do not come so equipped. But who can get off on shooing flies? It is not at all satisfying, for aim is not involved and they come right back.

zen

nothing exists
outside of the mind
shooing flies

Since I am often unsure of what my own translation means, it stands to reason that I would have trouble with reading the originals which, for all I know, sometimes escaped the understanding of their authors. One finds Nothingness in Buddhism as the single character pronounced *mu;* but, for all practical purposes, Japanese lacks the equivalent of the "nothing" so commonly used in English, as if it were something. I mean, can "nothing" *ever* exist?

emptiness is
the mind of a man
shooing flies

I love aphorisms and when I find the kernel of one in any haiku, turn on the stove, shake it up and turn it into popcorn. For some reason, this reminds me that *flies* and *fly-swatting* are, we ought not forget, summer themes. Is there not something of summer in this mindlessness?

summer time
(and the living is easy)

nothing else
in the heart, just
shoo fly, shoo!

But, for all the above, the grammar of the poem suggested a *fly switch* itself and not the shooing.

no fly switch
in the world outside
of your mind

Berkeley is too obvious for Zen. After writing the above, I went back over my notebooks and found that the poem was "made for a picture of a fly switch" (usually animal hair bundled and tied on a stick, properly called a *hossu* 払子の絵を書てこれに物かけといふ人に). Trying harder to keep the switch as the unquestioned subject:

the fly switch
hurts no flies but mind
has made it so

That is the fly switch equivalent of a right-wing Zen saying: *guns don't kill people, people do*. As haiku, it is no better than the last.

~~~~~~

I was flailing away when translator friend Mihoko saved Seibi's poem for me by observing it could be read as a praise of seihin, *something we might call* immaculate poverty, *the ideal state in which a sage (or haiku poet) lives. One finds inventories in* haibun *which might be called proof of poverty, where a poet might boast of owning nothing but a brush, ink, paper, a pot and half-a-sack of rice (obtained as a gift). I suppose poems could be read rather than written down and a poet could eat out.*

a fly-switch
everything else is
in his head

It is fun to imagine a poet's hut with nothing but a fly switch – possible in the summer but not the winter – and what is fun to imagine is usually the correct reading of a haiku. My other translations are almost surely wrong. Moreover, my own belated research showed that the hossu, *or fly switch, was a standard symbol of the Buddhist preacher inherited from Chinese Zen. The idea, which will be elaborated in the* Shoo Fly, Shoo! *chapter, is that the* sine qua non *of the meditative life is the ability to shoo away myriad everyday distractions. Instead of a guardian deity, Zen has the* hossu.
~~~~~~

a fly-switch
nothing else outside
of the heart

Switch may be exchanged by flap and if we read shoo *as a verb, in which case it modifies* kokoro (*which would then be pronounced* gokoro) *the poem may be read:*

..

nothing at all
outside of the desire
to shoo flies

Desire is, of course, bad. *But what about* the desire to rid oneself of desire? *One reason for my inability to guess what was what (if it is what was what) was that my reading of Seibi's intent was influenced by the well-known poem of his that follows.*

~~~~~~

蝿打てつくさん(つくさむ)とおもふこゝろかな　成美
hae utte tsukusan (tsukamu) to omou kokoro kana – seibi (d. 1816)
(fly/ies hit/ting, exhaust-would thinks heart/mind tis)

Killing flies,
I begin to wish
To annihilate them all.

– trans. Blyth

Swatting flies
There comes the urge
To kill them all.

– David

..

This last comes from the internet: "Shiki.archive.9507: Re: "skinny cats" – rules and symbols." David (DL, you by any chance?) introduces it only as "a haiku (loosely translated);" but someone adds that it "is not a haiku, IMHO." My not so humble opinion says it *is*, for it reflects something Seibi may well have thought while swatting flies, a *bona fide* summer theme. IMHO does have a point, though. Without the first-person, which is, after all, not explicit in the original, David's translation approaches aphorism and the chuckle at the human condition called *senryû.* But, the truth is that there are many old Japanese haiku (by virtue of their being by haiku poets and in haiku collections) that could *also* be classified as *senryû* and vice versa. I can't help recall a certain potato chip advertisement and add a modern title:

"you can't kill only one"

swat a fly
and soon you would kill
all of them
~~~~~~

The underused first-person "you" (my term for it) is my favorite way to English an aphoristic haiku. It has the active feeling of the Japanese yet does not really specify the person.

open season on *musca maledicta*

swat one fly
and before you know it
the sky's the limit

If the government ever runs out of things to do and flies are an endangered species, it could always have us take out yearly licenses with bag limits for flies. Seriously, by hinting at a "season," I arguably increased the haiku quality of the poem.

killing flies
my mind desires total
annihilation

The oppressively high humidity of the Japanese summer could create a strong urge to shake off all sweat, all dirt . . . all flies. So maybe the season was there all along.

..

swatting a fly
my mind would clean
them all up

The verb translated above as "exhaust/annihilate," "*tsukusu,* is by no means limited to destructive activity. It is one of my favorite Japanese words, for *mono-wa-zukushi,* or "thing-exhausting" refers to the charming Japanese literary practice of listing types of things, such as "adorable things," "despicable things," "foolish things," etc.. This wonderful game of divergent creativity began in China – where it apparently became extinct before it got a name – and forms the heart of the *Pillow Book* of the outrageously stuck-up 10th Century diva of good taste, Sei Shônagon. Blyth wrote that Seibi describes "a blood-lust," a "tendency in human nature to go to extremes." I prefer to call it an *urge to be thorough* that in Japan, as mentioned in the Foreword, is strongest in cleanliness-related matters.

秋の蝿殺セドモ猶尽キヌカナ 子規　明治 34
aki no hae korosedomo nao tsukinu kana – shiki (d.1902)
(autumn fly/flies, kill [it/them] but exhaust-not !/ah/?)

autumn flies
you kill them and still
it doesn't end

Shiki's haiku is unclear as to whether he means that even killing fall flies is not the end of them or whether, for all the swatting that went on all summer long, they were still around in the Autumn. Lacking any indication of number leaves the haiku open to another, singular reading:

an autumn fly
i kill it but they
keep coming

But the larger problem is deciding exactly *what* does not end. Are we just talking flies? The "heart/mind" is not mentioned in Shiki's poem, but if he is playing off Seibi's poem, he may mean:

no satisfaction

though i kill
the autumn fly i cannot
kill my mind

Before Autumn has even finished filling her Cornucopia, the poet begins his spiritual hunkering down for Winter.

no closure

i kill
an autumn fly
but still
it is not over

..
It is hard to *amen* a world without end. It is also hard to find the Zen in this poem or the last several poems. Seibi confesses to being as far from enlightened as a man can get. And yet, just as an unbeliever – Recall the Lake Woebegone girl who was "a Lutheran atheist" (*because it was a Lutheran God she did not believe in*)? – stinks of the believer, Seibi's and Shiki's confessions are ultimately Zen. Would the desire to swat a fly *matter* to, say, a Christian? Kerouac aside, I think not.

蝿をうつ時は小き心哉　梅室
hae o utsu toki chiisaki kokoro kana – baishitsu (d. 1852)
(fly[obj] swat-when small heart/mind 'tis)

the focus

when swatting
a fly, how small
my mind

To Chinese, a "small heart" is a good thing, for it means to be cautious and the Chinese have traditionally put a positive value on timidity. But the Japanese think a "small heart" is a bad thing, something indicating a lack of courage and what we might call "small-mindedness" – this, despite their alleged tendency to concentrate on detail reflected by grammar that modifies down from large to small in such a remarkable manner (the *ocean's island's beach's crab* in one poem being the usual example) that even a Korean speaking a tongue with a similar syntax was inspired to write of the "shrinking mindset" of the Japanese (Lee O-young: *Chijimi shikô no nihonjin*: 1984. The English titles, "Smaller is Better" and "Compact Culture," fail to reflect the active nature of the original.). So we may guess that Baishitsu's poem is not a recipe for successful fly-killing but for critical introspection:

concentration

when i swat
my heart is as small
as the fly

Like so much in haiku, this introspective attitude goes back to one of the fathers of haiku, Teitoku, whose very name – for all his silly wordplay and risqué poems – has the character for "morality" in it. While the flies are not mentioned, could I leave out the following haiku?

~~~~~~

In retrospect, Yes, very easily, *for all three of my readings failed to find the heart of the haiku, which has nothing to do with Zen, or for that matter, haiku! I leave it in this chapter, for I have found a lesson to peg on the end.*

~~~~~~

蚤蚊をも殺さで殺せわが心　貞徳
nomi ka o mo korosa de korose waga kokoro – teitoku (1571-1653)
(fleas, mosquitoes[obj] too killing-not-with/ by, kill! my heart/mind)[?]

without killing
mosquitoes and fleas
kill my mind!

The tricky thing here is who utters the imperative "kill" *korose.* No one is mentioned. If Teitoku were only a Christian, we could make it "Lord, kill my mind!"

no bloodshed

oh, heart of mine!
kill yourself, not these
mosquitoes and fleas!

..

Since there are no postpositions (the Japanese equivalent of the preposition found in Indo-European languages), the heart/mind can be read as object *or* subject. A clear address to the heart is not found in the original, but the subjectlessness of the previous translation, while normal enough to pass unnoticed in Japanese, is just not quite right in English. No matter what the translator does something is betrayed. Let me make one more try, following the improbable reading of *korose* as an abbreviation of *koroseba,* "kill-if," which would mean "if I only could" or, by semantic extrapolation, "I would" (Some old songs used *~se* where *~seba* would seem likely). If you think it correct, call it a translation. If not, call it a paraverse:

'squitoes and fleas
how i would i could kill
without killing!

This reading, where the desire is not killed but admitted, seems less Buddhist but more Zen, both for its honesty and for its *koan* quality. But even, then, there is a maudlin concern for morality that is not Zen with a capital "Z." Some way or another, this chapter, that began with a haiku by a Zen priest, lost its way. Kyoshi, a healthy, happy man who some think deserves more credit than his friend Shiki for putting modern Japanese haiku on sound footing, can bring us back. The following poems were written toward the end of his long and productive life.

~~~~~~

But, first, let me set you straight on Teitoku's poem as I have been set straight by haiku friend, Hagizuki-san. Here is what it really *means:*

..

too sweet to kill
mosquitoes and fleas, please
kill my longing

As Hagizuki-san points out, it could mean "**you** who would not kill a mosquito or flea" or "you who look too sweet to kill a mosquito or flea." *Male artists enjoyed depicting women burning mosquitoes. Their expression, secretly glimpsed in the light, was not what one might expect in a gentle lover. Hence, without any stated subject, we can guess Teitoku addresses a woman and has, shall we say, night-time thoughts. In ancient poetry, it was common to beg someone to "kill" one's love/longing (koi). One possible solution has been expressed best in English by Willie Nelson:* If you can't say you love me, say you hate me . . . ." *More commonly, the lovesick man or women wanted the other to meet and sleep with them* (*As a country song* not *by Willie Nelson puts it,* Let's burn up our passion and sweep up the ashes in the morning!) *and be done with it! Damn. I do not know anyone who has read more old Japanese love poems than me, and I knew well that haikai collections once included sections that were about* love and sex *rather than* seasons, *yet I failed to properly read Teitoku's poem! There is a lesson here:* Zen is the Way. Look for it and you will lose it.

~~~~~~

蝿叩とり彼一打我一打　高濱虚子
haetataki tori kare ichida ware ichida – kyoshi (1875-1959)
(fly-swatter/s pick up: he one hit, i one hit)

sharing

one fly-swatter
he takes a swat and
i take a swat

A healthy lack of concern manifested by not even expressing lack of concern for the life of flies is Zen, right? The smart whacks are indirectly highlighted by the simply stated repetition. I assume the *he* is the bedridden Shiki, for fly-swatting and sickness come together. Here is Kyoshi paraversing himself.

蝿叩に即し彼一句我一句　虚子
haetataki ni sokushi kare ikku ware ikku – kyoshi (1875-1959)
(fly-swatter/swatting suitable/instantaneously he/him one poem i/me one poem)

fly-swatting

with each kill
one haiku by him
one by me

There is no postposition, the equivalent of our preposition in the original. I was tempted to write "*for* him" and "*for* me," as if the poets took a life and received a haiku; but that would be too precious. If Issa, with his folk Buddhist background, came up with a blessing after each fly swatted, Kyoshi reminds us of the Chinese tradition of so many poems per drink and the *haikai* tradition that changed those drinks into flowers. A fly is far from a peony, but what the hell! This poem reflects Kyoshi's unique sanity and exuberance.

fly-ku

with each swat
he writes one poem
i write one poem

The only verb in the original is the one that does in the fly. There is nothing about "writing" or "saying" or "reading" the haiku – neither is there a postposition. But try to do without a second verb. "He one haiku" "Me one haiku." *Nope*. By avoiding specific verbs, I came up with more readings I like, though I doubt Kyoshi would have appreciated the titles.

swat team

each dead fly
gets one haiku from him
and one from me

tribute

each fly swat:
one *ku* from him and
one from me

~~~~~~

I quizzed two Japanese friends on this poem which is ambiguous with respect to being about swatting flies *or the* fly-swatter. *One Japanese friend thought it the former, another the latter. The second friend adds that "fly-swatter" would be normal* (futsû) *and that, even if it were a swatting poem, it would be about fly swatting not each fly-swat event because the idiomatic* "~ni soku-suru" *is different from the Buddhist usage of* soku *I was familiar with.*

just right for
a fly swatter, us two,
each, one ku
~~~~~~

The Buddhist "soku" *indicates the immediate translation of one thing into another whereas the idiomatic phrase means* apropos *to something. I would like to go with the first friend, but I fear the second friend is right.*

poems to fit
a fly swatter: one his
and one mine

The idea of poems that are right for *a fly-swatter bears a certain charm, especially if you think of how such poems suit a sickbed. This reading makes it a fine poem of friendship in and through haiku and, thus, probably a better poem than the more active* one-swat-each *reading.* Moreover *some Japanese fly-swatters could, like fans, actually be written on . . .*

~~~~~~

Where is the Zen! I can hear your beef. Unless Zen is about making people chuckle, my translations kill it; and, notwithstanding what I have just written, I cannot shake the suspicion that these haiku (the first, *one-swat-each* haiku, at any rate) by Kyoshi are self-consciously the opposite of maudlin, the opposite of what he felt giving up that well to the morning glories meant (I think Kyoshi – and, before him, Issa – was dead wrong on Chiyo's morning glories, but that is another story!). Being self-consciously anti-maudlin is, of course, a *no no*. So what would be a pure unadulterated Zen *fly-ku?* I think a dozen or so may be found scattered through chapters about various *fly-ku* sub-themes. Of these, I think Issa who was not Zen wrote the best one. In the standard pocketbook anthology of Issa (Maruyama ed.: Iwanami bunko), as I wrote before, the following poem is only treated in a footnote as a variant to his better known "swat 'em and bless 'em" *ku*. OK, I know I am being pushy, but, damn it, I think young Issa wrote a masterpiece (one of the best 10 haiku ever written) and *insist* upon an encore. This poem should be famous:

蝿一つ打ては山を見たりけり　一茶
hae hitotsu uchite wa yama o mitarikeri – issa (1763-1827)
(fly one striking/striked-as-for, mountain look[perfect+emphatic])

every time
i hit a fly i saw
the mountain

i swat a fly
and look out at
the mountain

i swat a fly
and look out on
the mountain

and each time
i swatted a fly my eyes
met the mountain

Unfortunately, my skill in Japanese and English is not sufficient to adjudicate the meaning of the poem or do it justice in translation. I believe we have a sequence (kill followed by looking), but cannot rule out a parallel (both at once) reading.
~~~~~~

日本人の読者よ。先の句は、傑作と思わない？いったい何故無名句でしょうか？

After the Zen Talk, or *When Fly-flaps Signify*

蝿打のありて留守なる庵かな 櫻魚
hae-uchi no arite rusu naru iori kana – ôgyo (19c? 20c?)
(fly-swatter's has absent-is hut/studio 'tis)

there is a swatter
the master is out
of his hut

the master out
a fly-swatter remains
in the hut

a studio with
the master absent: there is
a fly swatter

Had I not learned about the fly-flap (*hossu*) being the symbol of protection against desire, I would have thought less of this poem. Strictly speaking, a fly-swatter is not a device for shooing flies, but I cannot help making the association. I see the master (another assumption, for why would one write about anyone's hut?), going out without his metaphysical protection.

蝿蝿蝿蝿蝿蝿蝿蝿蝿蝿蝿蝿蝿蝿蝿蝿蝿蝿蝿蝿蝿蝿蝿蝿蝿蝿蝿蝿蝿蝿蝿蝿蝿蝿蝿蝿蝿

the bard's fly

What dost thou strike at, Marcus, with thy knife?

Marc. At that that I have killed, my lord, a fly.

Tit. Out on thee, murderer! thou kill'st my heart;
Mine eyes are cloy'd with view of tyranny:
A deed of death, done on the innocent,
Becomes not Titus' brother. Get thee gone;
I see thou art not for my company.

Marc. Alas my lord, I have but kill'd a fly.

Tit. But how if that fly had a father and mother?
How would he hang his slender gilded wings,
And buzz lamenting doings in the air!
Poor harmless fly,
That with his pretty buzzing melody,
Came here to make us merry! and thou hast kill'd him.

"One must admire" writes Blyth, "the brilliant insincerity of this, exactly contrary to the attitude of Issa, who is pretending to be insincere, pretending to be humorous when he is deeply compassionate." Yet, Titus' insincerity contains a truth: someone who is too quick to kill flies does have an axe to grind with the world.

蝿蝿蝿蝿蝿蝿蝿蝿蝿蝿蝿蝿蝿蝿蝿蝿蝿蝿蝿蝿蝿蝿蝿蝿蝿蝿蝿蝿蝿蝿蝿蝿蝿蝿蝿蝿蝿

the fly that was N*ot* T*here*

and the fly that was not then

蝿ハにげたのにしづかに手をひらき　柳樽
hae wa nigeta no ni shizuka ni te o hiraki – yanagidaru bk 16
(fly fled/escaped-though , quietly hand[obj] [he/she] opens)

opened with care
his hand shows the fly
is not there

This senryû is from the same series that I believe gave form to Issa's famous *fly-ku.* I use the third-person because when the subject is explicit in senryû, it is almost always *that* person. A simple translation, right on syntax, might be *"the fly escaped yet he quietly opens his hand."* Blyth's translation was sober yet hyped up with a double adverb: "The fly has escaped / But he opens his hand / Very, very slowly." I prefer to play around with the idea. More paraverses:

fly gone
he carefully opens
his hand

a fly is
seldom found in the hand
slowly opened

the emptiness
of a hand that should have
held a fly

his slowly
opened hand reveals
no fly

The first paraverse is in a straight senryû-style. The next is aphoristic, a style rarely encountered in senryû or haiku. If you have experienced that *emptiness*, you know that the third can be read as a haiku. The last completely reverses the syntax of the original, changing it from a description of how men act to a logical (as in logos-based) joke. Strictly speaking, it is neither haiku nor senryû. I think I got the idea from reading of a North Florida toe-bidding party where a man, finding the dish he hoped to eat gone, quipped that he was not interested in chicken-*was* but chicken-*is* (or something like that in Zora Neale Hurston's ethnographic and literary masterpiece *Of Mules and Men* or autobiography *Dust Tracks on a Dirt Road.*

老の手や蝿を打さい（へ）逃た跡　一茶
oi no te ya hae o utsu sae nigeta ato – issa (d.1827)
(old hand: fly hits-though, fled after/spot)

my old hand
hits the very spot
the fly was

Let's face it, killing flies is not like killing mosquitoes or (with a trap) mice. We have a moving target not only live but lively enough to manifest a *there! not-there!* quality worthy of quantum physics. Would I be wrong to guess that for all people who did not enjoy the satisfaction of hunting, fly-swatting must have been *the* game in the days before video and other electronic skill-games. In fact, we might call fly-swatting the prototype for all that Sony *et al* come up with. The first *Gamestation©* was the fly-swatter. It, too, was able to command the total mindfulness=mindlessness of the player. Now, the one rule for all games is that we cannot win all the time (This has been tested on all sorts of birds and beasts: they are more persistent if they are not allowed to succeed every time).

~~~~~~

In other words, if we never missed, fewer flies would be swatted. Yet, there are not as many misses recorded in haiku as one might imagine. Issa boasts the lion's share of them. But before I cough up another, let me play a bit more with the last:

my old hand
even when it takes a swat
the fly is not

the old hand
when it swats it swats
the fly that *was*

an old hand
swats the fly, all right
where it *was*

this ole hand
don't miss – it
swats right
where fly *was*

my old hand
not that it
misses the fly
just moves!

right place
wrong time –
an old hand
after a fly

I am not just trying to be clever with my "was" stuff and other shenanigans. A peculiarity of English is responsible for my forced translation. In English, an animal (or machine) has a *trail* or a *track*, or leaves a *mark*. The Japanese term *ato* (homophonic with another heterographic *ato* meaning "after/following/next") is more versatile, for it means all of these and also can mean something we can only describe as "the place where something was." In other words, the fly *was* there but not *then.* I am guessing the slow hand is Issa's, but it could be someone else's. Here is that *ato* again.
~~~~~~

群蝿の逃げた跡を打つ皺手哉　一茶
murebae no nigeta-ato utsu shiwade kana – issa (d.1827)
(swarm[of]flies' fled-after/spot hits wrinkled hand[subj])

the siege

a wrinkled hand
strikes where there was
a swarm of flies

striking where
a swarm of flies was,
a wrinkled hand

The first translation shows English flows best not following the original word order. In this poem we feel the helplessness of the old man walked all over by a whole swarm of flies more than in the last. *Poor Issa!* Can you guess where this is going?

打て打てと逃て笑ふ蝿の声　一茶
utte utte to nogarete warau hae-no koe – issa (d.1827)
("hit [me]! hit [me]!" dodging laugh/s fly/ies' voice)

fly with an attitude

hit me! hit me!
taunts the fleeing
housefly

par-*annoy*-a

hit me! hit me!
i hear the fleeing fly
laugh outloud

It is a fact that the fastest houseflies (in Hawaii called *banzai flies* if I recall) the solidly built speedsters that zip back and forth even when they are not chased, can drive anyone – including fly-lovers like me – crazy, are very loud. One of those flies almost blinded my co-habitant when Han-chan (usually, the world's most farsighted and, therefore, careful cat: *Han-chan's Dreams* will be published as soon as I can afford to publish something with color illustrations) lost his patience, leaped and, missing, left a four-inch *ato* in the form of a scar on her forehead with the lowest part reaching well into the eyebrow. But even quiet flies can irritate those who would, but cannot, swat them.

蝿にくし心のさきを（へ）立まはる（廻り）　焼台
hae nikushi kokoro no saki o(e) tachimawaru(i) – gyôtai (d.1792)
(fly/ies [is/are] hateful: heart/mind ahead of leave-go-around)

spiteful flies
moving fa*sss*ter than
my mind

flies are spiteful
they move about faster
than my mind

i hate flies
reading my mind and
acting on it

the spiteful fly,
flying about one step
ahead of me!

Shiki would later write practically the same thing. I do not know if it was sheer coincidence, or if he knew of Gyôtai's poem and wanted to specify what exactly the mind/heart was thinking.

蝿憎し打つ気になれば寄りつかず　子規　明治 25
hae nikushi utsu-ki ni nareba yoritsukazu – shiki (d.1902)
(fly/ies [is/are] hateful: hit-feeling-become-if/when, approach-not)

spiteful flies!
when you would swat them
they stay away

how i hate flies!
when you would swat, they
keep their distance

The hateful flies;
When I wanted to kill the things,
They wouldn't come near me.

trans. Blyth

Issa observed (or *invented*) what seems to be the exact opposite phenomenon, flies that *ask to be* swatted. Blyth did the above when he still favored 17 syllables.

打れても／＼来るや膝の蝿　一茶
utarete mo utarete mo kuru ya hiza no hae – issa (d.1827)
(hit-though/still hit-though/still, [it/they] come! lap's fly/ies)

a persistence of flies

swatted again
and again, the fly comes
to my lap

suckers for punishment

though hit again
and again, the flies come back
to my old lap

flies

swatted
back they come
to my lap

The poem is a good example of a case where the ambiguity with respect to number in Japanese irritates this translator. Are we talking about one fly Issa keeps missing? Or is this an instance of the "comeback of flies" I would prefer to save for the next chapter? If it is the former, maybe Issa misinterpreted his own fly. Who sez it does not *want* to be killed and *that* is why it rubs its little hands and feet? I am kidding. The reality is a diversity of flies. The country flies of Shinano may just be duller than those spitefully quick flies Shiki complained of. A smart city fly would only come back once or twice, not over and over (I am just guessing. This is something I hope will be taken up by scientists: Are there flies that can learn to avoid danger quickly while others can not?) The 20th century wanderer, the begging poet Santôka suggests that geography – and *genes*, for Darwin made it clear that isolation and evolved difference are related – may count:

うつ手を感じて街の蝿うまくにげた　山頭火
utsu te o kanjite machi no hae umaku nigeta – santôka (d.1940)
(hitting-hand/s[obj] feel/sense/s town-fly/ies[subj] skillfully fled/escaped)

city slicks

the flies in town
skillfully read and
beat my hand

The past tense – in ordinary vernacular, something rare in haiku – may mean the wandering poet has just passed through a town and, finding a fly that does *not* flee so quickly, looks back on the flies in the city. A few paraverses:

urbanity

reading my hand
the town-fly makes
a great escape!

adaptation

sensing hands
town-flies are adroit
at escaping

sophisticate

the town-fly:
an adept in the art
of escape

Familiarity may not breed contempt, but it does create caution. We all are very aware of the difference between animals familiar and unfamiliar with man. Unless tame, those that know "us" flee, and those that do not are curious, then dead, usually.

生き残る蝿がわたしをおぼえている　山頭火
ikinokoru hae ga watashi o oboeteiru – santôka (d.1940)
(surviving fly/ies-the me[obj] remember-are)

the flies
that survive
remember me

Santôka's poems do not come to a head with the *fly/flies*, in the manner of many more traditional haiku where everything else in the poem would modify the same. Paradoxically, by turning the fly into the subject of a prosaic *sentence* and, instead, focusing on the behavior, Santôka avoids making it the subject of the *poem* — while ending the sentence with the verb as anyone might in ordinary Japanese speech without so much as a nod toward haiku convention – which would, at the very least, put some haiku-esque conjugation on the verb. His second poem about "the flies that survive" appear to hypothesize upon the mechanism for the natural selection of smart city flies in his previous poem.

昼もしづかな蠅が蠅たたきを知つている　山頭火
hiru mo shizuka na hae ga hae tataki o shitte-iru – santôka (d.1940)
(daytime/afternoon-even quiet fly/flies fly-swatter[obj] know/s)

the fly that is quiet
in broad daylight is aware
of the fly-swatter

flies quiet
even at mid-day know
about swatters

Flies are generally quick right when we are ready for a siesta. Again Santôka recognizes the intelligence of some flies. Not all flies, *some* flies. Intelligence is individual.

蠅打をのがるゝ蠅の命かな　潤李　明け烏
hae-uchi o nogaruru hae no inochi kana – junki (1773)
(fly-swatter[obj] avoid/ing fly's life 'tis)

the life
of a fly that escapes
the swatter

flies that
escape from the swatter
have a life

Okay, flies escape. It is no big big deal for the man who feels chagrin (unless it is a tse-tse fly, but Japan has no such killer-flies). But, for the fly, that feels nothing – Or, are we wrong? *Could it feel exhilaration?* – it matters. This haiku by a little-known poet, is a good example of the typical Japanese style where the entire poem is a modified subject that comes at the end of the original – where the poem comes to a head. The first take reverses the order to preserve the flow, or relationship of the words in the Japanese. The second comes closer to the original word order, but ends up turning the original subject, *life*, into *flies*.

蠅の替りにたたかるゝ畳哉　一茶
hae no kawari ni tatakaruru tatami kana – issa (d.1827)
(fly/ies' instead of, is beaten: tatami 'tis)

scapegoat

the tatami
takes a good beating
for the flies

Issa reminds us that the swatter and the fly are not everything. *Something* always gets hit, even if it is only air. We cannot miss. Note the rich internal rhyme (*a-a-i // a-a-i*) and alliteration (*k-t-t-k-t-t-k*). When Santôka writes about striking the flies and *himself* (pg. 56, *The Hit-man*), we can't help but suspect a touch of philosophy. Here, Issa gives us what would seem to be a straight unlayered haiku. No allusions. But it does follow one of his favorite patterns, the *proxy* poem. In most cases, a creature takes *his* place (Blyth translated some of them, including my favorite about a crow [or sparrow] bathing in cold "young water" – Issa hated the cold – to start the year off right and that is why, I think, Richard Wright was so taken by them). Let me try another translation:

proxy

thwacked
instead of housefly
my tatami

Japanese poets spent most of their time seated on the tatami, their floor. Desks and tables were usually tiny and close to it. Few of our flies die on the floor. Most of Japanese ones do, or, rather, did. (Today, most Japanese still have tatami underfoot, but probably spend more of their time in chairs.)

見逃しているとも知らぬ秋の蝿　久夫（当てずっぽう）
minogashiteiru to mo shiranu aki no hae – hisao (date?)
(overlooked know/s-even-not autumn-fly/ies[subj])

ignorance is bliss

unaware that
men overlooked them
autumn flies

the autumn fly
does not know
i overlooked it.

– trans. Blyth

..
Blyth does not title his translations, but, with respect to this *ku,* he commented that "even in the world of flies, ignorance is bliss." *Sounds good; but who knows if it is true?* That is why, I would prefer to use such commentary as a title, thereby gaining poetic license hard to grant to prose. My translation keeps the fly/ies in the proper order (at the end of the poem) and Blyth's keeps the flow of the original by reversing the order. Either is an equally valid translation. My "men" could be changed to "I" or "we," as you prefer. But why *autumn* fly? Is it because the fly was thought to have survived since summer thanks to its good fortune? I doubt such a long view was intended. The fall fly is simply slower than the summer fly, more likely to alight and, being less numerous, recognizable as individuals (not necessarily by details but because of patterns of behavior or by the assumption it *must* be the same fly though it might not be). People notice specific flies and this poem, while denying the fly recognizes the relationship, indirectly makes us think of it.

out of it

the autumn fly
does not even know
i let it go

Or was the intent of the poem rather to describe a fly that is not sharp and aware of what is happening around it like those healthy summer flies that can supposedly read our mind? Either way, the fact that Fall signified the beginning of the end made the unknowing fly a foil to the all-too-knowing poet.

払っても、払っても。。。

知らぬが仏

••

払っても、払っても。。。

<u>Shoo fly, Shoo!</u>

the difficulty of ditching flies

達磨忌や払子にさはる蝿もなし　乙由　麦林集
darumaki ya hossu ni sawaru hae mo nashi – otsuyû (d.1739)
(bodhidarma-[death]day: hossu-to touching fly-even not)

dharuma day!
today not a fly touches
the *hossu* hair

Flies were not always *swatted*. They were also *shooed*. We saw the shooing device, usually called *hae-barai*, where it did not rightly belong, in chapter 6, the *<u>Zen of Swatting</u>*, where I called it a "fly switch," though switches are hard and thin while *hae-barai* are not. The *hossu,* a *hae-barai* identified with Buddhism, is made of bundled hair, (horse, cow, yak) or, occasionally, hemp. It is talismanic for the Buddhist Law's protection against sin and simultaneously can actually shoo, rather than kill, flies. (Is there a term for such usable symbols?) Dharuma Day is the day the Bodhidharma (the Mahayana Buddhist saint who left India to found Zen in China in the early 7th Century) *died*. In the Sinosphere, *death*days are widely celebrated; they mean more than birthdays (see TOPSY-TURVY 1585). The heart of the enlightened Daruma (Dharuma, Dharma, as you like) would not be plagued by flies=desires, his mind would not be cluttered with crap=flies; he would have been beyond vigilance. Then, again, Dharuma Day is at the start of Winter, when we would expect the last flies to have vanished. There is wit in this, as there is wit in Zen.

よの中はかくして過せ蝿はらひ　成美
yononaka wa kakushite sugose haebarai – seibi (d. 1816)
(world-within-as-for, thus[like this] live[spend our days]! fly-shoo)

a fly-shoo
live just like that
in this world

in this world
this is how to live
a fly-shoo!

in this world
here is how to live
a fly-shoo!

The original *ku* may, like Seibi's *a-fly-shoo-and-nothing-else* poem in the Zen chapter, be intended for a picture of the device. I hope the reader will forgive my neologism, *fly-shoo.* There are old words such as *flapper* and *fly-flap* for devices used to drive away rather than kill flies. Charles Darwin mentioned "the tail of a giraffe, which serves as a fly-flapper" in the *Origin of the Species*. Centuries ago, a "fly-flapper" was a low-class body-guard, someone hired to keep away the riff-raff. While these words are not yet obsolete (dictionaries still use these words to translate *hossu* and *hae-barai* and one can still find an occasional usage on the internet), "flap" insists upon being *flat* and that is unsuitable for a tubular cluster of hair. So, at first, I used "switch" but, in this chapter *on shooing,* keep the original word, *hossu,* literally "exorcize[shoo-away]child/thing" and translate the more secular *hae-barai* ("fly+shooer/ shooing/exorcising"). Because English lacks a simple *verb* for "away" ("banish" and "vanquish" are specialized; the Usanian slang "to off" means "kill.") such as *harau/harai,* I made what I hope is a transparent term: "fly-shoo."

追やれは殖るや蝿の後戻り　嵐外
oi-yareba fueru ya hae no atomodori – rangai (d.1845)
(chase [them] off-if/when, [they] increase!/: flies' back-return)

a comeback of flies

chase them off
they multiply – flies
always return

If swatting includes the possibility of missing, shooing included the even higher probability of those flies returning. Issa's contemporary Rangai put it well. The idea that the more you try to shoo them away, the more flies come to stay, is easy enough to English, but the punch-word *atomodori* is a challenge because it means both that the flies return *and* that the human agenda suffers a "set-back." It will not do to use the Latinate "retrogression" here (*chase them off / they multiply: fly / retrogression*), for it has no literal sense. So, for the above translation, I had to trade the idea of *our* setback for *their* making a comeback. The title employs a device not available to Japanese, a newly coined collective term (eg. *an exaltation of larks*) for flies.

"go back to start"

you shoo the flies
surprise, surprise! they bring
back their friends

it's a fact

shoo 'em away
and more come back to play
house flies

The one on the left is obviously forced. *Surprise, surprise!* should be pronounced as it was by Gomer Pyle in that inane television program that includes my name.

秋の蝿追へバマタ来ル叩ケバ死ヌ　子規 明治34
aki no hae oeba mata kuru tatakeba shinu – shiki (d.1902)
(autumn flies chase-if/when again come, strike-if/when die)

autumn flies
chase and they come back
swat and they die

chase fall flies
and they come back: swat
and they die

autumn flies

they come back
when you chase them and die
when you swat them

A century earlier, Issa tried another approach, the direct poetic appeal. This type of haiku is found more in Issa than any other *haijin* I know of. Classic poets appealed directly to clouds to lay off the mountain peaks they wanted to see and begged the wind to hold off on the blossoms. Well, Issa has poems brusquely demanding the cuckoo calm down, the geese land immediately before him, and the sea cucumber float up, and so forth.

とく逃げよにげよ打たれなそこの蝿　一茶
toku nigeyo nigeyo utare na soko no hae – issa (d.1827)
(quickly flee! flee! get hit-not! get hit-not! over-there fly)

caveat musca

beat it!
flee! don't get yourself
killed, fly!

you, there!

better flee!
quickly, fly, fly!
don't die!

♪ if the swatter
don't kill you ♪

flee, fly, flee!
fly away and live
until you die!

un-safe here

quick, fly
beat it! don't die
for me.

last plea

flee, fly!
don't make me
kill you!

if Mother Goose
(rather than Kiku)
had a fly-swatter

Flee, fly! Fly away!
Come back to play
another day!

I was tempted to guess and write "don't let *him* (or *her*) kill you!" Issa could have been laughing at a bloodthirsty friend or an extermination campaign by his wife Kiku. This seems more likely than warning the fly against staying near to him (unless he has been drinking too much and wrote this under the influence). Moreover, Issa has a similar poem where he tells an escaped bird to quickly get lost in the spring mist.

出よ蝿野には酢い花甘い花　一茶
ideyo hae no ni wa sui hana amai hana – issa (d.1827)
([let's] go out, fly/flies! field-in-as-for, sour flowers, sweet flowers)

advice for a six-legged friend

hit the road, fly!
the fields are full of flowers
sweet & sour

a beautiful day	*a day to go out*
flies, out you go! find yourself a sweet flower or a sour one!	flies, let's leave! flowers of every flavor fill the fields

The form of address in this *ku* is charming. Half-command and half-appeal, I believe it leaves open the possibility of including the poet-as-fly (convincing himself) in the number of the flower-eaters. This is a refreshing child-like poem that deserves to be more widely known (it is not included in the Iwanami classic collection of the top 2000 of Issa's haiku). Thinking about the flavor of the flowers is a stroke of genius and/or proof of Issa's having a bug's-eye view of the world.

~~~~~~

One way to make flies leave is not to invite them in the first place. It helps not to eat, defecate or sweat. But you can never be clean enough, for flies can even sniff out dirty thought:

(清談) 心清ししばらく蝿もよりつかず　子規　明治三十
"seidan // kokoro kiyoshi shibaraku hae mo yoritsukazu – shiki (d.1902)
("clean talk" heart/mind clean/pure: for a while, flies-even approach-not)

pure mind

clean to the core
for a while even flies
stay clear

The idea that cleanliness comes from the heart literally taken seems ridiculous, but imagine Shiki had just bathed, or been bathed and lay on fresh linen. A bath can refresh the mind, the flies may have been unable to sniff him out for a while and he may have exchanged only the most pleasant of words with a visitor (the title of the poem which I did not incorporate in the translation was "clean-talk"). So, as an epiphany, the poem is believable. Sick Shiki must have been feeling absolutely wonderful when he noticed something familiar was missing . . . the flies. The *shibaraku,* or "a while" recognizes that such immaculate moments when even flies keep their distance are fleeting.

~~~~~~

If cleanliness is the most humane way of getting rid of flies, what is the second kindest method? Turn the page:

蝿の捕捨所にこまってる　初代川柳
hae no tori[?]suteru-dokoro ni komatteru – early era senryû (~1700)
(fly/flies' capture: throw-away place-about, troubled over)

live garbage

catching flies alive
the hard part is finding
a place for them

his dilemma

catching flies
where, then, does he
throw them out?

next door?

catching flies
where, then, do you
throw them away.

the problem
is ditching the fly
you catch

~~~~~~

Ah, but it is wrong to think we are always in demand. We just feel that way because we notice the flies that stick around. Here is a modern *ku* as good as Issa's best.

蝿の来て我見て彼岸へと戻る 坊城俊樹
hae no kite ware mite higan e to modoru – bôjô toshiki
(fly comes me sees, other bank-to returns)

a fly comes
looks me over and returns
to the other shore

The original has a magical quality for the literary expression *higan,* meaning other bank of a river (the literal significance here) also means the other world of (Buddhist) Enlightenment which is celebrated on the Equinox. "Bank" would read better, but, following the advice of friends,[1] I use "shore" because it preserves the *possible* religious implications. If the poet were mortally ill when he wrote this poem, it might mean he was not called yet. If the poet were well and standing on the ugly (developed) side of a stream, it might mean that he has managed to view a fly as a part of natural paradise, perhaps cleaner than humans.

1. Advice of Friends. My first printing had "bank" and no explanation. I did not want to sully the poem with *anything* after it. But, I was challenged by two friends, one Usanian and one Japanese. They were right, my readers would not have guessed the paradisical allusion unless they already knew about the Higan celebration.
~~~~~~

。 。

don't B*other* me!

how flies get under our skin

頬を蹴て手をもむ蝿のにくさ哉　蘭秀　類題発句集
hoho o kete te o momu hae no nikusa kana – ranshu (1774)
([our] cheeks kick, [then] hands[obj] wring flies' spitefulness 'tis)

musca maledicta

kicking our faces
then wringing their hands
spiteful flies.

The American fly-phobic Ogden Nash feared July "when tickle-footed walks the fly" (*Summer Serenade*), but this face-kicking business is something else again! I haven't seen it in any other haiku, but 700 years earlier Sei Shônagon, in her *Pillow Book* came close:

> The fly should have been included in my list of hateful things; for such an odious creature does not belong with ordinary insects. It settles on everything, and even alights on one's face with its clammy feet (trans. Ivan Morris)

Another point unique to this fine haiku – together with Issa's, the only one I know putting the fly's hands and feet (implied in the "kick") to work – is the verb *momu* ("wring"). Unlike Issa's *fly-ku* and most other Japanese fly poems, where the original is *suru* and the only "wringing" of hands going on is in the English translation, *here, it is in the original.* The fly is not praying but, confound it, *pretending it is sorry* for what it will do all over again! This fly-as-malefactor idea is found in a more recent senryû:

昼寝の顔を踏み付て蝿仕合　柳樽
hirune no kao o fumi-tsukete hae shiawase – yanagidaru 120-33
(afternoon nap's face[+obj] tread-upon fly/flies happy/joyful)

stepping on the faces
of afternoon nappers, how
happy these flies!

flies in heaven:
stepping all over the faces
of men napping

A Japanese for whom everything has gone right, i.e., married the perfect spouse, found and moved into the perfect house, and is blessed with health and bright, good-looking, and caring children is *shiawase.* To be *shiawase* is to be not just happy but happy down to the soul. Flies find true contentment in walking on our faces.

世の中は蝿にとどかぬ牛の首　竿水（誤植？）
yo no naka wa hae ni todokanu ushi no kubi – kansui (竿秋= kanshu d. 1772?)
(world-among-as-for, flies-to reach-not cow/ox's neck)

what is this life?
an ox neck too short
to reach the flies

If a mere aphorism is not a haiku, this haiku is not a haiku unless we can picture the poet sitting there feeling for a cow that is shrugging its head in vain to catch the flies and suddenly realizing that this was his and all of our lives. Let's see some more poems on the uninvited bodily contact that, more than anything else, sours Japanese on flies.

~~~~~~

*T*ouching F*lies!*

初旅の娘なぶるや馬の蝿　如友藤首途
hatsutabi no musume naburu ya uma no hae – nyoyu (?)
(first-travel's maiden bully: horse's flies)

taking advantage
of a maiden on her first trip
the horse's flies!

The maiden is on her way to get married (after which she will have to put up with much tougher bullying on the part of her mother-in-law). It is her first trip and her last. Were the maiden, rather than the flies, the focus of the poem, this would be a senryû. The verb *naburu* suggests "bullying," "pestering," or "making fun of" with an element of physical intimidation or horse-play. The horse's flies may or may not be horse-flies. The same *naburu* in another form is found in this old *fly-ku:*

剃り立のあたまや蝿のなぶりもの　嵐中？
soritate no atama ya hae no naburimono – ranchû (?)
(just-shaved head! flies' play-thing)

usefulness

a shaved pate
something for the flies
to play with

buddhist hazing

freshly shaved
my head is a plaything
for the flies
~~~~~~

The poet may well have taken Buddhist vows, but the shaving might just be an attempt to lose lice. Issa did not use *naburu* or *naburi* in any of his *fly-ku.* But one comes close –

そり立てのつぶりを蝿に踏れけり　一茶
soritate no tsuburi o hae ni fumarekeri – issa (d.1827)
(just-shaved head's crown-obj/though: flies-by treaded on [emphatic])

cleanly shaved
my crown is trampled
by the flies

flies treading
upon something new
my shaved pate

If I read the rhetoric of the *o* after *tsuburi* (crown) correctly, the subject of the first part of the poem is *betrayed* by what happens in the second part. Issa's shiny skull, purified of hair ("hair," or *ke,* is a homophone for "pollution/uncleanliness/impurity/ defilement" i.e. metaphysical dirtiness and desire, in colloquial Japanese called *kegare*) has paradoxically drawn flies to dirty it. Issa almost wrote this:

i shave my head
the flies can now tread
every square inch

a shaved pate
now the flies can walk
all over me

Heads without hair were considered troublesome for flies. A bald crown was called a *hae-suberi,* or "fly-slide." There is even a haiku from an early collection:

はげあがるあたまや蝿のすべり道　久任 ゆめみ草
hage-agaru atama ya hae no suberimichi – kunin (1656)
(bald-rise head:/! fly's/flies' slippery-road)

a receding hairline
makes a slippery road
for the flies

this bald ascent
up my brow, for a fly
slippery going

Apparently, *shaven* pates are paradise for flies, while genuine baldness is hell. Add the oil Japanese men used on their hairdo to the natural oiliness of the bald pate without the stubs for friction and you get the true *hae-suberi.*

僧正の頭の上や蝿つるむ　一茶
sôjô no atama no ue ya hae tsurumu – issa (d.1827)
(high-priest's head-on-top!/: flies mate)

profanity

on top of
the high-priest's pate
flies mate

flies mate
on the crown of
our bishop

The lack of specific terms hurts poetry in translation. The problem, of course, is that specific terms tend to favor one's own culture. The order of the words in the "bishop" version is also contrary to that of the original, something that changes the punch-word (Is that unforgivable?). The Buddhist high-priest probably has a shaved head rather than a genuinely bald one. The flies did not risk slipping off in the middle of their nuptials. Issa, following Buson, has a high-priest taking a "field-shit" (*noguso*), so we can assume the same stark contrast of the ornately robed man of religion and animality. When I used the word "bishop" in the second translation, I imagined flies doing it upon the little round tip on top of the bishop's hat as it is found on a chess piece! Be that as it may, Issa's *ku* seems more *like* a senryû than the following post-Issa senryû.

昼寝の面を踏付て蝿つるみ　柳樽
hirune no tsura o fumitsuite hae tsurumi – yanagidaru bk. 131-2
(day-time-nap's face/s[obj] step on flies mate)

noon-nap
(haiku-style)

flies mating
step all over the face
of a sleeping man

noon-nap
(senryû-style)

flies mate
standing on the faces
of sleeping men

The senryû style is more general and tends to depend upon more obvious contrast. I have only read one senryû and one haiku where the victim of flies' unsolicited touching is not human. First the senryû, which was popular enough to be reprinted in several volumes of *Yanagidaru*:

蝿が来てからかって居る猫の耳　柳樽
hae ga kite karakatte-iru neko no mimi – yanagidaru bk. 122-4, 125-36, 127-95
(fly/ies come, making fun of cat's ear/s)

twitchery

a fly comes
and makes fun of
the cat's ear

my cat's ear
a laughing-stock
for the flies

While a healthy and well-groomed cat's ear with its thousands of neat hairs each coming to a fine tip is one of the marvels of natural engineering – and a simulacrum of the more finely ordered microscopic world – most cats are not perfect specimens, and there are secretions in and around the ear that draw flies. Sei Shônagon includes "the inside of a cat's ear" in her list of "Squalid Things." Be that as it may, it is amazing how quickly a cat's ear can flick when touched by a fly. Had this poem been written by a *haijin*, it would been admired (by some, at least) as a haiku, for this facetious zoomorphizing is as acceptable as the facetious anthropomorphizing of Issa's famous fly-ku.

蚊に喰れ蠅にせせられ時鳥　嵐流
ka ni kuware hae ni seserare hototogisu – ranryû (?)
(mosquitoes-by eaten, flies-by picked, cuckoo!)

summertime blues

eaten by mosquitoes
and picked on by flies
cuckoo!

Cuckoo driven cuckoo. The verb *seserare* suggests a relentless picking or digging away at something, such as . . . a stuffed nose. The cuckoo was alleged to put its all into its song, or, rather loud call, until blood poured out its mouth. It was also the harbinger of mid-summer, as its *lhude* singing relation was for the early summer in the West. Here, it sounds like it lets rip its call, which is the same as its name (*ho-to-to-gi-su*), out of desperation while being tortured by summer bugs. This may well be allegorical, for the *hototogisu* flies in from the mountains/forests and in traditional poetry stood for a commuting lover (Perhaps this belongs in the "love and flies" section). The blood Emerson said we pay the bugs for a walk in the woods, lovers paid for romance. I think that may be best for the poem, but it is hard to know where to stop. We could go even further: the mosquito could stand for bothersome bonzes (begging for money?) and flies for likewise annoying *wakashû,* or young gay men propositioning for sex (蠅若衆に蚊坊主). Because of the inability (for someone like me, at least) to settle upon a single reading, determining which of the above two poems is senryû and which haiku is not possible. After such a poem, one with no allegorical or romantic possibilities is welcome:
..

病中　秋の蠅かうべむやむや足せせり　秋之坊
"byôchû" aki-no-hae kôbe muyamuya ashi seseri – akinobô (d. 1718)
("sickness-during" autumn fly/ies head *muyamuya* [mimesis] legs peck-at)

sick-bed nausea

autumn flies
picking away at my head
with their feet
..

Without the psychological mimesis, *muyamuya,* I fear the poem dies. I am not surprised the expression is not even included in the 2000 page Kenkyusha Japanese-English dictionary. It is in my 10-volume Japanese-Japanese dictionary, which explains it combines discomfort approaching nausea with relentless repetition. The most common usage was for a heart sick with jealousy. Perhaps I should find a way to include the adjective Morris used to translate Shônagon's fly feet: *clammy.* The poet may also be allegorizing himself as a fall fly who may be rubbing his legs on his own head, too (in Japanese, it could be read this way, too).

病中作　活きた目をつつきに来るか蝿の声 子規
"byôchû-saku" ikita me o tsutsuki ni kuru ka hae no koe – shiki (d. 1902)
("sick-in composition" living eyes jab/needle-to/for come? fly/ies' voice)

the sick-man lives

i hear you, fly!
you've come to vex
still living eyes?

I must admit that I got the splendid "vex" from Blyth, who translates a visual, and perhaps more natural version of the same poem, with fly/ies' flying (*hae-no tobu*) rather than "fly/flies' voice (*koe*):

On a Sick-bed

Have you come to vex
My still-living eyes,
Criss-crossing fly?

trans. Blyth

Not only the "vex," but the "still-" and the "criss-crossing" are all fine improvements for a difficult poem to translate.

i saw the deadman
impatiently brush away
the flies from his mouth

Richard Wright
(my decapping and centering)

Is a memory of the dead man when he was alive being contrasted with the patient (helpless) corpse? Or did Wright imagine he saw the deadman react to the flies? Ambiguity is no monopoly of the Japanese. Neither are good haiku. I find Wright's haiku – this individual one, and the body of his work – superb.

蝿蝿蝿蝿蝿蝿蝿蝿蝿蝿蝿蝿蝿蝿蝿蝿蝿蝿蝿蝿蝿蝿蝿蝿蝿蝿蝿蝿蝿蝿蝿蝿蝿蝿蝿蝿

how to write "bothersome" in japanese

There is a Japanese word pronounced *urusai.* It means "bothersome," "troublesome," "irksome," "pesky," "annoying," "noisy," "a pain in the ass," "noisy," . . . . It is also used as a command without an imperative. That is to say that by hissing, growling or barking *"Urusai!"* a superior can shut up an inferior without actually saying "shut up." In the soap operas, at least, this would seem to be the most common expression used by Japanese husbands to avoid communicating with, that is, to muzzle, their wives. It is also commonly heard coming from the mouths of drunks who would shut up others with opposing views. Be that as it may, the most *interesting* thing about this word that is itself annoying, is how it is written with three Chinese characters having no relation to its pronunciation whatsoever: 五月蠅い= *five+month +fly* (an early fly). The fifth month is now May, but *was* mid-June to July under the old calendar. This usage dates back at least to Natsume Sôseki (late 19c), and is literal proof of how annoying Japanese find and have found flies.

Here, a contemporary wife evens the *urusai* balance:

蠅叩きなんかで私を呼ばないで　とっき
haetataki nanka de watashi o yobanai de – tokki
(fly-swatting something-for me[obj] call-not!)

don't you
call me to swat a fly
or something!

As one fellow poet explained, the poet is not necessarily upset with her husband and such a poem may, rather, reflect their exceptionally pleasant joking relationship. (from Ukimido's Fly-ku Fest = *Haeku-kai*).

蠅蠅蠅蠅蠅蠅蠅蠅蠅蠅蠅蠅蠅蠅蠅蠅蠅蠅蠅蠅蠅蠅蠅蠅蠅蠅蠅蠅蠅蠅蠅蠅蠅蠅蠅蠅蠅

Next to touch, the biggest complaint, and I think the most valid, is that the flies either won't let the poets take their daily naps or interfere with them. Who is to say whether this need to nap derived from a high carbohydrate diet fitting the long Japanese intestine (or vice-versa) – I paraphrase a Japanese explanation for the number of people sleeping in commuter trains – from the copying of the dreamy lifestyle of ancient Chinese, or from the advanced age of some of the haiku poets.

蝿いとふ身は［を］故郷に昼寝哉　蕪村
hae itou mi wa[o] furusato ni hirune kana – buson (d.1783)
(fly hate/hating body/person-as-for[though] hometown-in noon-nap 'tis/!/?)

a fly-hater
trying to take a nap
back home

Unlike Issa, whose happy early years was followed by a miserable childhood and a less than happy relationship with his town, Buson's images of childhood and home are all good. But when an adult who made it big in the city goes home, there are some things that may not have bothered him as a youth – no child is a fly-hater – that he now finds hard to take. Buson's slightly older contemporary Yayu probably did not mind flies, for he chuckles:

..

蝿が来て蝶にはさせぬ昼寝哉　也有
hae ga kite chô ni wa sasenu hirune kana – yayû (d.1783)
(fly/flies come/came, butterfly-to-[become] allows-not nap 'tis)

my afternoon nap

a fly comes
and won't let me become
a butterfly

A mid-day nap:
He won't let me become a butterfly, –
This fly!

– trans. Blyth

I suspect this is a case where the poet cannot fall asleep or cannot enjoy that light sleep at the tail-end of the nap particularly rich in dreams. The allusion is to the famous Chinese philosopher's dream of being a butterfly dreaming it was him dreaming . . . . Speaking of dreams, here is the only haiku I know that *welcomes* flies into them:

うきゆめのあるとき嬉し蝿の声　失名 俳懺悔
ukiyume no aru toki ureshi hae no koe – lost name (1790)
(float-dream have/some time delighted: fly/flies' voice)

buzz of prosperity

the sound of flies
a delight when you dream of
being down & out

guardian angels

a dream of dying
called back from the dead
by houseflies

distraction

when your day-dreams
are blue, what's good for you?
the sound of flies

sweet nothings

we are delighted
with the sound of flies
in a wet dream

The "floating dream" (*uki-yume*) is not found in my largest Japanese dictionary. Perhaps it is a contraction of *ukiyo-no-yume,* "dream of a floating world," something sadly ephemeral in classic literature but more broadly blue later. My best bet is that it was a dream of poverty: *The bzz of flies / delightful when dreaming / of one's debts. Why?* Flies, like mice, could symbolize prosperity. But the floating world, identified with prostitutes, also has lively connotations. Perhaps, it is about the whispering of lovers or a wet dream, though frogs would make a better sound-track for that!

蝿が来ていやいやさせる昼寝の子　柳樽
hae ga kite iya iya saseru hirune no ko – yanagidaru 165-12
(fly/ies come/s, no! no! make/force day-nap child)

flies turn up
and force themselves upon
a napping child

flies come
and make a child balk
at napping

Because this is a senryû, the flies may allegorize men molesting a child, unless my second reading is possible. This next is pure haiku, I think.

蝿に怒る目に力なき昼寝哉　子堂
hae ni ikaru me ni chikara naki hirune kana – shidô (1777)
fly-at anger eyes-in strength-not day-nap 'tis

powerless
eyes rage at flies
nap-time

Some way or another, the Japanese manages to share some of the powerlessness with the *nap* as well as the *eyes*; but I could not pull it off in English. I imagine this is talking about an exhausted elderly person. This next is far lighter.

蝿が来て昼寝の顔を皺にする　柳多留？
hae ga kite hirune no kao o shiwa ni suru – yanagidaru？
(fly/ies come napping face[obj] wrinkles-into makes)

a fly comes
and wrinkles the face of
a napping man

..
By this logic, flies bring us grey hairs even when we are not conscious of it. There are also a number of haiku on flies *not* bothering the sleeper. I save them for later. Now it is time to wake up.
..

松風のひるね破れて蝿の声　成美
matsukaze no hirune yaburete hae no koe – seibi (d.1816)
(pine-wind's afternoon sleep broken, fly's/flies' voice)

the noon nap
of the pine wind broken
the sound of flies

flies buzzing
disturb the noon nap
of the pine wind

Before I replaced it with the above *ku*, I had one by Shikô, a poet of Bashô's generation, here. It read as follows: "noisy flies!/ for today, my nap / is through" (*hae no koe kyô wa hirune no shimai kana*). There was one problem. I misread. The *fly* was a *cicada* (*semi*!). The old characters for both are quite similar. Unlike cicada, who can make enough noise to challenge traffic on a busy road and are said to create "storms" of noise (*semi-arashi*), flies are rarely loud enough to disturb sleep unless one is expecting a horse-fly and the searing pain that overlooking a visit can bring. But the wings of flies can still disturb those who would listen to the sound of silence. The aesthete poet Seibi, who noticed that the pines were *not* making any noise (unless I am wrong and he just means he is taking a pleasant nap in the cool pine scented breeze) may well have been disturbed by flies. People meditating or praying also tend to be easily distracted and Donne complains in his Sermons that: "I neglect

God and his angels for the noise of a fly." Once, I might have said *Amen* to that, but now, suffering from tinnitus, have not a second of silence to enjoy and am always happy to have cicada or flies (anything!) to camoflage the unceasing noise from within! (For readers without tinnitus, let me add that, in the same way one may lose track of the radio when distracted sufficiently by thought, I do not always hear it. Yet, I also never hear *the sound of silence* and perhaps never will until my last second of life when, heart stopped, my blood-pressure will drop suffciently to stop pushing those noisy cells through the capillaries where they do not belong. I will, finally, rest in peace.) But flies, I am afraid, are not be loud enough.

独りすむ昼すさましや蝿の声　沾峨　(沾山?)
hitori sumu hiru susamashiya hae no koe – senzan (d. 1758) or senga?
(alone-live, day-time appalling/dreadful/tremendous: fly/ies' voice)

the sound of silence

living alone
flies flood the afternoon
with noise

clean-up crew

living alone
what a dreadful racket
the flies make

bachelorhood

living without
a wife, the houseflies
make a racket

I have memories of life before tinnitus and the type of thing described in this old haiku: a quiet house where not only flies but clocks seem to be plugged into amplifiers? Or, one that has turned into a den of flies without the little missus around to clean up and keep order? (When the cat is out, mice are not the only things that will play.)

酒飲のうるさがるなり蝿はぢき　乙二
sakenomi no urusagaru nari hae hajiki – otsuni (d.1823)
(sake-drinker/ing's disturb/ing-become fly swatting/swatter/s)

our drinking
disturbed by flies? – no,
by fly swatters

Otsuni, reverses the identity of disturbance and flies in this *ku.* I cannot find a fly *hajiki* in the dictionary. A *hajiki* is any type of spring-gun (or device for *offing* something or someone) today, but who knows what Otsuni referred to! Was someone perhaps throwing the pennies (*zeni*) at them on the table?

~~~~~~

*D*irty F*l*ies*!*

After the defiling touch and the interference with sleep that is largely noise, one major area of complaint remains: *flies as dirty things.* By this, I do not mean in the modern sense of being unhygienic. They stick on things and get in the way.
~~~~~~

染飯の蝿追ふてゐる祖父哉　涼菟
somehan no hae o ôteiru sôbu kana – kyoki (d. 1717)
(dyed rice's flies[obj] chasing grandfather[subj] 'tis)

coming of age in japan

red rice today
her grandfather chases
after the flies

The menarche was celebrated by rice cooked with tiny reddish beans, a tradition which has lasted to the present day. Apparently, the symbolism isn't accompanied by much talk, for senryû and movies enjoy focusing on the totally mystified younger brother. Despite the fact this girl will no longer be allowed to visit Shinto Shrines for seven days a month, menarche, or *hasshio,* "first-tide" was an auspicious occasion. The dirty flies bring out the paradox and foreshadow suitors.

~~~~~~

We are talking about extraneous matter, the fly itself, its remains when squashed and, something Japanese call *hae-no-fun* or *hae-no-kuso*: "fly shit." Growing up with bugs with mouse-size droppings – that is to say, the scat of large cockroaches – I am embarrassed to say that I never even noticed the toilet habits of flies!

蝿打ていさゝか穢す団扇哉　几董
hae utte isasaka yogosu uchiwa kana – kitô (d.1789)
(fly/ies[obj] strike, slightly stain/dirty fan 'tis)

swatting a fly
it gets a bit soiled
my fan

Japanese has many words for fans. This one, *uchiwa,* refers to one that is solid – does not fold up – and looks more than a bit like a fly-swatter. Still, it is hard to push a lot of air *and* swat a fly. Does this poet *slice* into flying flies? Here, the dirtiness can not be blamed on the flies, who did not swat themselves. But flies could be – or were believed to be – dirty. A pre-Bashô haiku – part of a series of theme verses about "white and black" things (白黒) – has "flies shitting on" the white "summer-robes" of some one forced to stand around waiting (*natsukoromo tachii ni hae ga fun o shite* 夏衣立居に蝿がふんをして). A more entertaining poem by a poet who strongly influenced Issa:

..

一ッ家や蝿で塗たる酒の升　素丸
hitotsu ie ya hae de nuritaru sake no masu – somaru (d.1795)
(one house 'tis: flies-by painted wine-box[square wood sake cup])

their house?
this wine-box finished
by flies
~~~~~~

~

looks like shit!

behold my shack!
a veritable wine-box
painted by flies

That "wine-box" stinks. But what can a translator do? A *masu* is a small square box made of polished but unpainted wood, usually cedar, which is standard for drinking good cold *sake,* or rice-wine. Any description, such as "square cup," brought into the poem would ruin it. In the original, the only difficulty is deciding whether to read it straight or as a metaphorical description of the poet's quarters. But to translate it in the latter capacity, I had to add a lot. This is a good example of a poem that makes learning a foreign language worthwhile, for you sure can't bring it home! It is possible I am mistaken about the shit, and *somaru* means that the *masu* is painted not by, but *in* (i.e. covered over with) flies.

..

蠅蠅蠅蠅蠅蠅蠅蠅蠅蠅蠅蠅蠅蠅蠅蠅蠅蠅蠅蠅蠅蠅蠅蠅蠅蠅蠅蠅蠅蠅蠅蠅蠅蠅蠅蠅蠅

The "bar flies" are not in a double-column box because MS-word kept *insisting* upon changing the entire book into two-columns, so I gave up the format.

*B*ar-f*l*ies

bar-flies

busy, curious,
thirsty fly! drink with me
and drink as I

This is a fly-ku'ed version of the first stanza of *On a Fly Drinking out of a Cup* by William Oldys (1696-1761). Issa would have liked it.

旅店　富士の雪蝿は酒屋に残りけり　其角？（五元集）
ryôten // fuji no yuki hae wa sakaya ni nokorikeri – kikaku? (d.1669)
(travel-store/restaurant // fuji's snow, fly/flies-as-for, drink-room-in remain)

roadside pub

snowy fuji
the flies remain
at the bar

Sometimes, when the wind is right, one can feel the cold coming from the air, as one does the heat from the sun. I guess the flies were happy to exchange the view for the heat. A far less pretty *senryû*:

酒呑の屎に酔てる下戸の蝿　柳樽
sakenomi no kuso ni yotteru geko no hae – yanagidaru, bk 156-22
(sake-drinker's shit-by, drunken teetotaler fly)

solid moonshine

a dry housefly
plastered on the shit
of a drinker

a tale of two flies

housefly abstains
but still gets drunk
on bar-fly shit

watch your diet, boys!

non-drinking
musca maledicta piss'd
on bar-fly stools

Who is corrupting whom! I love this. It probably would be true if puke were involved. No matter. It is the idea that counts. Whichever direction the bad influence goes, bars and flies, drunkenness and flies are associated. More on this later.

蝿蝿蝿蝿蝿蝿蝿蝿蝿蝿蝿蝿蝿蝿蝿蝿蝿蝿蝿蝿蝿蝿蝿蝿蝿蝿蝿蝿蝿蝿蝿蝿蝿蝿蝿蝿

蝿のふん色紙の歌の仮名違ひ　柳樽（九）別上４
hae no fun shikishi no uta no kana-chigai – yanagidaru (18c)
(fly shit: colored-paper's [poem-card]'s song[prob. waka or kyôka]'s letter-difference/mistake)

classic touch?

fly shit
the letters of the song
read wrong

cacography

some fly shit
changes the reading of
an old poem

The *shikishi* is a square piece of paper or cardboard upon which poems or "songs" as most poems longer than haiku are called, are written with freely parsed lines. As these "songs" were generally more elegant than haiku, the sacrilege (therefore, humor) would have been greater. Judging from a *haibun* of Bashô's translated in William J. Higginson's *The Haiku Handbook,* these "poem cards" were generally pasted to the wall. When I introduced this senryû to WJH, he promptly came up with a good syntax-precise translation and a playful modernized version, reproduced respectively and respectfully below:

fly shit
the letters on the poem card
are changed

fly shit –
the poem on the broadside
typo'd

Japanese has a number of syllabets in its phonetic syllabary that could be changed by a tiny speck of fly shit. A "shi" (し) could be changed to an "i" (い), a "tsu" (つ)

turned to "u" (う), and almost any hard sound *ka* →*ga* (か→が) *shi*→*ji* (し→じ), *ta*→*da* (た→だ) converted to a soft one or, as Japanese call it *nigori,* a clouded or muddled one. In the case of English, our letters are relatively safe, but as Ambrose Bierce – who clearly had the eye of a senryû poet, and is much appreciated in Japan (despite the lion's share of his wit being lost in translation due to the different syntax) – flies could still find a way to cooperate by *punctuating* our text (see below). But Japanese flies could do that, too:

点一ッ蝿が打たる手紙かな　一茶
ten hitotsu hae ga uchitaru tegami kana – issa (d.1827)
(point [punctuation mark]one fly strikes/written letter 'tis)

the fly strikes
a punctuation mark
in my letter

my letter
gets punctuated once
by a fly

The reader may recognize *utsu* (*uchi*), the same verb used for striking flies is used for writing in punctuation. Japanese is a bit more consistent than English when it comes to *striking.* In English, only context can tell whether striking a line is drawing it in or effacing it. Even with the slight humor of a fly being the one doing the striking, the poem is too simple. I wonder if Issa recalled reading the earlier *Yanagidaru* senryû.

蝿蝿蝿蝿蝿蝿蝿蝿蝿蝿蝿蝿蝿蝿蝿蝿蝿蝿蝿蝿蝿蝿蝿蝿蝿蝿蝿蝿蝿蝿蝿蝿蝿蝿蝿蝿蝿

a *P*unctuation of *F*lies.

– according to *the devil's dictionary* of ambrose bierce –

FLY-SPECK, n. The prototype of punctuation. It is observed by Garvinus that the systems of punctuation in use by the various literary nations depended originally upon the social habits and general diet of the flies infesting the several countries. These creatures, which have always been distinguished far a neighborly and companionable familiarity with authors, liberally or niggardly embellish the manuscripts in process of growth under the pen, according to the bodily habit, bringing out the sense of the work by a species of interpretation superior to, and independent of, the writer's powers. The "old masters" of literature – that is to say, the early writers whose work is so esteemed by later scribes and critics in the same language – never punctuated at all, but worked right along free-handed, without the interruption of the thought which comes from the use of points. (We observe the same thing in children today, whose usage in this particular is a striking and beautiful instance of the law that the infancy of individuals reproduces the methods and stages of development characterizing the infancy of the races.) In the work of these primitive scribes all the punctuation is found, by the modern investigator with his optical instruments and chemical tests, to have been inserted by the writers' ingenious and serviceable collaborator, the common house-fly – *Musca maledicta.* In transcripting these ancient MSS, for the purpose of either making the work their own or preserving what they naturally regard as divine revelations, later writers reverently and accurately copy whatever marks they find upon the papyrus or parchment, to the unspeakable enhancement of the lucidity of the thought and value of the work. Writers contemporary with the copyists naturally avail themselves of the obvious advantages of these marks in their own work, and with such assistance as the flies of their own household may be willing to grant, frequently rival and sometimes surpass the older compositions, in respect at least of [sic] punctuation, which is no small glory. Fully to understand the important services that flies perform to [sic] literature it is only necessary to lay a page of some popular novelist alongside a saucer of cream-and-molasses in a sunny room and observe "how the wit brightens and the style refines" in accurate proportion to the duration of the exposure. (*The Devil's Dictionary*: 1911)

Following Bierce's logic, Japanese flies apparently flew straighter than ours, because Japanese commas are straight, rather than curved.

蝿蝿蝿蝿蝿蝿蝿蝿蝿蝿蝿蝿蝿蝿蝿蝿蝿蝿蝿蝿蝿蝿蝿蝿蝿蝿蝿蝿蝿蝿蝿蝿蝿蝿蝿蝿蝿

から紙のもやうになるや蝿の屎　一茶
karagami no moyô ni naru ya hae no kuso – issa (d.1827)
(chinese paper's pattern/design-as/into becomes!/: fly shit)

natural design

a pattern
like chinese paper ?
fly specks

musca decorativa

fly droppings:
more fancy paper
coming up!

fanciful design

my stationary
decorated a l' chinoise
by fly shit!

The association of fancy paper and fly poop is pleasant enough, but this haiku, too, is not dense enough to enjoy reading over and over. "Chinese" here may reflect a touch of nationalism. Chinese things to the Japanese resemble French things to Usanians.

塗盆を蝿が雪隠にしたりけり　一茶
nuribon o hae ga settchin ni shitari-keri – issa (d.1827)
(lacquered tray[obj], flies toilet-as/into make[it] [vague+emphatic/perfect])

a lacquered tray
turned into a toilet
by the flies

the houseflies
turn a lacquered tray
into an outhouse

This, too, is a pretty sorry haiku. But Issa may have chuckled as he wrote it. Here is why – a haiku he wrote five years earlier:

ぬり盆にころりと蝿の辷りけり　一茶
nuribon ni korori to hae no suberikeri – issa (d.1827)
(lacquered tray on, tumble/quickly fly/ies slip[emphatic])

a lacquered tray:
the flies fall down
and slide about

the lacquered tray
a fly takes a hard spill
and slips about

houseflies
on a lacquered tray
lose their feet

all of the flies
slip and lose their feet
a lacquered tray

a lacquered tray
have you ever seen flies
fall on their ass?

Lots of tries, but the mimetic adverb for taking a quick spill, *korori,* is just too good to be matched in translation. Regardless, the tray-as-toilet haiku is greatly improved by the existence of this haiku on flies in trouble which suggests the former might be titled, *"Revenge of the Flies."* Another poet jokes about a mess of flies:

馬糞紙は蝿の都の御製哉　朧意 東日記
bafunshi wa hae no miyako no gyosei kana – ryûi (1681)
(horse-shit-paper [cardboard?]-as-for, fly/ies' capitol's honorable[imperialism]-make 'tis)

cardboard
marble for the capitol
of the flies

packing-paper
for imperial poems of
a fly capitol

I only just now (2004/9/14) learned from Tenki that the "gyo" 御 in "gyosei" 御製 was not just an unEnglishable honorific (usually pronounced "mi" or "on") but together with "*sei*" means a poem made by a member of the Imperial family! In other words, *the second translation is the correct one.* I fear I could not find a good word for the "horse-shit-paper." It is often translated as "cardboard," but it was not always that. It was a cheap dark rough paper. (*Does anyone know a good word for such paper in English?*) Because this *ku* was in a *Danrin* (chat-woods?) anthology, I *imagine* it an Osakan view of a ticky-tacky Tokyo (then, Edo), but this awaits confirmation by a historian.

しこつ蝿火入の灰を又浴る　一茶
shikotsu hae hi-ire no hai o mata abiru – issa (d.1827)
(filthy fly! stove-pipe ashes[obj] again bathe)

air pollution

you filthy fly!
back for another bath
of stove-ash

the hearth monster

you, bad fly, you!
bathing yourself again
in my stove ash

This is Issa's only haiku where he seems downright angry at the flies for making a mess. It is not about their toilet habits, unless we include toiletry in the broadest meaning of the word. If my recollection is right, Issa's insulting adjective *shikotsu* is found in Japan's oldest book of poetry, "Ten Thousand Leaves" (*Manyôshû*). A distraught lover uses the colloquialism three times in a single poem damning the person, house and bed of an unfaithful mate. Literally meaning "piss," it might be translated as "filthy," "damn," or, if you are English, "bloody."

蝿の身も希ありてや灰浴る　一茶
hae no mi mo negai arite ya hai abiru – issa (d.1827)
(fly/ies body/self too, wishes/petitions have/!: ashes bathe/cover)

ablution

flies, too
petition the gods
ash-bathing

the petitioners

covered in ash:
so, houseflies have things
they wish for.

The Japanese have long been big on ablution, not only to purify themselves, but carried to excess – such as letting a waterfall fall upon one's head for hours –to petition the help of the gods for serious matters. Flies, Issa seems to say, do the same thing by bathing in ashes. The translation is hurt by the lack of a good verb in English for the act of showering and covering oneself with a foreign substance. The closest verb we have is "dust," but to speak of dusting oneself with ashes is stylistically awkward. Perhaps old Issa's anger with ashen flies in the previous poem mean that he thinks he knows just what the flies want: a dead body, *his*. One of his last fly *ku* seems to give credence to this interpretation:

無常鐘蝿虫めらもよっくきけ　一茶
mujôgane haemushimera mo yokku kike – issa (d.1827)
(impermanence[funeral]-bell fly-bugs[+insulting suffix], too, well listen!)

the bell tolls
for all of us, listen up
you damn flies!

the bell tolls
all you fucking flies
better listen!

What does one do with an insulting suffix with no particular meaning? [1] I thought about "wretched" rather than "damn" or "fucking," but it just didn't sound right. Said bell as a "funeral bell" is not in my 10-volume dictionary, but *mujô-kemuri* means the smoke one sees after a cremation, so it can hardly mean anything else. Flies, here, might also be metaphor: people obsessed with survival who rub their hands = pray = beg for a long life. If, however, Issa really means "flies," the idea might be that "you guys seem to really enjoy corpses and funerals, but, hey, the bell doesn't toll for humans alone."

1. Dearth of Meaningless Emotion in English. As I revise today (2005, Jan. 12), I heard of a famous musician describing the "bad word" (which upset the censors) he used while accepting an award, the "percussive part of English." If he spoke Japanese, the musician could have expressed his excitement to the full, enjoyed a whole drum solo, without any words considered "bad." To someone who speaks Japanese, the way English cannot be evocative without upsetting the religious or sexually repressed is amusing.

• •

a T*ransport* of flies

– how they hitch-hike, get under your hat and ride piggyback –

蝿をうつして代る関守　武玉川
hae o utsushite kawaru sekimori – mutamagawa
(flies transferring change border-guard)

transferring flies
a change of guard
at the check-point

見附番蝿をうつしてかハリ合　柳樽
mitsukeban hae o utsushite kawariai – yanagidaru 2
(guards, flies transferring, changing-meet)

as the guards
exchange their duties
flies transfer

Japanese cities had few solid walls but abounded in mandatory checkpoints. People had to show travel passes and get the proper stamps. Religious travel was favored, so haiku professionals like Issa tended to travel as lay monks. Rubbing their hands to get permission to enter a country, they were, as we have seen, compared to flies. The senryû are sweet if you only think of real flies; but I fear senryû lovers and border-guards reading it would envision a back-up of supplicants at the gate.

梁の蝿を送らむ馬の上　其角
utsuwari no hae o okuramu uma no ue – kikaku (d.1706)
(beams' flies[obj] send/deliver-would horse-on-top)

take with you
the flies on the rafter
by horseback

on horseback
then take with you
the rafter-flies

Kikaku, a rowdy Zen monk half-disciple and half-competitor of Bashô, wrote the above, prefaced with these words: "as a farewell gift for someone begging leave to go to Shinano," [信濃へ参らるる人暇乞せらる截に] which, you might recall, is Issa's country. The "rafter-flies" (*utsuwari-no hae*) pun on "rafter dust"(*utsuw/hari-no hai*), an allusion to a fine singing/reading voice that made dust dance in the rafters according to a Chinese tale; and may hint at "rafter-swallows," known for close family bonds. So we have a complimentary send-off, with a possible dig at Shinano (*owls to Athens, coal to Pittsburg, and flies to Shinano?*), all in an untranslatable fly-sized haiku.

昼顔にしはしうつるや牛の蝿　几董
hirugao ni shibashi utsuru ya ushi no hae – kitô (d.1789)
(convolvulus-on/with, a while transfer: cow's/s' flies)

siesta

for a while
they visit a day-glory
cow flies

high noon

moving for a while
to the bindweed bloom
the flies on the cow

Scientific names for the plant (*Calystegia japonica* or, more loosely, *convolvulus*) will not do for a poem. Bindweed isn't much better, for "flower" or "bloom" must be added. In Japanese, *hirugao* joins the "morning-face," and "evening-face" – respectively *morning* and *evening glories* – as a "day-face." An old poem about moving flies: "Wild pink / flies coming from the stables/teamsters of yotsumachi (*nadeshiko no hae wa yotsumachi-no umaya kana* 石竹の蝿は四町の馬屋哉　沾徳) Sentoku (d.1747) plays on the *Dianthus superbus* standing for maidens, and teamsters had the reputation of being womanizers. The day-glory *may* be a person out at mid-day, but it is unlikely.

..

唐迄もうつり行らん蝿の足　焼台
kara made mo utsuriyuku ran hae no ashi – gyôtai (d.1792)
(chinese/candy-until-to, transfer-goes! fly's leg/s)

a ticket to ride

from host to host
all the way to china!
flies get around

My first reading of this poem was far crazier than the correct one. It was this:

the candy-man
carries out of town
a fly's leg

I first supposed the character for "China" used here (唐) was shorthand for another (糖) meaning "sugar" or "sweets"(such abbreviation is not uncommon) in which case, we would be talking about a tiny fly leg stuck onto a traveling piece of candy. Perhaps a Chinese candy-seller in Nagasaki failed to sell all his wares and . . . But it is almost certain Gyôtai's *ku* concerns mobility: *legs* are idiomatic for modes of transport in Japanese (as *arms* are for weapons in English). I can't help wondering if there is an earlier poem ending on the legs of rain (*ame no ashi)* – meaning the rain seen falling down from a cloud – "rain" and "candy" are both pronounced *ame* – for such a borrowing +allusion would make this poem wittier.

~~~~~~

Later. As it turns out, this leg idea was not entirely my invention. There *was* such a poem, a senryû written about a 100 years later. I had read and even marked it :

飴の蝿足一本を置てにげ　柳樽
ame no hae ashi ippon o oite nige – *yanagidaru* bk. 99-93, 100-144
(candy's fly leg one[obj] stuck, leaving-flees)

the candy-fly
fleeing, one leg is
left behind

Now, put this next to the candy-man poem pulled from my memory masquerading as creativity, and we have a fine stereo effect! This type of thing makes me glad to
~~~~~~

have so imperfect a memory! (And it is why I do not think most borrowings are plagiarism: I assume other poets were and are as scatter-brained as I am).

~~~~~~

..

Flies are not loners. If they can find anything to hang on to, they do. Here is a haiku about flies meeting up with people.

我背にもつくか旅行く冬の蝿　百明
waga se ni mo tsuku ka tabiyuku fuyu no hae – hyakumyô (d.1784)
(my back-to-even stick? traveling-go winter fly/flies)

would you, then
stick to my back, travelling
winter fly?

I tried, but failed to find a translation that would make the poem interesting. But, then again, the original is not very interesting. The next works better:

人々にすかり付けり舟の蝿　志硯　心一つ
hitobito ni sugari tsukikeri fune no hae – shigan (1791)
(tpeople-people-to, clinging attached[emphatic-perfect]: boat's flies)

each finds
a person to keep
boat-flies

boat-flies
each hangs on
to someone

boat-flies
each finds itself
a passenger

~~~~~~

Issa has written more on the transport of flies than everyone else combined. And all of them are about the thing itself, honest-to-goodness flies. Not only does this make them genuine haiku, but far easier to translate. His earliest traveling fly is suspiciously close to the older day-glory and wild-pink poems:

蝿負ふや花なでしこに及ぶ迄　一茶
hae ou ya hana-nadeshiko ni oyobu made – issa (d.1827)
(fly/ies-carry [on back] flowering wild-pink-to reach-until)

service

i carry
a fly all of the way
to the wild-pink

taxi cab

i drop off
my houseflies
at the wild-pink

a favor

carrying flies
i take them all the way
to the wild-pink

Has Issa read old haiku, and pretending to take them literally, thinks flies will enjoy such flowers? Or has he noted that his flies ditched him when he passed by a young woman? The verb *ou* has no match in English, It means to carry something or somebody on one's back. Because it is the way young children or decrepit parents were carried, the poem is warmer in the original. This concept is later made explicit in one of Issa's cutest poems.

親しらず蝿もしっかりおぶさりぬ　一茶
oya-shirazu hae mo shikkari obusarinu – issa (d.1827)
(parent-not-knowing fly, too, securely piggybacks)

the natural

never knowing
a parent, the fly rides
piggyback

another mystery

not even knowing
its parents, flies ride well
piggyback

The Europeans have long carried their babies in front, costing parents the use of their arms and, because it takes far more strength to carry a child in one's arms than on one's back, making it impossible for tiny tots to carry babies, much less play at the same time, as Japanese children did (See *Topsy-Turvy 1585*) Lacking the practice, we lack a basic word for it and must make do with the comical "piggyback."

~~~~~~

Issa usually did not have to piggyback his flies; they hitched a ride inside his hat. This does not mean that the flies were trapped inside like ours occasionally are. Japanese hats are a cross between an umbrella and an upside-down salad bowl. Called *kasa* – exactly what umbrellas are called (only the Chinese characters differ) – they are held on by various harness arrangements rather than clinging to the head and trapping hot air as our cold-weather designs do. The flies are free to fly in and out or cling on wherever they want and share the ample shade with the poet.

笠の蝿も（う）けふから（は）江戸者ぞ　一茶
kasa no hae mo[mô] kyô kara [wa]edomono zo – issa (d.1827)
(hat's fly/ies too[already] today-from[as for,] [you are] edoites!)

sombrero fly
from today you too
are an edoite!

sombrero flies
from today, you
are edoites!

An Edoite is a resident of Edo, the largest and most prosperous city in the world during Issa's lifetime. Issa spent most of his life on the outskirts of the mighty city now called Tokyo. This is not just a nominal change of identity. Issa wrote a number of poems about Edoites, with their quick-to-quarrel and extremely active character.

..

今日からは田舎の蝿ぞ道の駅　AQ
kyô kara wa inaka no hae zo michi no eki – akyû (ukimidô fly-fest)
(today-from-as-for, country-fly/flies! road station)

the rest stop
fly, from today you're
a country fly
~~~~~~

AQ's poem did pretty well at the Ukimidô Fly-fest. He was aware of playing with Issa, but the other participants probably were not. Back to Issa. In the last *ku*, he came from the country. In the next, he lives in it:

..

帰庵　　笠の蝿我より先へかけ入ぬ　一茶
"kian" kasa no hae ware yori saki e kake-irinu – issa (d.1827)
("return[to]-hut" hat's fly/ies: me more-than before-to, hasten-enter)

coming home

the flies
in my hat
beat me in!

I thought of the opposite, too: *going out*: "The flies / beat me / into my hat!" But Issa wouldn't have written *that* for it would not be true. A dog might anticipate a master's going out, but a fly? *Hardly!* What Issa wrote, however, could be true. If the house looked cooler than Issa, a smart fly could well beat him into it.

雨止ぞ立て行 / \ 笠の蝿　一茶
ame yamu zo tatte yuke yuke kasa no hae – issa (d.1827)
(rain ends! take off! go! go! hat's fly/ies)

the rain's over
take off! hat-flies
go! go! go!

One more of Issa's many fine imperative haiku. An older haiku by a poet Issa liked:

払ふ手にはかなや蝿の雨やどり　大江丸 kzg
harau te ni hakanaya hae no ameyadori – ôemaru? (d.1805)
(brushing/shooing hand-by impermanent/sad: fly's/flies rain-shelter)

a shooing hand
fly's shelter from the rain
is no longer

a shooing hand
the poor fly takes
a rain check

Issa doesn't always specify how the flies accompany him. Sometimes they just come and go with him or his guests.

我庵の蝿をも連て帰りけり　一茶
waga io no hae o mo tsurete kaeri-keri – issa (d.1827)
(my hut's fly/ies also/even in tow, go/es back[+emphatic/perfect])

shinano here i come!

i'm going home
the flies of my shack
for a retinue

the popular poet

heading back
the flies from my hut
in tow

god speed!

with the flies
from my hut in tow
back he heads

My first two readings are based on the fact it was written in the year Issa headed back to Shinano for good; I added a third in case Issa was writing about a guest, though it is unlikely. Regardless, we can bet Issa is conscious of Shinano. Remember Kikaku's poem? Issa's self-deprecation builds upon poetic precedent.

我出れば又出たりけり庵の蝿　一茶
ware dereba mata detarikeri io no hae – issa (d.1827)
(i leave/left-when, again leaving/left[emphatic], hut's fly/ies)

companionship

when i leave
out they go again
my hut-flies

when i left
out they went again
my hut-flies

This is just a plain ole haiku (except for the conjugation of the verb that does not really English and suggests that *whatever he does, the flies do too*) but you have to admire a man for paying such close attention to his flies! In Issa's time, such plain poems were far rarer than today, when they are a dime a dozen. So I give it a scarcity value, as well.

客人のおきみやげ也門の蝿　一茶
marôdo no okimiyage nari kado no hae – issa (d.1827)
(guest/s [from? to?] parting-gift becomes: gate/door's fly/ies)

a keepsake
from my honored guest
these door-flies

Marôdo is a beautiful classic term for guest, not just any guest, but a rare one, entertained for the first time. According to anthropologists they were sometimes mistaken for gods in the old times. It is why I added the adjective "honored." Could Issa have remembered a verse by Teitoku? "Leave a bird or two / for a keepsake, won't you! / returning geese!" (*ichi ni wa mo okimiyage ni seyo kaeru-kari.*) But the poems are not *that* close and I am not certain why Issa uses the classic term.

And sometimes the flies come all by themselves, but that is the subject for the next chapter.

..

EXTRA: *A fly has come here too* Santôka (d. 1940) 蝿も移つてきてゐる 山頭火 (*hae mo utsutte kite-iru*). "The poet has come from another place and the fly too that's all" – TK

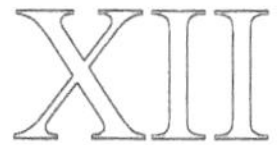

Living with flies

issa's playmate, *musca benedicta*

起て見よ蝿出ぬ前の不二の山　一茶
okite miyo hae denu mae no fuji no yama – issa (d.1827)
(get up, see: flies appear-before fuji-mountain)

(*the poet's advice to himself*)

up and rise!
see mount fuji before
the houseflies

Night is a country that belongs to the mosquitoes. Day belongs to the flies. By getting up early, we can witness the flies retaking the world every day. Or, someone in East Japan can simply enjoy the unsullied snow-cap of Mt. Fuji. Could Issa allude to people engaged in *Fuji môde*, the Fuji-climbing pilgrimages common in his day.

蝿のもち蝶から先（に）来たりけり　一茶
hae no mochi chô kara [yori?]saki ni kitari-keri – issa (d.1827)
(fly/ies' sweetrice-cake: butterfly-from[before?] come/came[+emphatic/perfect])

dibs

my sweetrice cake
belongs to the flies who
beat out the butterflies

property rights

the flies own
the rice-cake – they beat out
the butterflies

Issa has more poems about swinishly hungry butterflies than flies, but here, he suggests that the flies tend to get there first. Another version goes "The flies' rice-cake / i don't think they are / calling the butterflies" (~蝶に来よとは思ぬぞ ~ *chô ni koyo to wa omowanuzo*). I am not sure if I get it.

飯欠もそまつにせぬや御世の蝿　一茶
meshikake mo somatsu ni senu ya miyo no hae – issa (d.1827)
(table-scraps, too, they waste-not: honorable-era/nowaday's flies)

frugal times

even scraps
from the table not wasted
by our flies

frugality

even table-scraps
are not taken for granted:
this age of flies!

This was written in Bunka 12, the year after Issa married, and would seem to be a comment on the times, for his *miyo* is a common feature in dozens of such poems of his. The next *ku* was written in Bunsei 8, after he has buried his wife Kiku and all their children, remarried and divorced. It was a drought year, which Issa spent almost entirely on the road.

くれておく飯（に）かまはず宿の蝿　一茶
kurete-oku meshi[ni] kamawazu yado no hae – issa (d.1827)
(received meal [at], troubled-not, inn's fly/ies)

don't look

the inn-flies
don't mind if their food
is a handout

beggars can't be choosy

we inn-flies
don't mind if our food
is a handout

a gift-horse

it's a hand-out:
who cares if the food's covered
with inn-flies

in the mouth

hey, i'm happy
to feed all the inn-flies
with my free meal!

Who is the happy party, Issa, the flies or beggars at the inn! I really don't know. Here's a food-sharing *fly-ku* written in better times:

世がよくばもひとつとまれ飯の蝿　一茶
yo ga yokuba mo hitotsu tomare meshi no hae – issa (d.1827)
(world if/being good, one more alight meal/rice's fly/ies)

when prosperity smiles

good times:
one more fly, land!
on my rice

the host

times are good!
i welcome yet another
fly to my table

invitation

a good year, this!
come join us for dinner
one more fly

good news

prosperity's here
our food can take another
fly with cheer!

Sometimes it is hard to tell if the Japanese is a supposition or not. I chose "when/being" over "if" here, but it would be possible to do this:

si fuera rico
yo diria a las moscas
venid! yo invito!

(trans. by josé vicente anaya)

direct translation	*loose translation*
if [i] were rich i'd say to the flies come! i invite [you]!	if times were good i'd say "flies, i invite you to share our food!

Anaya has many fine a-b-a translations of classic haiku. Note his *rico* and in*vito,* a Dickinsonian vowel-centric rhyme, is similar to Japanese internal rhyme and better than my "good/food." We used to call our food either "bread" (*our daily bread*) or "meat" (*one man's meat . . .*) and still call it our "meal" (ground grain). The Japanese, likewise conflate their meals with "rice" – not uncooked rice which is called *kome, okome, junmai,* and so forth, but cooked rice: *gohan,* or *meshi*, as in the above poem. Issa was combining a couple ideas in this poem. First, "flies above a meal" (*meishi no ue no hae*) was an idiom for a boisterous swarm of anything. (We, too have: "the common people swarm like summer flies" – Henry VI 2-6). Second, Issa associated boisterous flies with prosperity. He has 3 more such poems, all written in his last decade of life.

草の葉や世の中よしと蠅さわぐ　一茶
kusa no ha ya yo no naka yoshi to hae sawagu – issa (d.1827)
(grass/weed- leaves:/! world/times-among friendly and flies active/noisy)

leaves of grass:
when times are good
the flies clamor

out in the bush
a frenzy of flies when
things go well

Kusa is "grass." But it is a broader category in Japanese than English and includes much that we might call weeds. Indeed, "weeds" are *zasô,* or "sundry-grass," and "weeding" is *kusa-tori,* "pulling grass." Most herbs are *kusa*, or more strictly speaking, *yakusô,* "medical grass," flowering plants are called things like *sakura-sô* = "cherry-grass" (primrose) or *fukumigusa* = "deep-look-grass" (peony), etc.. Here, I use expressions from the weedier side of *kusa* because the emphasis on the "leaves of grass" suggests that Issa may well be alluding to the behavior of the common folk.

豊年の声を上けり門の蝿　一茶
hônen no koe o agekeri kado no hae – issa (d.1827)
(bountiful-year-voice/s raise-up gate-flies)

a bountiful year:
the flies by the gate
raise their voices

I wonder if the original's "bountiful-year-voice" would work in German translation? English, unfortunately, came apart at the seams over 500 years ago. I think there is a good possibility that Issa is alluding to visits from beggars and/or bonzes here.

田がよいぞよいぞとや蝿さはぐ　一茶
ta ga yoi zo yoi zo to ya hae sawagu – issa (d.1827)
(field is good[+emphatic] good[+emph.]:/! flies clamor)

the crop's good!
good! good! how
the flies clamor!

In this poem, Issa may be making an observation that extends far beyond his gate. These flies may be the poor – the real poor, not the poet who occasionally had to tighten his belt, but was not really in danger of starving – for this was a time of rice-riots (wealthy merchants and wholesalers sacked by crowds) and other unrest, some of which even our liberal "peoples poet" thought went too far.

~~~~~~

Lest you think the fly-feeding I seem to have strayed from was a monopoly of Issa's, here is an older poem by one of Bashô's disciples that I think deserves recognition as a particularly fine classic *fly-ku*:

顔に付飯粒蝿にあたへけり　嵐雪
kao ni tsuku meshitsubu hae ni ataekeri – ransetsu (d.1707)
(face-on stick rice-grain fly-to give[+emphatic-perfect)

the report

a grain of rice
stuck on my face – i gave it
to a housefly

alms

i give the flies
grains of rice picked from
the master's face

feeding the world

i give the rice
stuck on the cat's face
to the flies

An dying person would often eat white rice (uncommon enough for all but the wealthy to have been considered a delicacy), hence "the master's face" in the second reading. There also is a *senryû* with no flies, but a grain, or grains of rice stuck on the whiskers of a cat, or cats, making love. I cannot recall the date, but it suggested my third reading. But, I imagine that Japanese men a few hundred years ago did what Japanese men do today, namely, shovel rice into their mouths from the bowl which is lifted up to rest against the bottom lip. That would explain the rice on the face, so the first reading seems the most likely to me. After finishing the meal, sipping some tea and/or sucking on a final salted plum, the poet feels that piece of rice on his cheek and . . .
~~~~~~

飯粒の 一粒づゝに蝿とまる　子規 拾 明治27
meshitsubu no hito-tsubu zutsu ni hae tomaru – shiki (d.1902)
(meal/rice-grain's grain-each-on fly rests)

each grain
of rice has one
fly on it

I doubt that this is a bowl black with flies, for such a sight would not create a pleasant poem. I think it is about a table top after a boisterous meal with grains of rice here and there, each with its 6-footed owner.

むれる蝿皺手に何の味がある　一茶
mureru hae shiwade ni nan no aji ga aru – issa (d.1827)
(swarming flies, wrinkled-hand-to what flavor/taste is?)

the old salt

swarming flies:
what flavor is there
in an old hand?

attractive

swarming flies
is my wrinkled hand
that tasty?

This was written less than four years before Issa's death. It is a great improvement of one of his first *fly-ku:* "the flies at my shack / what the hell makes them / hang around?" (*io no hae nani o uro-uro nagarafuru* 庵（の）蝿何をうろうろ長らふる). Issa has many such second or even third or fourth poems. Like this one, they almost always taste better than the earlier ones. Unfortunately, few of the good poems Issa wrote in his last years make it into anthologies. Japanese haiku scholars, turned off by the large number of rough haiku he wrote at that time, tend to throw out many of his best babies with the bath-water.

~~~~~~

Food-related poems tend to be personal and subjective, far from what the haiku establishment thinks good. The next three fly-ku are of a more conventional style. They observe. Still, such fine observation indirectly suggests how close Issa was to his flies. Reading them, you feel he really did appreciate their being around.

出始の蝿やしぶしぶ這畳　一茶
dehajime no hae ya shibushibu hau tatami – issa (d.1827)
(appear-first's fly: gingerly creeps-tatami)

the first to come
treads lightly – flies
on tatami

the first fly
treads gingerly
on the tatami

the first fly
timidly walks
the tatami
~~~~~~

the first fly
creeps cautiously o'er
the tatami

Seeing this alone, one might think it is the first fly of the year. But it might only be the first of the morning. In the afternoon, they swarm like sharks in a blood frenzy, but all begins with one timid fly. In the original, the psychological mimesis *shibushibu* makes the poem. I tried 4 different adverbs, but am not confident any work.

初蝿や客より先へ青だたみ　一茶
hatsu hae ya kyaku yori saki e aodatami – issa (d.1827)
(first fly: guest/s before, green/new tatami)

the first fly
beats the guest in!
fresh tatami

fresh tatami
the first fly enjoys it
before my guest

The beauty of this *fly-ku* can only be appreciated by one who has lived for years on *tatami*. New tatami smells like freshly mown grass and is literally green in color. Old tatami not only turns brown, loses its shininess and gets frizzled on top like old carpet, and – if one has the acquaintance of cats – inevitably houses a thriving colony of fleas. When people move, the tatami is always changed.

青畳音して蝿のとびにけり　一茶
aodatami oto shite hae no tobinikeri – issa (d.1827)
(new/green tatami: sound makes fly flies off)

new tatami
a fly makes a sound
taking off

new tatami
the fly leaves behind
a sound

New tatami would echo better than a soft or packed-down old tatami. But this is not the sound made by the wings. It is the one made by the disengagement of the fly's sticky feet from the crisp surface of the new mat. I have a vague memory of this sound accompanied by a deep and slow breath in and the soothing scent of the straw.

~~~~~~

Issa tells off a fly

In life, but particularly in the literary arts, I have my doubts about people who don't hate. People who say they like *all* birds really don't appreciate any. If they *always* welcome their singing, then, they hear little of it. Likewise for *anything.* I think the following *fly-ku* is splendid.
~~~~~~

さはぐなら外がましぞよ庵（の）蝿　一茶
sawagu nara soto ga mashi zo yo io no hae – issa (d.1827)
(disturb [others] if, outside is better [+!/: hut's fly)

ultimatum

if you want
to horse-around, then,
housefly, leave!

house rules

if you want
to zip about, housefly,
go out!

if you would
horse around, outside's better
fly of my hut

the bouncer

act rowdy,
fly, and you'd best
get out!

house-mates

act up, fly,
and, by god, you'd best
get out!

The rambunctious fly mentioned is probably one type that sometimes comes into the house and rips about like a racing car on a basketball court. I don't know if housefly is right. "Hut's fly" doesn't work, as can be seen from the middle translation, "fly of my hut" is too long and ludicrous.

~~~~~~

Flies by Themselves

So what do houseflies do when they are not at home, which is to say with us? A good question:

夜の蝿人を忘れて何処へか　之房 新選
yoru no hae hito o wasurete izuko e ka – shibô (1773)
(night's fly/ies, people[obj] forgetting, where to?)

mystery

forgetting men
where in the world do flies
go at night

flies without people

where
do our flies go
at night

the question

flies at night
where do they go
without us
~~~~~~

蝇蝇蝇

The F*ly*-hunter's Complaint,
or, an anti-Issa who loves to hate flies!

Eventually, the Occupation and the Editorial writer at *Asahi Shinbun* had their way. Today, Japan is no longer a Paradise for Flies. This rant found on the net googling 蝇蝇蝇蝇 reflects the change and touches upon the Japanese attitude toward flies. I translate+digest (reducing by 80% in the process) eight articles written anonymously, for good reason. Be prepared for something rare in Japanese, bad language (And I cut 90% of it!). Believe it or not, *the Fly-Hunter* – as I think we should call him because he resembles our large-game hunters who would preserve nature to have something to shoot – had the same line of flies 蝇蝇蝇蝇蝇 I use to mark the edge of special items (蝇を数匹並んで Google すれば、この恐ろしい蝇狩り大痔もち男のサイトに行ける).

~~~~~~

1

Where have all the shit-faced flies gone? [The original, shit-jerk-flies (*hae-no kuso-yarô*) suggests *kusobae* or dung flies to me]. Recently, you don't see any. The reasons are clear enough. It is because the garbage pick-up is frequent now, and because of the circumstances: Japan quickly became a hygienic country in the 1980's and to realize its ideal of artificial cleanliness used large quantities of agricultural chemicals, and increasingly effective insecticides. Be that as it may, we have become obsessed with the illusion of cleanliness (*seiketsu*) and the fly as a symbol of dirtiness has been shut out of our lives. Soon, the existence of flies and other such may even be vanquished from our minds. . . .

When was the last time I saw a fly? I got to thinking about how quickly the flies disappeared and I began to feel lonely. I missed them.

> "So what! It's better not to have them around!"
> "What! You like flies? Yu……ck!"

Come on! Who says I *like* flies? I just think it would have been better not to wipe them all out like that. It is absurd to see humans chasing furiously after dung flies. Can such a species be called grown-up? Humanity should be ashamed of itself!

Isn't it dandier to have a fly or two buzzing about your room?

2

Today, there is no longer any demand for fly-paper. To me, a town without fly-paper is boring. It is still manufactured in South-east Asia, but when you go to a hardware store or home-center and chase it down in a dusty corner – it used to be in the front – it is as likely as not absent and available only as an order from the warehouse. Asking for it seems an inconvenience to the clerks busy selling more expensive things. Like the fly it is treated as a nuisance.

3

Hearing how I miss both flies and fly-paper, readers might say

> "Sure enough, you are a fly-loving pervert (このハエ好きの変態男)!"

I never cared for people who disparage others, so this makes me feel like rolling up a newspaper and swatting these human-flies on the back of the head, but to continue with the fly-paper, I remember liking the sound and feeling of unrolling it and how it is white when you hang it up in the morning and black with flies by the evening. Many are still alive and you can poke at them with toothpicks . . . I think I'd like to try that one more time.

And I think I will have that chance, for once we fill up our surroundings with garbage that cannot be processed and increased immunity to insecticide creates superflies, they will be back. Of course, they can keep making stronger insecticides to kill stronger flies, but that cannot go on for long because anything that strong would kill us. Trust me, they'll be back. Nature always rocks back on us. Call it the revenge of the fly on humans who denied them symbiosis.

Humans and flies back on a level playing-field. I welcome it. Just like in old times, we can enjoy a good fight. Hey, you shit-faced flies, are you waiting for me? I'm waiting for you!

4

To me, a fly is something that you shoot as soon as you see it. The best ammunition is made from a 5 centimeter-square piece of paper tightly folded up and shot from a rubber-band strung between the index finger and the thumb. I still recall the thrill I felt knocking off a fly with a perfect shot.

With flies few and far between, one hesitates before killing them, but when there are so many they are coming out your ears, there is no need for concern. I really would like to once again enjoy the excitement of picking off flies. And let me add, it must be flies. No other bug will do. Why?

The fly is the most evolved of all the world's flying creatures. Even the most advanced of our planes cannot match them. The closest we can come to their style of flying is the UFO. Disregarding gravity, they can land on walls or ceilings, take off without a runway and zip every which way at low or high speeds! They are boundless, exceeding even our imagination.

That is what makes killing a fly so wonderful. That is
~~~~~~

what makes you so excited. At 40, I reflect. And I think, my feelings about flies were right on.

When you hear that buzz of a fly in the air, your sleeping attack-instinct immediately awakes and your mouth automatically voices "that shit-dripper! [m. f__ker!]!" and if you get him with that first shot, you cannot help but grin from one side of your mouth. Yes, when I see a fly, a forgotten primordial power wells up inside.

5

No, it is not just hate, my feelings toward flies are more complex and include rivalry based on grudging admiration and perhaps, even, jealousy. And I feel irked that they make me feel that way for they really aren't that great at fleeing. Compared to the untouchable cockroach, they are downright familiar with us, touchable. . . . There are books on the cockroach, but flies never get more than a few pages. They are always *second best.*

6

But, oh you damn flies (*hae no kuso-baka-tareme* – lit. fly-shit-fool-dripping-jerk)! You could stay outside on dog-shit, but you dare come in here!

Of course, I shoot you with my rubberbands. Still, I am a gentleman, a samurai or knight to the end and will fight you fairly. If you met up with my mother, you would not have a chance. She has no philosophy whatsoever. She will just kill you on sight. To her, you are nothing but an object to evoke her killing instinct or a stimulus that evokes a response with whatever weapon she has on hand. It shows in the merciless eyes that even look spooky to her children. She doesn't realize it, but all the frustrations of marrying into a different household have been taken out on the flies for generation after generation. And, boy do women build up that frustration. It is like the shit you hear that some women can keep in for 10 days. No man can get that full of it! But will human frustrations ever be satisfied with the bodies of flies? No. It is like trying to fill the sea with pebbles.

~~~~~~

Note: This description of mothers and women, while it may hold a kernel of the truth, could use some balance. Here is a haiku that did quite well in the Fly-ku Fest (*haekukai*) put on for me by Ukimidô:

暮れ際の蝿叩き持つ母無敵　亜子
kuregiwa no haetataki motsu hahamuteki – ako
(dusk-edge's fly-swatter holding mama no-enemy)

mom invincible
holding her fly-swatter
in the sunset

I can not help viewing this next to the Hero-mother's of the USSR or our Rosie the Riveter, but it is more a depiction of a good old-fashioned mother selflessly giving her everything to protect the family as seen through the eyes of a little child.

~~~~~~

But, flies it will be. Hitting mosquitoes is bloody business and cockroaches splatter you with innards that smell worse than shit.

7

While I think of flies as shit-bugs and hunt any that come near, I do not always kill them. That is because I am a man of ideas and rules. Mine could not be more different from the mindset of my mother who, as I said, will splat a fly instantly.

I could, for example, be seated at the kotatsu (a low table in the middle of the room) and take a pot-shot at a fly in the far corner with the weapon described earlier. This takes great skill and concentration, and even then you frequently miss. But do I close the windows to prevent the fly from escaping? *No.* I had a childhood friend who would rush to close the open windows and gleefully laugh, *Hah! Now, we've gotcha!* I never did that and I should say that this same kid would take things without permission from my desk and, if you ask me, the two behaviors are doubtless related and show he had a character as ugly as a bloody dogshit. Fair men and boys do not want to shoot bound flies.

8

With me, the fly is always free to leave. And if I miss it, then that was the fly's good luck and if it flees it is that fly's victory. It is not that I sympathize for the shit-sucker. Rules are rules. On the battleground, we respect our adversary. That is what bushido and chivalry is all about.

With my mother – I repeat myself yet again – flies are but germs to be wiped out or tools for the relief of stress. You make think this is a piddling point of difference, but it destroys our original symbiotic relationship, where we thought of flies as spiteful bits of flying shit and they flew buzzing about drawing our attention to show they exist. This was fun, healthy and natural.

When I hear someone say, *"Oh, don't kill it. Flies are cuter than you think."* or *"Oh, look, can't you see it rubbing its little hands? Isn't that sweet?"* I feel like picking up a cat's hairball on the end of a stick and shoving it into their face. Anyone who could seriously say something like that is a nauseating shit-faced shrivel-prick with serious problems of impotence and ….[Editor: I apologize for the bad language, but leave it because it shows how far Japanese will go to prove they are hardboiled and the extent to which Issa's *fly-ku* as generally construed infuriates the macho-man. そういうセリフを平気で吐くヘドうんこのチンポちょびれは、感性の愚劣なアンポンタンの底抜けマンキンタンであると同時に、ビラビラおまんちょの汚れギンタマでもあると言えよう。] People who release fish they have caught are just as bad. If you catch a fish, then *eat it!* And some one who would "ririsu" (release) a fly they had in hand is such a fool he is only good for braining with the lid to the toilet bowl.

The ideal 21st century society is one where people have no

qualms whatsoever about killing the flies they encounter but just do it, naturally, one where we co-evolve in a swat-and-swatted relationship. Our modern age where circumstances do not allow this is as painful and sick as these sentences you read. *What our society needs is more shit!* and *more flies!*

9

The cockroach.

They are pure wariness. Their will-to-live infinitely exceeds ours, they reproduce like crazy, they can bite if you pick them up (one bit my finger as a child and I must admit that it traumatized me into letting them alone). They have the confidence of having lived with the dinosaurs and they will still be here if we kill ourselves with atomic weapons.

And how they stink! It is too much to bear. I feel like using darts or arrows on them, but so far have managed to forbear and make-do with slippers.

~~~~~~

Note: Mr. Cockroach summed up in a haiku:

御器噛追ひ詰めおいて助け呼ぶ　高沢良一
gokikaburi oitsume oite tasuke yobu – takasawa yoshikazu
(cockroach/es chase-corner place/leaving, help call)

dial 911?

big cockroach
after cornering it, she calls
for support

Not the most precise translation, but you get the idea. This is no bug to mess with . . . Another:

髭振りつ次はどうでる油虫　高沢良一
hige furitsu tsugi wa dô deru aburamushi – takasawa yoshikazu
(*whiskers/moustache waving/waging, next how act, cockroach*)

reading 1

whiskers move
what is coming next?
the big roach

reading 2

whiskers moving
cockroach considers
his next move

reading 3

his whiskers move
so what will be
the roach's?

duel with a roach

so what is
the whiskered wag's
next move

I did not feel up to disturbing Takasawa-san to ask exactly what his poem meant, so I have translated the possibilities. Back to the Fly-hunter.

~~~~~~

But the main thing that disgusts me most is that the way they slip around, something magnified by the fact they prefer the night. Compare that to the fly that boldly presents its face, and in the daylight. Now, I used to work as a reported for a financial paper and if there was one thing I didn't like, it was the corporations that were not open with their figures. I always felt that they were up to no good. This is supposed to be a democracy, is it not? And this was particularly true for Japanese companies. The foreign ones tended to be more up front**. . .**

~~~~~~

Note: There is a haiku that expresses the diurnal nature of most flies by foil:

罪深く夜を寝ぬ蝿や瓜の皮　几董 (d.1789)
tsumibukaku yo o nenu hae ya uri no kawa – kitô
(sin/crime-deeply, night sleep-not fly/ies! melon skin)

the sin is deep
flies awake at night
on melon rind

Or, if the fly is really a human melon thief – he or she might eat some melon on the spot, leaving rinds which real melon flies could enjoy,

up at night
a fly is up to no good
melon rind

Back to Fly-hunter's essay ↓

~~~~~~

The fly has something the cockroach lacks, *kakugo*. Resignation. It is prepared for death. That sounds grand, but I guess it comes down to this. The cockroach is the big jerk you wish to avoid and the fly the little jerk you want to bop.

Yes, the fly is a shit-faced piece of trash. You shouldn't let them sucker you. There are those bug-freaks who claim they are cute and misunderstood, and I say those freaks are themselves full of shit. Look, not only do they sit right on your face sucking your oil, but their very existence takes all of us for suckers. To praise them is to say you are a fool.

So Kobayashi Issa with his affectionate haiku about them rubbing their feet was a capital fool (*bakatare ni naru*).

People like that are flies, that think they themselves are cute and lovable. Well, I say, pick up a fly-swatter and swat those guys. They will love it.

10

Flies and toilet bugs (*senchin-mushi*), not long ago we had both in abundance.

In my old house, the toilet bugs came crawling up from the tank every day and I would pick them off one at a time with my pee and yet they never gave up; they would keep on coming,. They were magnificent. They were like the salmon that fight their way upstream to spawn and, worn out, die. They were like a certain boxer in the 1970's who kept getting knocked down only to stand back up to fight. Yes, we all knew toilet bugs back then. You might say that in the harsh post-war times, the toilet bugs provided us with both a perfect model of perseverance and a way to blow off steam, for what boy or man did not enjoy blasting them one at a time off the side of the toilet.

Indeed, doing that and shooting flies were my only real childhood pleasures.

蝿蝿蝿

EXTRA! EXTRA!

Is This Maudlin?

かうまでよりすがる蝿をうたうとするか　山頭火
kô made yorisugaru hae o utô to suru ka – santôka (d.1940)
(this-until cling-to/depend-upon fly[obj] hit-would do?)

would i swat
a fly that has become so close to me?

was i about to swat
a fly so much in need of me?

Is it strange to sometimes feel for a fly? How do we explain such compassion? As a "monk," Santôka could just parrot the line about all life being valuable, but instead dared to think about his relationship with a fly. The "Fly-hunter" would laugh at him. Would *you*?

And What About This?

蝿打つてさみしさの蝿を見つめけり／山頭火
hae utte samishisa no hae o mitsumekeri – santôka
(fly swattting/swatted, loneliness's fly/flies[obj] stare[at][+emph])

fly-swatting
staring at the fly
of loneliness

I thought it had to be *"Swatting flies / my loneliness ends up / staring at them."* But a Japanese friend wrote "the loneliness is the fly's, i think." Note: Santôka does not write of "a lonely fly."

Weak & *Dying* flies

fall and winter are another story

The fly by itself with no other indication of seasonality in the poem is a sign of summer. Needless to say, flies are found in other seasons. While the Spring fly is too rare in haiku to have developed any character to speak of, the Fall and Winter flies deserve a chapter, for they offer something different from the swarming and bothersome bane of summer.

~~~~~~

THE *LINGERING* FLIES OF *FALL*

蠅ならふはや初秋の朝日かな　野童（葛松原）
hae narabu haya aki no asahi kana – nodô (1692)
(flies lining up [across], already fall's morning-sun 'tis/!/?)

flies in a row
greet the sun: the first
day of autumn

a row of flies
it is already a fall
morning sun

秋の蝿障子を明けて追い出しぬ　野童
aki no hae shôji o akete oidashinu – nodô 17c.
(fall fly/flies paper-door open chase-out)

autumn flies
you open the shôji and
chase 'em out

引きとめらるまゝ逗留して
(held [prevented from leaving] –as-is-staying on)
追はれねは立つことしらず秋の蝿　也有
owareneba tatsu koto shirazu aki no hae – yayu (d.1783)
(chased-not-if, take-off/leave know/s-not fall fly/flies)

when invited to stay longer, i do

unchased
they never leave
fall flies

will stay put
unless you pursue it:
an autumn fly
~~~~~~

Issa has a poem about the clouds of summer, how they start the day in a neat row. I think most of us have observed that and thought it interesting. Not so many of us have observed the way the fall flies line up (across in rows – our English verb for "line up" assumes a column unless otherwise noted) on the paper doors and windows. Because the morning sun shining over the horizon, whether far off or the neighbor's roof, lights up the paper from the top first (or middle, if the eaves block the top) the tideline (?) of light would be horizontal and, at first, a narrow band. These flies, unlike the ones making a quick stop in midday, would be sitting head up in that band, I think.

人中で生まれたやうに秋の蝿　梅室
jinchû[hitonaka] de umareta yô ni aki no hae – baishitsu (1852)
people/man-among-at was-born-as-if, autumn-fly

they act as if
they were born among us
autumn flies

飛んで来て直ぐに打たれし秋の蝿 石川風女
tonde kite sugu ni utareshi aki no hae – ishikawa kazame
(flying come, immediately hit[passive] autumn fly/ies)

it flies in
and is instantly killed
a fall fly

or,

as soon as they land
autumn flies are swatted

Has human skill improved over the summer, while the flies slow down in the cool air? The modern haiku by Kazame is perfectly dispassionate. It has neither pity, nor hate. But it seems a pity for the autumn fly to be treated like that. A *ku* by Otsuni (d.1823) on what I take to be early summer flies makes my point in reverse: *"gathering all at once, the flies are hateful things."* Or,

..

集れは一度に憎し物の蝿　乙二
atsumereba ichido ni nikushimono no hae – otsuni (d.1823)
(gather-if/when, one-time-on, spiteful-thing's fly/flies)

when they gather
flies suddenly become
musca maledicta

Fear and hate would appear to have a "critical mass." Fall flies have dispersed. Few enough for observation *as individuals*, they seem closer to us. But, like the summer heat, some of the antagonism we – or some of us – feel lingers on, and when there are few enough to be individually spotted coming in, they may be picked off.

振上げた我手眺（詠）めつ秋の蝿 桃李 続明烏
furiageta waga te nagametsu aki no hae – tori (1776)
(waving-raised my-hand staring-at fall-fly)

the fall fly
just watches
my raised hand

手をもみて立ちかねにけり秋の蝿　家風 新類題発句集
te o momite tachikane-ni-keri aki no hae – kafû (1793)
(hand/s[+obj] wringing, take-off-cannot[+finality, fall-fly]

wringing its hands
unable to take-off
the autumn fly

..

I recall a bullfight in Mexico City. The bull was not in the mood. It even forgave the first few goads of the picadors and walked straight over to the TV camera and licked it. If I were rich, I would have stood up and offered to buy its life. The *momite,* or "wringing" in the second *ku,* is more anthropomorphic than the *suri,* or "rubbing" in Issa's famous fly-ku, because human behavior is explicit in the original denotation.

いくほどぞ日向追行秋の蝿　琴風　続の原
ikuhodo zo himuko oi-yuku aki no hae – kinpu (1688)
(how many?! sun/day-facing pursue-go autumn-fly)

the autumn fly
how many sun-chasing
days remain?

how many left
of the sunlight-chasing
autumn flies?

人去て畳の上を秋の蝿　五来 新類題
hito sarite tatami no ue o aki no hae – gorai (1793)
(people leaving/left tatami-on, autumn fly/flies)

autumn

no humans
the tatami is tread
by fall flies

people gone
upon the tatami
walks a fly

everyone out
fall flies walk about
on the tatami

Because the shôji, or paper sliding-doors, brighten with sunlight, flies shut in at night would be on them in the morning warming their bellies. And, whether there, on the tatami, or on your desk, the fall fly needs to be prodded to take off. The "o" in the last haiku suggests contradiction *and* walking (at least not flying) and I thought the lonely mood would be helped by adding that "walk" rather than simply writing "a fall fly" for the last line of that last *ku.* This is the type of haiku I could do ten takes on, but I will leave that to the reader and proceed to a haiku that combines a feeling I think of as modern with a touch of old grammar:

うたすともよかったものを秋の蝿　風後（恒誠）
utazu to mo yokatta mono o aki no hae – fûgo (c.1800)
(hit-not good-would-have-been [+particle of regret], fall-fly/flies)

why did i
have to swat him!
the fall fly

in retrospect
i should not have swatted
autumn flies

autumn flies
we really did not need
to swat them

The question here is whether the regret in the original is for striking a fall fly or of seeing the state of flies in the fall, then regretting the swatting of the previous month, at a time when it felt necessary if flies were not to take over the world. (風後の事もっと知りたいが。。。)

馬の尾にふり捨行や秋の蝿　虚白
uma no o ni furisute-yuku ya aki no hae – kyohaku (d.1847)
(horse's tail-by shake/fan-throw-away-go:/!/? fall-fly/ies)

whisked off
by horse tails, the flies
of fall go on

left behind
the horses, i mozy on
an autumn fly

tossed off
by tail after tail, the life
of a fall fly

At first, I ignored the grammar and made the horse's tail a subject: *Tossing them off / a horse's tail proceeds! / autumn flies.* I further imagined this scene: *Autumn flies / whisked off and left / by horse tails* (unlike summer flies, too weak to pick themselves us and rush back after the departing horse, . . .). I even did so making the tail the *only* subject: *The horse tail / leaves behind a trail / of fall flies.* The problem is that *ni* (by) does not permit such a reading. I have properly tried to feature the flies but, as you can see,, the translations are not very interesting. I imagine an aging poet allegorized his regret being left behind on some expedition, but who knows!

秋の蝿　蝿タタキ皆破レタリ　子規　明治34
aki no hae haetataki mina yaburetari – shiki (d.1902)
(fall flies, fly-swatters all torn and stuff)

autumn flies
and the fly-swatters
all broken

The *-tari* pegged on the verb in the original, leaves the claim open. In this case, it means not only *yabure* (broken or torn) but otherwise damaged in one way or another (eg. old and stained, too flexible, twisted, etc.). The closest I could come in English "and stuff" wouldn't make the poem, so I used "broken." Shiki wrote many poems about fall flies. Identity perhaps? With the swatter out of commission:

病室や窓アタタカニ秋ノ蝿　子規　明治 34
byôshitsu ya mado atataka ni aki no hae – shiki (d.1902)
(sick-room: window warmly autumn's fly/flies)

sanitarium

my sick room
basking in the window
an autumn fly

fall

my sick-room
the fly in the window
looks warm

a sick-room
the window is warm
autumn flies

The "warmly" in the original is hard to interpret for it is an adverb with no verb. In the last reading, I see Shiki sharing some of the sun and identifying with the fly/flies.

わがからだ ぬくしととまる秋の蝿　山口誓子
waga karada nukushi to tomaru aki no hae – yamaguchi seishi (mod.)
(my body warm if/and/therefore land/alight/stop/stay fall-fly)

a fall fly
my body's warm
so it lands

as my body
is warm, it stops
the fall fly

A good *ku.* In my reading copy of this book, I wrote *"We can appreciate what olde haiku missed by lacking the female perspective. Not only were there less women in haiku, but the subject of flies (like sea cucumber) was particularly short-changed."* Unfortunately, the well-known modern poet Yamaguchi Seishi happens to be male!

富士高く海低し秋の蝿一匹　西東三鬼
fuji takaku umi hikushi aki no hae ippiki – sanki (d.1962)
(fuji highly ocean lowly autumn fly one)

fuji high
ocean low, one
fall fly

I have no idea what this poem means. The grammar is just too vague. All I can do is imagine a fly in that blank space one finds in paintings between Fuji and the sea. In haiku, the fall is associated with air as clear as the water in the Bahamas. Even a fly could be seen a hundred miles… .

秋の蝿辿る海図の緯度経度 大島民郎
aki no hae tadoru kaizu no ido-keido – ôshima tamirô (modern)
(autumn fly reaches marine-chart's latitude-longitude)

the coordinates
on the marine chart where
the fall fly stops

an autumn fly
on my marine chart: note
the coordinates

Another Japanese-style poem-as-a-modified-noun. This is rare in English, although the first translation shows it is possible. The question is whether the shift of the subject from the end to the start ruins the poem or not. I think the snappy conclusion of the verb "stop" saves the poem, one enjoyed by every Japanese reader I know of.

(閑寂の地にして句を思ふに便ありと人々入つとへば)
俳諧のあまみを追ふや秋の蝿　成美
haikai no amami o ou ya aki no hae – seibi (1816)
(haikai's sweetness[obj] pursue:/!/? fall-fly)

(people say that a quiet place is
good for thinking up poems)

this pursuit of
haikai sweetmeat:
autumn flies

If I am not mistaken, the preface implies that a lonely abode would be a good place for an old haijin to retire. By "old," I do not mean real old, but 45 or 50. Japanese, as noted in item 3-21 of T*O*PSY-TURVY 1585, tended to hand over their fortunes and businesses to their children and retire early. Like the fly mentioned as a metaphor for a solitary existence, the poet would be in the Fall of his life.

~~~~~~

W*E* ARE W*INTER* FLIES
THE FLY AS M*ETAPHOR*

十月や冷たき蝿の顔へ来る　古巌
jûgatsu ya tsumetaki hae no kao e kuru – kogen (?)
(*tenth month!/?/: chilly fly/flies' face-to come*)

the 10th month:
a very chilly fly
comes to my face

The 10th month is the start of winter, late November or early December (the 10 still in its name, too) in "our" Gregorian calendar. The Shinto gods all go to Izumo and the flies call on the poet's face? The poem is refreshing for I tire of the following:

憎まれてながらふる人冬の蝿　其角
nikumarete nagarafuru hito fuyu no hae – kikaku (d.1706)
(hated-while long-remains-person, winter-fly)

the geezer

despised
but living on and on
a winter-fly

a term for us

men despised
live past their time:
winter-flies!
~~~~~~

This often reprinted poem was prefaced: "cold[-season]fly stove circles." (*kanbae ro o meguru* 寒蝿炉をめぐる). Harry Behn's translation of Kikaku's poem is "How can a creature / as mean as a winter fly / continue to live?" (MORE CRICKET SONGS) While I will grant his "mean" means *low-down* or *abject*, let me *pretend* Behn means "not nice" and answer his question. In Japan, it is sometimes considered healthy to be hated a bit, for spiteful people were thought to live long lives! Yet Kikaku's *ku* cannot be sugar-coated. A couple hundred years later Shiki wrote: "How depressing / to be alive too long: / a winter-fly" (うとましや世にながらへて冬の蝿 子規 *utomashi ya yo ni nagaraete fuyu no hae*). He uses the same verb: "long" (*naga~*) turned into a verb and put into a passive tense indicating that long-living was not done on purpose but foisted upon the poet. This reflects the typical Japanese view of aging. On the one hand, old people were respected so much that the age of highly admired people was overestimated. (Matsuo Bashô, the God of haiku, is often depicted as an old sage of perhaps 80. He died at age 51.) On the other hand, Japanese hate to trouble others with their care, and the Buddhist idea that it was selfish to hang on to anything, including life was bolstered by the samurai tendency to make light of death. Living a long time was circumstantial evidence of fear.

今は世をたのむけしきや冬の蝿　旦藁 (pre-1740)
It looks like / *this* is the time to pray / winter flies. – Tankô
It looks like all / i can do now is *pray* / a winter fly [or "we" or "flies"]
住はてぬ姿成けり冬の蝿　文水 新選＝俳諧新選ならば ↓
So this is what / the end of life looks like: / *a winter fly.* – Bunsui (1773?)
百とせの後なき人や冬の蝿　嘯山
Before long/ i'll be a 100: now *that* /is a winter fly. – Shôzan (d.1801 at 84)

These three *ku* are better than Kikaku's famous one. Unfortunately, I found them too late to squeeze them in without repaginating. Full treatment must await the next edition. But, good or bad, Kikaku's poem does raise an interesting question. The author of a book of famous haiku wrote that it came to mind when he "looked at a fly by the stove moving about with no energy and saw a hated old man living long" and that "daring to verbalize this bold thought is the Kikaku style and very interesting." My 10-volume dictionary also gives Kikaku's haiku as *the* example of the winter-fly as metaphor. *Did Kikaku's haiku create the idiomatic "winter fly?"* Or, can an earlier instance be found? And come to think about it, *how much Japanese trope (metaphors that have become idiomatic) has derived from haiku?* (研究者諸君：「冬蝿」などの慣用句が俳句に語源あるかどうか知りたいが。)

~~~~~~

べんべんと何をしなのゝ冬の蝿　一茶
benben to nani o shinano no fuyu no hae – issa (d.1827)
(idly/indefinitely what shinano/do-nothing's winter-fly)

day after day
shinano's up to nothing
winter flies

day after day
a shinano up-to-nothing
winter fly

Without the pun on the name of Issa's country, Shinano, as "nothing-doing," the poem is worth nothing. Unlike the case with Kikaku, where *hito,* or "(other) person" is mentioned, Issa is probably deprecating himself.
~~~~~~

冬の蝿貧女が髪にむすぼるゝ　白雄
fuyu no hae binjô ga kami ni musuboruru – hakuyû (also shirao d. 1791)
(winter-fly/ies poor woman's hair-in tangled up)

a winter-fly
tangled up in the hair
of a poor woman

子守女のねくたれ髪や冬の蝿　大谷句仏
komori-me no ne-kutare-gami ya fuyu no hae – ôtani kubutsu (d. 1943)
(child-guard[nursemaid]'s sleep-disheveled hair:/!/?-winter-fly/flies))

the nursemaid's
sleep-disheveled hair
a winter fly

Could the use of horse manure under straw-strewn floors to naturally heat the hovels of the poor have drawn flies which in the nevertheless cold room were too weak to keep themselves from becoming entangled? The first poem by a famous poet is famous, the second is not. It lacks a clear link between the hair and the fly or flies.

蝿一つわれをめぐるや冬籠　焼台
hae hitotsu ware o meguru ya fuyugomori – gyôtai (d.1792)
(fly-one me circle/seek: winter-confinement)

A single fly
hangs round me;
Winter confinement.

wintering in
with this one fly
circling me

The first, syntax-wise correct translation, is Blyth's (*History of Haiku*). My circling fly brings out the lack of movement of the poet, himself a winter-fly.

冬の蝿火鉢の縁をはひありく　子規　明治 28
fuyu no hae hibachi no en o hai-ariku – shiki (d.1902)
(winter's fly hibachi's edge crawl-walks)

that makes two of us!

the winter fly
creeps along the edge
of the hibachi

文机の端まで歩く冬の蝿　夏井いつき
fuzukue no hashi made aruku fuyu no hae – natsui itsuki (mod.)
(letters-desk's edge-until walk winter-fly)

a winter fly
walks to the far edge of
my writing desk

Thank goodness *hibachi* is English now and I need not write "charcoal brazier." The thin edge of the hibachi is a fine line between the numbing cold and the roasting heat. I added the title because one of Shiki's legs went lame as a result of his long illness. He knew such a metaphorical reading could not be overlooked by his readers even if he had *only* depicted a fly. The modern poem probably has no such allusive possibilities and only shows something that happens.

行燈の糊につたふや冬の蝿　大江丸
andon no nori ni tsutau ya fuyu no hae – ôemaru (d.1805)
(lantern-glue-on/to depend-on/go-from-one-to-next: winter-fly/ies)

winter flies
go from lantern glue
to lantern glue

going from
lantern glue to glue
winter flies

Not only is it cold but there is little to eat. This poem is not, however, quite as clever as its predecessor:

綿帽子の糊をちからや冬の蝿　許六
watabôshi-no nori-o chikara ya fuyu-no hae – kyoroku (d.1715)
(sateen-cap/s' starch/glue-for energy: winter's fly/ies)

cap-starch
it gives some backbone
to winter flies

a winter fly
the starch from my cap
keeps it going

This poem is wonderful as fact or as possible metaphor: have you ever noticed how old people like starchy clothes, collars that hold themselves erect and surfaces that do not even suggest wrinkles? My Japanese dictionary gives "cotton satin" or "sateen" for the material the cap is made of. Elsewhere, I have seen the material called "floss," and in Japanese as "silk-crap." But, eventually, the starch runs out:

冬の蝿耳にささやく最後の語　西東三鬼
fuyu no hae mimi ni sasayaku saigo no go – sanki (d. 1962)
(winter-fly/ies ear-into whisper last word/s)

winter flies
like last words whispered
in the ear

a winter fly
its last words whisper
in my ear

a winter fly
whispers its last words
in my ear

the soft bzz
of winter flies
last words?

Mid-20th century haiku could be very spare with particles of speech. I have no idea whether the surreal simile of the first and metaphor of the last readings or the real (aside from the anthropomorphism) of my double column readings was intended.

脚ちぢめ蝿死す人の大晦日　西東三鬼　冬の蝿
ashi chijime hae shisu hito no ômisoka – sanki (d. 1962)
(legs shrinking/shriveling, fly/ies dy/dies on ny-eve)

legs shrivel up
a fly dies on the last
day of the year

on the busiest day
for humans, the fly dies
legs shriveled up

For Japanese, NY eve is associated with hectic running about to settle accounts before the New Year. The "legs" (*ashi*) figure big in prose and poetry concerning the *ômisoka* (in Japanese "legs" not only get one around but are synonymous with *money*). Yet the best dead fly haiku of all is not by a Japanese poet. It is by the American beat Jack Kerouac: *In my medicine cabinet / the winter fly / has died of old age.*

~~~~~~

Add.

冬蝿のたふとき命砕くなよ　林翔　　俳句年鑑 2005
The life of a winter fly is precious: Let it be!　Hayashi Shô (modern)

~~~~~~

envoi

日の当たるところにじっと冬の蝿　福岡県 橋中２　古賀 幸
hi no ataru tokoro ni jitto fuyu no hae – koga sachi
(sun-striking place-on/at still/constant winter-fly/ies)

staying put
on the sunlit spot
a winter fly

in a sunny spot
the winter fly
stays still

Sometime, somewhere over the past year, I came across a premature haiku of mine, written for a junior high school English assignment:

in the glades
a great white egret
standing still

I reduce it from 17 cramped syllables to 7 clean beats, but for me the idea was an eternal silence of white bird against black water. The above haiku, by a Japanese (Fukuoka Prefecture) junior high school student the same age I was, puts the fly in a different but similar place, forever. *Winter flies never die. They just fall off the wall.* An old haiku is closer to my metaphysical juvenilia (and not as good as the student's):

白壁に氷遠にとまれる蝿を見き　白泉
shirakabe ni eien ni tomareru hae o miki – hakusen (?)
(white wall-on, eternally/forever-for stop fly[obj] saw)

i saw a fly
that sits forever
on a white wall

Sundry flies

DAY AND *NIGHT* FLIES

蝿と蚊の入替りけり暮の鐘　一柳 西華

hae to ka no irekawarikeri kure no kane – ichiryû? 1699

(flies and mosquitoes' exchange/transfer[+emphatic/perfect]: dusk bell/s)

Vespers clang: the flies and mosquitoes have changed guard!

the mosquitoes
take over from the flies
the vesper bell

time for the flies
and 'squitoes to change guard
the evening bell

Japanese temple bells clanged the moment the sun sunk from view, or would sink had the clouds not been in the way. I like the word *vesper* and hope it not too Catholic. My "change of guard" is also hard to defend, but look at this later *ku* –

鐘鳴や蚊の国に来よ／＼／＼ と　一茶

kane naru ya ka no kuni ni koyo koyokoyo to – issa (d.1827)

bell/s ring/s: mosquito-country-to "come! come! come!"

the bell clangs
come! come! come!
to mosquito country

the vesper tolls
come! come! to the country
of mosquitoes

The use of the Chinese character for "come" as part of an invented onomatopoeia (*koyokoyokoyo*) for a bell-sound is clever and the substitution of a change in *time* with one in *space* brilliant. As dusk falls, everything outside your mosquito net suddenly becomes *Mosquito Country!* I took this poem to the office (I worked for a publisher) in Japan and was shocked that no one really got the poem. I guess you have to have lived it (as I did on Key Biscayne in the 1950's, when the mosquitoes could be so thick their collective din filled the air). Movement through that foreign land required custom duties, paid in blood. But, let us leave mosquitoes for another book. Here, I would only add that the bell also signals leaving the Country of the Flies, as suggested by the earlier haiku. Of course, there are exceptions, flies in a foreign land:

行燈の蝿の寝耳にさはりけり　沙月 改造社歳時記

andon no hae no nemimi ni sawarikeri – shagetsu?

(portable lamp's fly/flies' sleeping-ears-to touch[emphatic])

the flies from
the night-lamp touch
sleeping ears

I was always so overwhelmed by mosquitoes that I did not notice if any flies stayed around at night. And I never really thought about what that *meant* until reading the essays of the Fly-hunter appended to the last chapter where I discovered the immoral melon-fly. The above haiku suggests that there are flies that hang out after dark if a light is on. I suppose that only a grocer could tell us if these night-lamp flies are melon flies (which might be what Japanese call all fruit-flies) or some other type. If there were any on Key Biscayne I would have seen my geckoes eat them, but since day-flies are very rare, my chances for a fly by night – excluding the tiny fruit-flies which do not seem like proper flies – are not very high.

..

燈ともせば畳を這ふや秋の蝿　山法師 俳句大全
hi tomoseba tatami o hau ya aki no hae – sanbôshi (?)
(lamp light-when/if tatami-on crawl/s:/! autumn fly/flies)

light the lamp
and they crawl on the tatami
autumn flies

Could they have discovered that it was warmer in the light at night than in the day? Or, was the occasional night-fly not noticed in the warmer months when moths and mosquitoes made the stronger impression? For a poet – something I am not – there is no reason this must be known. Not knowing can create a better poem:

おのれらも寝られぬ事か夜の蝿　素檗 俳人藤森素檗
onorera mo nerarenu koto ka yoru no hae – sôbaku (d.1821)
(you[from other'spoint of view+plural] too sleep-able-not thing? night-flies)

so, you, too
have trouble sleeping?
night-flies

Sôbaku, in his day, was better known than his fellow Shinano poet Issa. Like Issa, many of his *ku,* like this one, directly address the non-human.

~~~~~~

ONE ON ONE

人一人蝿も一ッや大座敷　一茶
hito hitori hae mo hitotsu ya ôzashiki – issa (d.1827)
(person one/alone [person], fly too one: big parlor/room/hall)

..

In the large room
one person
and one fly

trans. Addiss and Yamamoto
~~~~~~

There are three words beginning with *hito* in the original. The first means "person," the second, "alone" (in this poem written with two Chinese characters 一人 "one+person," but also written in other ways meaning "lone") and the third, the number "one." The long words *hitori* and *hitotsu* fill the space in this haiku with a kernel of information itself as small as a man and fly in a large room.

the meditation hall

a man
and a fly
alone

solitude

a big room
just one man
and one fly

guest

a large room
i sit and wait
with a fly

luxury

one man
and one fly:
big room

The way that room is just plopped on to the end of the poem in the original may not work in English. I tried with the last reading.

睡足りて姑く蝿と相対す　尾崎紅葉
nemuri tarite shibaraku hae to aitaisu – kôyô (c.1903)
(sleep suffices [for a] while fly-with/and mutual-facing)

a sound sleep
i wake to find myself
facing a fly

soft time

waking up
i find i'm face to face
with a fly

close up

still drowsy
a fly and i share
a magic moment

sleeping my full
i wake and for a while
commune with a fly

Repeating the "ing" was a problem when translating this poem. The first line of Blyth's translation (*Sleeping my full, / For some time facing each other, / A fly and I*) which I borrowed for the last reading cannot be excelled. Blyth gave this "pre-1903" haiku a tantalizing preface: "Depth is potential, but never realized." That is a little too deep for me. Keigu remembers it – a similar(?) experience – like this:

夢醒めて目の前に目を摺りたる蝿　敬愚
yume samete me no mae ni me o suritaru hae – keigu
(dream-waking, eye-before eye-rubbing fly)

a waking dream
i face a fly rubbing
its drowsy eyes

~

waking from a dream i saw a fly rubbing its eyes

You know you do not know what the fly is doing, but you also know what you feel you are seeing, and that is a fly as drowsy as you are. And judging from the way their little paws? sweep over their eyes like a cat cleaning its forehead, it really does *seem* that flies also know the sandman.

蝿の初音うたたねの森にも読や　立吟 東日記
hae no hatsune utatane no mori ni mo yomu ya – rigin (1681)
(fly's/flies' first-sound's utatane [dreamy-half-sleep]-forest-in-even read/make!)

in the forest
of half-awake already
thinking of a *ku* for
the first sound
of the fly

This was my first reading of the poem, i.e., half asleep / haikuing the fly's / first sound. Tenki thinks it *unlikely* (polite for "wrong") because the character for "read" is not the one usually associated with making poems. But old poets were sometimes loose with characters. On second thought, it is more likely that we are indeed talking poetry *but the fly is the one making it*. I say so because the preface to the *Kokinshû* (c.905) – or, was it the *Shin[new]kokinshû* (c.1205)? – has nature (including frogs, some varieties of which have an elegant ring in Japanese) taking the lead with producing, i.e. singing, poetry. For a fly, a creature too base for these classics, to be credited with poeticizing would be very *haikai*. If the sea cucumber fits *haikai* by being grotesque, the fly does by being small and bothersome (haikai poets thought of themselves as renegades).

the first sound
of a fly in a sleepy glen
that, too, a *ku*

the woods stir
flies in may composing
their first songs!

If I can get confirmation from experts on my reading, i.e., *flies-as-haikai*, I think I might put this poem in the front of the book. 専門家にお聞きしたい。これは、古今集の蛙などの歌うことに対し、ハエの句作という俳諧てき発想になるかどうか、それとも、歌（和歌）を詠むこと（を茶化している）か、是非知りたい。)

~~~~~~
~~~~~~

A FLY *ALONE*

大床に人の絶え間や蝿ひとつ　百池
ôyuka ni hito no taema ya hae hitotsu – hyakuchi (1835)
(big-floor-on, people run-out-of/pause: fly one)

a pause in people
the temple hall plays host
to one fly

the ninja

one fly
in a large room with
no one

envoi

this fly is left
alone in a large room
wringing its hands

The large floor and the people "running-out" (which implies the opposite, a steady stream of people) suggests the location is a samurai's estate house or of a temple. My *envoi* is, of course, totally specious, but the idea of a fly continuing to behave anthropomorphically in the absence of men appeals to me.

~~~~~~

FLIES & OTHER *ANIMALS*

The two-legged and the six-legged were not the only life in Issa's home. The poet also depicted the relationship between his four-legged friends and the flies. Issa's earliest cat and fly poem is his most well known of these.

冬の蝿逃せば猫にとられけり　一茶
fuyu no hae nigaseba neko ni torarekeri – issa (d.1827)
(winter-fly let flee when/if cat-by caught[emphatic/finality?)

The winter fly i let escape, alas, is caught by cat!

karma

a winter fly
i let it go and my cat
catches it

life

my cat
kills the winter-fly
i let go

the breaks

the winter fly
i let go free? my cat
has killed it
~~~~~~

Recently I read that flies live for only a few weeks, months at most. Here, I firmly believed that a winter fly was a summer or autumn fly heroic enough to try to live until spring by hiding out in a warm place. Handicapped by the cold, they can't zip back and forth making us feel dull-witted. For this, I think, we feel grateful. For me, at least, it is hard not to feel affection for these slow flies who behave themselves. And with little other insect life around in the cool half of the year, their company is especially welcome to someone who works alone at home, as Issa still did at that date and I do now. Any *movement* in the room stimulates the senses and prevents the radiator in the brain from overheating. Here is a sort of reverse to Issa's last *ku* –

if i'd known you
were coming, spider, i wouldn't
have killed the fly

johnye strickland

Strickland explains "my own tribute to Issa (which I think I wrote before I read your essay ["The Zen of Swatting" chapter was published in *Simply Haiku*])." I have had relationships with spiders, so I trust Strickland's *ku,* but , at the same time, I wouldn't be surprised if she, too, once read the "pity the poor spiders" poem/chapter of *archy and mehitabel* where the sadness the human race causes the insect world is explained by a weeping middle-aged spider. Archy turns her complaint into song. One stanza:

curses on these here swatters / what kills off all the flies
me and my poor little daughters / unless we eats we dies

Three years later, Issa inherited half-a-house (which he shared with his step-brother) and married. I do not know if the cat in the following *ku* is the same cat.

我宿の蝿とり猫と諷ひけり　一茶
waga yado no haetori neko to utaikeri – issa (d.1827)
(my dwelling's fly-catching cat as sung-done)

the reputation

my cat
a celebrated
fly-catcher!

watch out!

the cat
in my shack: a known
fly-killer!

I must mention a beagle we adopted that was famous for hunting something even less likely: the ghost crab. Freckles, would walk down the beach, taking out one crab after another. He did not get very far, for the crabs lived in holes deep enough to swallow up his broken tail. I suspect one could write a book full of nothing but strange hunters. Somewhere out there is a dog that catches nothing but sandals or a cat that preys on praying mantises. But to return to our flies, the most avid, and successful fly-killer I have known was a fat stub-tailed female calico whose whiskers arched so far forward when sniffing a finger (most cats' whiskers move very little, and some actually retreat whenever the cat sniffs something) as to touch my hand. It would be fun to test for correlations between said whisker-movement and fly-catching ability. The next poem was written eight years later. Chances are Issa was into his second or third generation of pedigree fly-catchers by then.

安房猫蝿をとるのが仕事哉　一茶
ahô neko hae o toru no ga shigoto kana – issa (d.1827)
(foolish cat: fly catching [its] work 'tis!)

my fool cat
thinks that catching flies
is his work

my fool cat
thinks she has a job
as fly-catcher

I cannot "it" a cat, for the character of the respective sexes is very different. Moreover, "it" would weaken if not contradict the charming pretense "work." Japanese is so lucky to work well without pronouns! (It has them, but rarely needs to use them.) Issa has dozens of poems about the "work" of animals. Even the vicious little executioner, the praying mantis – whose hands rather than praying, like flies, hold tiny axes to the Japanese way of thinking – is only, according to our poet, doing its work. (Issa has himself work, too. As an old and infirm poet, he called *taking a nap on a hot day* his "work." But, strangely, he never called his *writing* work.) At any rate, this last poem and the next one are two of the most pleasant cat-*ku* ever written.

なぐさみに猫がとる也窓の蝿　一茶
nagusami ni neko ga toru nari mado no hae – issa (d.1827)
(consolation-for cat-the catch-does window's fly)

and the mice?

for solace
the cat catches a fly
in the window

consolation

the grounded cat
sits in the windowsill
catching flies

seeking solace
the cat goes to the window
and kills a fly

Buson, a poet midway between Bashô and Issa in poetic chronology, wrote of a cat that bit a morning glory for the same reason. Scientists talk about cats playing with their prey in order to unwind. But it is funnier to watch them unwind *elsewhere* when they fail to capture the intended prey. I do not think it is purely nervous overload. In *Hanchan's Dream* (to be published), I argue it can come from emotional causes. My first translation guesses this is the situation. But it might be the cat is a mother and her kittens were taken from her, or that she was prevented from going out and losing the heat or scolded for peeing in the house, or any number of things. Here is the only poem I know involving cats and flies that is not by Issa.

蝿打に猫飛出ル膳の下　汶江
haeuchi ni neko tobiideru zen no shita – bune?
(fly-swatting-to cat jump-leave table-below)

a fly-swatter
strikes the table and out
jumps the cat

So the cat is sometimes the victim in the fly war. I think of a modern *ku* that reads "Fly-swatting / up dances a needle / from the *tatami*" or (I do not have it straight yet), "A fly-swatter / the needle fails to dance up / from the *tatami*" (「畳より針をどり出ぬ蝿たゝき」斉藤俳小星). But, sticking to animals, here is an Issa *dog* fly-ku.

口明て蝿を追ふ也門の犬　一茶
kuchi akete hae o ou nari kado no inu – issa (d.1827)
(mouth open, fly chase-does gate/door's dog)

my watch-dog
chases after flies
open-mouthed

door-guard

open-mouthed
our watch-dog chases
the houseflies

porteus

mouth open
the old watch-dog
chases a fly

群蝿を口で追けり門の犬　一茶
murabae o kuchi de oikeri kado no inu – issa (d.1827)
(swarm-flies-o mouth-with chase[+emphatic] door/gate's dog)

a swarm of flies
chased by an open mouth
our watchdog

If, as Cervantes wrote, "a close mouth catches no flies," are we to assume an open mouth catches them? If you have seen a dog doing this, you have a clear image of what Issa sketches. You can see the dog tilting its head back and forth as it bats about the flies with open mouth, only occasionally making infuriated snaps. If you have *not* seen it, the sketch was probably insufficient. As far as the "gate/door" goes, Japanese dogs almost never stayed inside on the *tatami*, but spent their lives by the front gate which can be the front door, if no other gate is out there. I thought "watch-dog" would be a good loose translation for "gate/door's dog" because, whatever portal we are talking about, that is where you'd find such a dog.

馬の蝿牛の蝿来る宿屋かな　夏目漱石 明治三十年
uma no hae ushi no hae kuru yadoya kana – sôseki (1897)
(horse's/s' flies, cow's/s' flies come inn 'tis/!)

an inn visited
by the horses' flies
and the cows'

horse flies
and cow flies come
to this inn

There is something delightfully casual about the interspecies intercourse sketched by the great novelist-educator. Do not think "horse-fly" and "cow-fly" because you will read right past the heart of the *ku,* the literal connection of flies, hosts and inn.

FLIES DOING IT

Issa's flies did it on the high-priest's head (pg.93), so they were not so much doing it as exercising what Usanians call their 2nd Amendment Right; making a statement. I read that haiku somewhere in English (probably Blyth) before I read it in Japanese and got the mistaken idea the priest was any old Buddhist priest, that is to say a bonze. Then, still before I read the Japanese, I discovered that the seed pods on onion stalks are called "bonze-heads" (*bôzu-atama*) when they lose their flower and become smooth. *Aha!* I said to the farmer, *Issa's flies mating on that bonze's head was a pure haiku, after all!* But, I found the Japanese and the "bonze" (*bôzu*) was a "high-priest." No farmer calls said onion pods *shôzô* (high-priest). Issa's poem had no second layer. Here is a Meiji era senryû and a modern American haiku:

蝿の恋人は無情の蝿たたき　井上剣花坊
hae no koi hito wa mujô no hae tataki – kenkabô
(flies' love/s: people-as-for merciless fly swat/ter)

Human being's sadism
Striking the flies
As they copulate.

trans. Blyth

the inhumanity
of man: striking flies
as they copulate

blyth+me

mating flies
the human fly swatter
is merciless

~

two flies locked in love
were hit by a newspaper
and died together

richard wright (decapped & centered)

mating flies
hit by a newspaper
die together

same (shortened to japanese size)

Issa has a long story including what he claims to be first-hand hearsay about a man who was cruel enough to kill entwined snakes. His son's stout manhood turned into a worm as cold as a fish on his wedding night and destroyed him and, with him, his family line! The following, by an early 20th century poet, is about flies doing it, period.

何と忙しくさうざうしく蝿はつるむなり　山頭火
nan to isogashiku sôzôshiku hae wa tsurumu nari – santôka (d.1940)
(how busy, brazenly, flies mating is)

how busy!
how fervid are flies
mating!

how busy!
how utterly brazen!
flies mating

Next, an even more recent and very different haiku on the same subject, by a woman. She is a modern poet. I cannot recall reading *any* olde *fly-ku* by women! True, not many women wrote haiku, or senryû until the mid-20th century. They generally wrote 31 syllabet poems called *tanka.* But it is also because of the subject. Olde haiku by women happen to be virtually free of flies. Had the subject of this book been "cherry blossoms," "heat," "coolness," "willow trees" or "beach-combing" etc., it would be a different story. [*Oops!* For a second time I have mis-sexed Yamaguchi Seishi a well-known *male* poet. Hey, it goes to show how few women wrote *fly-ku!*]

地の上に蝿重なれり日あたらし　山口誓子
chi no ue ni hae kasanareri hi atarashi – yamaguchi seishi (contemp)
(ground-upon, flies overlaying/coupling, sun new)

on the ground
in the morning sunlight
coupling flies

In Kodansha's large haiku almanac (Nihondaisaijiki), this is the featured haiku for the "fly" category. Despite the absence of allusion and puns such as found in so many old haiku, the poem is rich. As a good line in the 750-word (were it in English: Japanese *never* count by words) explanation points out, the location brings grandeur (the earth?) into the tiny act and the new sunlight makes a hymn of it.

two flies, so small
it's a wonder they ever met
are mating on this rose

j. w. hacket

..

While most *ku* introduced in Blyth's *History of Haiku* are, for obvious reasons, translations, he did include some English haiku, such as the above *ku* by a modern Usanian poet. I felt tempted to title it *"When an Atom meets an Atom."*

~~~~~~

WHEN *PEOPLE SLEEP*

馬方の蝿に曇りて昼寝哉　牧童
umakata no hae ni kumorite hirune kana – bokudô (d.1715)
(teamsters flies-by clouded over noon-nap 'tis)

teamsters
nap under a cloud
of flies

napping outside, grateful for the shade of the flies – keigu
~~~~~~

The original uses a term ordinarily applied to the weather. By "teamsters" I mean the people, mostly, but not exclusively, men, who carried people and goods by horseback. Since the teamsters cleaned their horses more than they cleaned themselves, they probably smelled horsier and drew more flies (笑). Please excuse Keigu for throwing in a *ku* for the hell of it.

おもひ寝の手を投げて置く蝿の中　武玉川
omoi ne no te o nagete oku hae no naka – mutamagawa 18c.
(longing/thinking-sleep's hand/s thrown left flies-among)

dreaming of her
he tosses out his hand
to the flies

dreaming of him
she opens her arms
to the flies

A direct reading of this early senryû in the original gives us a hand cut-off and tossed into a swarm of flies – gross and absurd (for flies don't gather like dogs waiting to be tossed things, but swarm things already tossed out) – but the slower, idiomatic reading tells us it is just someone sleeping, with a smile on his or her face suggesting romantic thought, while flies lick the sweat, or whatever, off his or her hand/s. The image is good enough, true enough to be a haiku. Poking fun at the romantic dreams of a poor person is, however, typical of senryû.

腹立てて蝿打ちまはる寝起哉　幾勇 皮籠摺
hara tatete hae uchi mawaru neoki kana – kiyû? 1699
belly-standing[anger] fly-swatter/swatting sleep-waking 'tis/!/?)

going about
angrily swatting flies
upon waking

If this is about someone awakened from sleep or a pleasant dream by insistent flies, it is amusing; otherwise, it is sad.

身動きに蝿のむらたつひるね哉 子規 明治２５
miugoki ni hae no muratatsu hirune kana – shiki (d.1902)
(body-movement-to flies swarm-rise day-nap 'tis)

every movement
rouses a cloud of flies
afternoon nap

This is a fine description. A man or woman napping, yet still affecting the world of insects with every unconscious movement. The following, earlier poem is not about sleeping. But it is similar.

織りやめばむらがる蝿や機の上　左籠
ori-yameba muragaru hae ya hata no ue – saryu (1777)
(weave-stop-when, gather/swarm flies: loom-above)

stop weaving
and flies coagulate
on the loom

she takes a break
how the flies gather
upon the loom

when i pause
the flies all race
to the shuttle

This is a fine haiku. The shuttle keeps drawing and scattering the flies until, like magic, they come together above the pausing loom.

~~~~~~

POOR PEOPLE

詩にあらず錦にあらず機の蝿　召波
shi ni arazu nishiki ni arazu hata no hae – shôha (d.1771)
([chinese] poetry-in are-not, [chinese-style fancy dress]brocade-in are-not loom-flies)

not in poetry
or chinese dress
loom flies

loom flies won't be found in chinese poetry or dress

When Japanese speak of their own poetry, they use words that indicate the various specific types of poems, such as *waka, tanka, renga, haikai, haiku, renku, senryû, kyôka,* etcetera. The word *shi,* "verse" or "poetry," by itself means Chinese poetry or, depending on the context, Western poetry. Brocade was not only associated with China but with success. To "return home wearing brocade" was *to make good.* This *ku* was written by Buson's plain-spoken but occasionally fantastical haiku friend Shôha (If you have read *Rise, Ye Sea Slugs!* you will recall his *sea cucumber talking to the moon-jellyfish*).

these loom flies
brocade and fancy poems
don't know them

While the syntax of this translation is far from the original's, substituting "don't know them" for the less emotionally charged "are not in it," brings out the significance of the poem, that is, if I have grasped it correctly.

Note: *Poor People Flies* was a category thought up late in the game, so I am afraid that most examples have already been assigned elsewhere. Otherwise, there would be more.
~~~~~~

~~~~~~

OTHER PEOPLE'S FLIES

蝿打や座頭の側に妻一人　東潮
hae-uchi ya zatô no soba ni tsuma hitori – tôshio (1694)
(fly-swatting/er: troupe-head next-to wife one)

wife #2

the troupe head
has a tail with two eyes
to swat his flies

A "troupe-head" was a blind man who managed a group of female musicians or massagers, and also sold their favors. Today, we might call them pimps and loan-sharks, but they had strong clout with the authorities thanks to a strong national organization which functioned as a union. They could afford more than one wife. Their ability to judge a woman's worth in bed was legendary, but there were some things they could not do well. Swatting flies was one of them.

寝すがたの蝿追ふもけふがかぎり哉　一茶
ne-sugata no hae ou mo kyô ga kagiri kana – issa (d.1827)
(sleeping form's flies-chasing today limit !/'tis)

the filial son

chasing the flies
from his sick-bed – today
it should be over

This poem is Issa's first *fly-ku.* It is fairly well-known, and was written either just before or just after his father died. A poet only slightly before Issa's time wrote:
..

蝿うつやしばし宿れる君がため　蘭更
hae utsu ya shibashi yadoreru kimi ga tame – rankô (d. 1798)
(fly swat: a while stay-can you-for)

"the guest is god"

i'll swat flies
for you who can but
stay a while

My title is a Japanese proverb reflecting the fact that Japanese, like people in many cultures, treated guests well and had tales of gods traveling incognito. This becomes "the customer is god" in a retail business context and "the client is god" in a
~~~~~~

professional one. This haiku might be about such an honored guest, another poet, for haiku poets, being constantly engaged in group link-verse events and teaching, traveled a lot. But, my guess – perhaps influenced from having read Issa's poems first – is that it refers to someone who is terminally ill. I thought this haiku, with its masterful simplicity would be famous – at least known well enough to be found by a simple internet search. Had it been written by, say, Kyoshi about dying Shiki, it would be out there accompanied by ample explanation. I couldn't find a thing. Here is another fly-ku by this classic *haijin,* who, I might add, kept a statue of Bashô at his atelier d' haiku named Bashô-dô, or Basho Shrine:

我夢も(を)驚かされぬ(しけり)蝿叩き　蘭更
waga yume o/mo odorokashikeri/~sarenu haetataki – rankô
(my dream/s[obj/also] surprised[+emphatic] fly-swatter/ing)

my dream
is surprised by
a fly-swatter

fly swatting
disturbs me and
my dreams

even my dreams
disturbed by those damn
fly swatters

The last is the *"mo"* (even/also) version. I feel there may be an allusion (even *my* dreams), but do not know what it is. The idea might be that me *and* my dreams are disturbed. Because Japanese used to entertain the idea of plural souls . . .

蝿追を二人供しけり未亡人　一茶
hae oi o futari gushikeri mibôjin – issa (d.1827)
(fly-chasers two equipped[+emphatic] widow)

double-tailed?
(with a nod to boccacio)

equipped
with two fly-chasers
a widow

This seems more a *senryû* about the category "widow" than a haiku. This type of poem never gets into the selections of Issa for that reason. But we need it to understand the poet and his environment. Here is a similar "haiku" by another poet.

うつくしき継子の顔の蝿打ん　紅雪 其袋
utsukushiki mamako no kao no hae utan – kosetsu (c.1700)
(beautiful stepchild's face's fly/ies hit-try)

she would strike
the flies on the beautiful
stepchild's face

I think Japanese would take this to mean that a jealous step-mother uses the flies as an excuse to whack the child, living proof the real mother was beautiful, too.

まめ人の人の頭の蝿を追ふ　一茶
mamebito no hito no atama no hae o ou – issa (d.1827)
(diligent person's [other] person's head's fly chase)

a diligent soul
in pursuit of flies
on our heads

diligence is
someone who shoos flies
from another's head

I could not do a good and accurate translation here. I do not think Issa means to be critical, for he praises his dead wife Kiku as *mame* (diligent) on other occasions.

看護婦やうたた寝さめて蝿を撃つ 子規 明治 30
kangôfu ya utatane samete hae o utsu – shiki (d.1902)
(nurse: [her]doze-sleep awakes, flies hit)

the nurse
nods off, awakes
kills flies

starting
awake, the nurse
swats a fly

the nurse nods
and wakes to kill
more flies

I think Shiki observes his own nurse waken with a start and swat a fly. But I fear my translations don't quite do it in English. I thought to add a title to the poem, "quick recovery," referring to the nurse, not the patient, Shiki.

眠らんとす汝静に蝿を打て 子規 明治 30
nemuran to su nanji shizuka ni hae o ute – shiki (d.1902)
(sleep-try-do: you quietly fly/ies hit!)

I want to sleep;
Swat the flies
Softly, please.

trans. Blyth

This is Shiki's best known *fly-ku.* I tried a number of translations, but think Blyth's cannot be excelled. There is no "please" in the original, but the "you" (*nanji*) is a very polite "you." In English, a *you* is a *you* is a *you.* So "please" it is.

~~~~~~
~~~~~~

& *H*ONORABLE *H*ORSE'S FLIES

武士[さむらひ]に蝿を追せる御馬かな　一茶

samurai ni hae o owaseru onuma kana – issa (d.1827)

(samurai-by fly[obj] make to chase honorable-horse!/'tis)

making samurai
go chasing after flies:
honorable horse

The samurai is in charge of his Lord's horse, whose welfare would, for him, be a matter of life and death. So, he goes chasing after flies to protect his charge. Issa haikus not only the blues of a poor man but those of the magistrates (who must ride in processions in bad weather to satisfy the Shôgun) and, here, the low level samurai. While Issa has many poems suggesting he is close to non-human animals, he was *also* attentive to social inequality and has haiku about the beautiful mosquito nets enjoyed by the horses of the nobility (as contrasted to his condition). So I think this *ku* alludes to his wretched self as contrasted to the pampered horse of the rulers, as well as the pitiful duties of the low-level samurai.

~~~~~~

*H*OT FLIES

草むらに燃え立つ蝿の暑哉　梅郊（梅隣?）

kusamura ni moetatsu hae no atsusa kana – baikô?

(grassy-place-in/at burn-rise flies heat !/?/'tis)

summer pastoral

from the weeds
flies rising like smoke
in dog-day heat

..

The "burn-rise" verb cannot be matched in English, so I substituted *smoke*, then got carried away and added the dog-day for effect. Haiku poets have long loved the theme of "hot things." Even Blyth, with his preference for subtle Zen haiku, was seduced by the splendid hyperbole – who doesn't like hyperbole! – that heat provokes, and included page after page of hot haiku in his anthologies of seasonal haiku. The heat fits the season but it usually has a psychological aspect, one of discomfort, coming from overworked horses, sick, skinny cows, carcasses, etc.. Had I closely followed the relationship of the words in the original syntax, rather than the order, the subject of this Japanese-style poem-as-modification-of-a-single-theme would have been clear. Here, then, is a relationship-based translation:
~~~~~~

the awful heat
of flies rising like smoke
from the weeds

In other words, it is not really a *fly-ku*, but a *hot haiku* served by the fly. I did add the "awful." If I had not, I would have had to write one of the following:

how hot to see
flies rising like smoke
from the brush

flies rising like smoke
from the field
hot indeed

Either way, there is 2-5 beat (equivalent to 5-12 syllabet) break in the first and a 5-2 (12-5) break in the second which is not found in the Japanese-style poem that only breaks at the very end. Here is another haiku less about *fly* than *heat* –

蒼蠅の魚の目せせるあつさ哉　池柳
aobae no sakana no me seseru atsusa kana – chiryû? (1725)
(bluefly's/flies' fish's/fishes' eye/s peck-at heat 'tis/!/loh)

blue flies
picking at fish eyes
what heat

this awful heat
pantry flies picking at
the eyes of fish

The character 蒼 can mean "blue" and "frantic" and also 倉 or "pantry." Because there is a "blue fly" but no "pantry fly" in the dictionary, the first reading is almost surely right. The original reads "the heat of pantry-flies pecking at the eyes of a fish," with the "heat" coming to a head as the subject at the tail of the poem. In contrast to the last two poems, the next poem really is a *fly-ku* and not a *hot haiku*, for it ends (in the original) with the subject, the fly:

立声の尚暑くろし瓜の蠅　嘯山 葎亭句集
tatsu koe no nao atsukuroshi uri no hae – shôzan (1801)
(raised-voice-still-hot-painful-melon-fly)

the melon fly
sounds even hotter
as it leaves

Even if I had found room for "painful/uncomfortable," the poem would be hard to comprehend. My *guess* is that because melons are identified with coolness (within the hot summer), someone who finds flies "hot=uncomfortable" to begin with, feels it all the more so in contrast with the melon. By the fact that the flies make noise as they leave, I learned that these melon-flies were real flies, as opposed to the tiny fruit-eating gnats(?) that come to most fruit left open and unrefrigerated in South Florida.

~~~~~~
~~~~~~

COOL FLIES

朝の間は蝿も新し魚の店　素芳
asa no ma wa hae mo atarashi uo no mise – sobo (?)
(morning-while, flies too fresh fish-shop)

in the morning
even the flies are fresh
at the fish-shop

Some flies might indeed come with the fish early in the morning. *Do they wake up that early?* If anyone has studied the hour at which flies awake, their opinion is welcome. I like the *ku* and regret to have to say that Sobo is not one of the 17 *haijin* whose pen names begin with 素 in my *Haikujinmeijiten*. (And I lost the source.)

~~~~~~

SMART FLIES?

魚舟のよれるか蝿の沖へとぶ　習先
uobune no yoreru ka hae no oki e tobu – shûsen (?)
(fishing-boat/s approach/ing? flies offshore-to fly)

does a fishing boat near?
the flies head out
to sea

I confess to having a weak spot for the part of ethnology called "animal intelligence." This poet has observed something interesting though it might be explainable by instinct. In the days before binoculars, flies might have taught us things.

~~~~~~

RAIN FLIES

雨の蝿畳の上を歩行けり　超波
ame no hae tatami no ue o aruki-keri – chôha (d.1740)
(rain's fly/ies tatami-upon walk-done)

it rains
and a fly treads
the tatami

a rain-fly
walks all over
the tatami

they're walking
on the tatami: flies
this rainy day

I can't quite get this charming poem right. The "rain" + possessive + "fly" cannot be translated as a "rain-fly" even if I did it once.

むら雨に蝿も見合すけしき哉　素外
murasame ni hae mo mi-awasu keshiki kana – sogai (d.1809)
(fall rain-to/in, fly/ies too give-up/cancel scene 'tis)

fall showers
the flies, too, take
a rain-check

fall showers
i see the flies, too
remain inside

I can well understand that. If I were a fly I, too, would stay in. How incredible that little bugs fly about with raindrops weighing more than they do falling from the sky!

たれこめて蝿うつのみそ五月雨　渭橋
tare-komete hae utsu nomi zo satsuki-ame – ikyô
(secluded, fly to swat only! five-month rain)

trapped at home

swatting flies
what else is there to do!
monsoon rain

monsoon rain
swatting flies is the only
game in town

swatting flies
i kill time – trapped
by monsoon rain

In Japanese, rain written "five-month-rain" can be pronounced either *samidare* or *satsuki-ame*. Only the proper length of the haiku taught me which to chose. I think that the later may allude to a murderous mood: *satsu,* as in "murder/kill" and *ki,* or "mood." Occasionally, to escape swatters, or warm up in the air by the ceiling, the flies lift off:

梅雨の部屋蝿みな宙をとべりけり 皆吉爽雨
tsuyu no heya hae mina chû o toberikeri – minayoshi sôu (contemp)
(plum-rain[early monsoon rain]'s room, flies all space fly[for good])

monsoon rain
all the flies in the room
are airborne

EXTRA

~~~~~~

走梅雨店に小さき蠅とんで　藤井正幸　藍生　*hashirizuyu mise ni chisaki hae tonde*

Pre-monsoon rain / a little fly comes / into the store – Fuji Masakichi (contemp)
~~~~~~

THE SOUND OF SWATTING

蝿を打つ音も厳しや関の人　太祇
hae o utsu oto mo kibishi ya seki no hito – taigi (d.1771)
(fly striking sound too, strict/harsh/rigorous: barrier's person/s)

the mind's ear

even the sound
of swatting flies is harsh:
barrier guards

Though one of the two most commonly anthologized haiku about the sound of swatting, this *ku* could just as well have been a senryû. Blyth's translation may be easier to understand: *Even the sound of fly-swatting, / By the officers of the barrier, / Is strict and rigorous.* The "by" is not specified in the original, but like Blyth, I felt it necessary to mention the officers/guards. The "barrier people" (*seki no hito*) refers to those who, waiting to be passed through one of the numerous internal checkpoints found throughout Japan in the Edo era, hear the swatting and shiver. Here is a less known haiku:

あさましく蝿打つ音や台所　召波
asamashiku hae utsu oto ya daidokoro – shôha (d. 1771)
(base/despicable/wretched/shamefully fly swat sound:/! kitchen)

this sound of
swatting flies so base
my kitchen

how base
the sound of fly-swatting
from the kitchen

The sound of an enlightened fly swatter killing flies without hate would be different. Here, however, someone (female?) is really upset, or so it sounds to the poet. No matter how it is Englished, the idea of *baseness* does not quite work. It is not an East-West thing. *Modernity* has made such a sensitivity archaic if not obsolete.

from my kitchen
that sound i know of flies
basely swatted

the base sound
of flies being swatted
in the kitchen

how vulgar
to hear fly-swatting
in the kitchen

Shôha's is an honest poem, perhaps, but not as good as this next *ku* by the same poet this section began with, Taigi (who, with 6 *ku,* was the most prolific pre-Meiji era (pre-Shiki) poet of sea cucumber, too). It is the other most commonly read haiku about the sound of swatting, and deservedly so.

蝿を打おとや隣もきのふけふ［から］ 太祇
hae o utsu oto ya tonari mo kinô kyô (kinô kara) – taigi (d.1771)
(fly striking sound: neighbor/s too, yesterday-from [also: yesterday, today])

neighbors, too,
the sound of fly-swatting
from yesterday

next-door, too
the sound of fly-swatting
yesterday, today

the sound of swatting
flies: next door, too
from yesterday

"It is strange what things unite (and divide) us" writes Blyth, who forgot to include the indispensable *mo* (also/too) in his translation (*The sound of swatting flies; / next door, / from yesterday*) [or, is the missing "too" a typo?]. The original does indeed break in the middle as per Blyth's translation, but parsing it so looks ugly. Contentwise, this poem is about as haiku as a haiku as can be. It marks the beginning of a seasonal phenomenon. Today, in the large haiku almanacs, flies and fly-swatting are usually separated by dozens if not hundreds of pages, with the former in the insect part of the animal (*dôbutsu*) section of summer and the latter in the human living (*seikatsu*) section of summer. In the older almanacs, fly-swatting and flies are a single theme.

ゑいやつと蝿叩きけり書生部屋 夏目漱石 明治二十九年
eiya! to hae tatakikeri shoseibeya – sôseki (1896)
(whoopee-with fly/ies swatted[+emphatic+finality?] student-room[dorm])

whoops and cries
for each fly swatted in
the dormitory

So the sound of swatting is not necessarily limited to the swatter's impact. The only other haiku depicting students by this name (*shosei*) I know of is equally hilarious. It is by Buson (d. 1783) and concerns their practicing acupuncture on a sea cucumber.

~~~~~~

FLY-*SWATTERS* IN USE & OUT

一匹の蝿一本の蝿叩 高浜虚子
ippiki no hae ippon no hae tataki – kyoshi 1954
(one *hiki=piki* fly, one *hon=pon* fly-swatter)

one on one

just one fly
and just one
fly-swatter
~~~~~~

I added the "just" to bulk up the poem a bit. Translation is hard, for English has no proper class pronoun, which is to say we don't say "one fellow fly" or "one stick fly-swatter." It did, however, seem the right haiku to start a section on fly-swatters.

蝿叩き持てば蝿叩きへ止り　花川洞
haetataki moteba hae tataki e tomari – kasendô
(fly-swatter had-if fly-swatter-to perches)

the best defense

the fly settles
on the fly-swatter
he picks up

life

pick up
a swatter and a fly
sits on it

It happens doesn't it! I wish I had a date on the poet or poem but I do not.

蝿をうつ其手枕のねふり哉　己百　花つみ
hae o utsu sono tamakura no nemuri kana – kohyaku? (1690)
(fly swat that hand-pillow's sleep 'tis)

the hand
that swatted flies
a pillow

Japanese can make almost any body part into a pillow, simply by sticking it in front, with occasional slight changes in the pronunciation. Japanese have "hand-pillows" (*ta-makura*), "arm-pillows" (*ude-makura*), "lap-pillow" (*hiza-makura*), and so forth.

蝿打を持て居眠るみとりかな　子規 明治30
hae-uchi o motte inemuru mitori kana – shiki (d.1902)
(fly-swatter[obj] holding-sleeps nurse/attendant 'tis)

fly-swatter
in hand, my nurse
fast asleep

clutching
the fly-swatter
nurse sleeps

my nurse
asleep, still holding
the fly-swatter

Mitori is an elegant word for someone who cares for someone. The translation might be titled *Garde-malade.* I first mistook *mitori* for the more common word *midori* (small child).

蝿たたき鍋取に柄を付にけり　喜清
haetataki nabetori ni e o tsukenikeri – kisei ( )
(fly-swatter pot-holder-on handle attach-done)

i stick a handle
on a pot-holder: voila
my fly-swatter!

There are as many ways to strike a fly as to skin a cat. My personal favorite is a pea-shooter, be that as it may.

すぐ出来て無雅無造作や蝿叩　榎村
sugu dekite mugamuzôsa ya haetataki – enomura? (pre-1925)
(immediately made/ready no-elegance-no-art fly-swatter/s)

made like that
crude and artless
a fly-swatter

made on the spot
there is no art in this
fly-swatter

山寺に蝿叩なし作らばや　虚子
yamadera-ni hae-tataki nashi tsukurabaya – kyoshi 1955, July
(mountain-temple-at fly-swatters not: make [them] were-to-if?)

no fly-swatters
at the mountain temple
let's make them!

Mountain temples are so cool that there are less flies and mosquitoes than in the town and field below. They are also the purist bastions of Buddhism, places where *ahimsa,* or "not taking life" was taken seriously. At the same time, some of these temples had Zen abbots like Ikkyu, who, beyond the ken of little matters such as life and death, would be happy to make use of a swatter.

出来たての蝿叩持ち蝿もゐず　星野立子
dekitate no haetataki mochi hae mo izu – hoshino tatsuko (contemp)
(freshly-made flyswatter carrying flies are-not)

no flies
me and my freshly made
swatter

walking about
with my freshly made swatter
where are the flies?

having just made
a swatter i look around
surprise: no flies!

walking about
with a brand-new swatter
no fly in sight

I cannot recall making a fly swatter, but I bought one recently at a garage sale. It served to kill the cockroaches that came up the drain for my bath-tub from the septic tank shared by . . . But I didn't buy it for that. I bought it because the screen part is shaped like a heart and when I saw it I thought, for a quarter I must get it because I am writing this book. I have heard of wearing one's heart on ones sleeve, but on the end of a fly-swatter? (Ah, yes. Traditional Japanese fly-swatters were typically made of hemp palm (shûro) leaves, cardboard on bamboo handles or iron screen (like ours?). I hope to have more information in a later edition.)

憎らしくやがて哀しい蝿叩き　美代子
nikurashiku yagate awareshii hae-tataki – miyoko
(spiteful/hateful, finally pitiful/sad fly-swatter)

a fly-swatter
in time, spiteful things
become pitiful

first spiteful
then pitiful in time
fly-swatters

As another *ku* sent to the Ukimidô fly-ku fest put it, like us, fly-swatters become bent with age. In senryû, *nikurashii,* literally, "hateful," generally means a cute boy or girl one is jealous of or cannot win; here it reflects the fact that there is something despicable about a cheap instrument for killing things. But it is also a word that women use a lot, so we feel the femininity of the poet.

~~~~~~

ANOTHER *USE* FOR A *SWATTER*

草の戸やささらになりし蝿叩　碧梧桐
kusa no to ya sasara ni narishi haetataki – hekigoto (d.1937)
(grass-door[humble-hut]!/: rustling-musical-instrument-becomes fly-swatter)

an old hut
the fly-swat serves for
a washboard

I am joking with that "washboard." You may substitute *sasara* for it. The *sasara* is a folk instrument made from a length of bamboo split into a dozen or so strips on one side (or strips of wood fastened together on one side) which is rubbed over a pole that is grooved to make a percussive sound that must be both grating and rustling (I have never heard one, but I am sure I would like it for this is a sound sadly missing in both classical and popular music that my ears thirst for).

~~~~~~

F*ANNING* FLIES

蚊と蝿につかはれて居る團哉　失名
ka to hae ni tsukawarete-iru uchiwa kana (lost the name)
(mosquitoes and flies-on used-is fan 'tis)

my fan
kept busy by flies
and mosquitoes

This is the type of fan that is shaped like a huge lollipop and does not fold up. It is the type of fan one would carry into the field or to an outdoor dance. This idea of the mover being moved is found in Issa's haiku about a butterfly raising a cat a few feet from the ground. Because it is witty, it is more common in senryû than haiku, though no examples come to mind at the moment, unless the above *is* a senryû. I am afraid I lost the source.

うつつにも団扇のうごく蝿ぎらひ　柳樽 2-2
utsutsu ni mo uchiwa no ugoku hae-girai – yanagidaru
(unconsciously/dreamily-even, fan's move fly-hater)

dozing off
the fly-hater's fan
still moving

Utsutsu is a state between sleeping and waking, such as when one has just woken from a dream. English lacks a word for it. This senryû could as well have been a haiku. Had Issa written it, it would be.

蝿打つていさゝか穢す団扇哉　几董
hae utte issaka kegasu uchiwa kana – kitô (d.1789)
(fly/flies-swatting/swatted dirty/sully/ing fan!/'tis)

a wee stain
from hitting a fly
my *uchiwa*

my old fan
slightly stained by
hitting flies

Fans, to my mind, are good for shooing but not for swatting. The only fan I have strong enough to kill a fly is East African. Since I live on a fly-less island, I cannot tell if it is fast enough (and if a fly *did* visit I would not swat it but serve it some food). I suspect it would work, for on numerous occasions *she* (The carving on the handle is female) has successfully batted large flying cockroaches back out the window through which they flew in. The fans I had in Japan would be very hard to swat a fly with. One would need to move them at a slice sharper than that proper for a serve in tennis and turn at the last moment. Did Kitô use skills developed from sword-play? Or did they have heavier fans? I have heard of great 16th century generals (Shingen, at any rate) using a "battle fan" to parry sword and halberd blows. A fan like that should be more than enough for a fly . . .

秋の蝿たゝむ扇にはさまるゝ　渉舟 新類題
aki no hae tatamu ôgi ni hasamaruru – shôsen (1793)
(fall-fly, folding-up fan-by squeezed)

a fall fly
is folded up in
a fan

This *ku* rightly belongs to the "fall fly" theme, for it is its character and not that of the instrument – the folding fan, a Japanese invention – that is developed.

~~~~~~
~~~~~~

CATHOUSE FLIES

吉原の蝿に投げうつ小判哉　成美
yoshiwara no hae ni nage utsu koban kana – seibi (1816)
(*yoshiwara's flies-at throw* koban (oblong Japanese coin)!/'tis)

yoshiwara flies
have gold coins
thrown at them

cathouse flies
are stoned with
silver dollars

The koban is slightly rectangular oval gold coin that poor people rarely saw. Issa's patron and at the time the more well-known poet, Seibi suggests that flies *did.*

~~~~~~

LOVE AND FLIES

高安の恋はさもあれめしのはへ　失出典
kôan (takayasu?)no koi wa samoare meshi no hae – (haiku? kzg (see *apologia*)
(high-low's love(takayasu romance?)-as-for however, meal/rice's fly/flies)

be it the love
of rich or poor, a dish
draws flies

takayasu love
lost because she went
to the rice

"Flies on food" is idiom for something troublesome you just cannot shake. The first reading of this 17th or 18th century haiku turns it into an epigram where the flies are pure trope for would-be lovers trying to join in the feast. The second reading guesses it refers to a *Tales of Ise* romance where the man is turned off by finding his lover (in Takayasu) served her own rice – went to it rather than having it brought to her. Does this "servant-like behavior" make her like a fly? *Takayasu* is in the dictionary, while *kôan* is not, so my second reading seems more likely.

蝿なくば一華折らん夏の菊　其角
hae nakuba hito hana oran natsu no kiku – kikaku (d.1706)
(fly/ies not-if one flower would-break[take], summer chrysanthemum)

gadding about

if not for flies
i'd have one summer
chrysanthemum

the confession

were there
no flies, i'd pluck this
summer mum

Kikaku, a physician who worked out of a temple as his father had, was a student of Bashô and also a student of masters of Zen, calligraphy and painting. He was thought of as the heretic of the haiku saint's "ten disciples" for he was anything but the austere asthete. His poems reflect his life, which was blessed with an excess of drinking and witty intercourse. In the mid-19th century, before Issa and Buson were
~~~~~~

popularly discovered, I believe he was, with Bashô and Chiyô (the top female *haijin*), the most well-known haiku poet. Today, almost all of his clever puns and abundant allusion requires explanation, so he is virtually unreadable. Had I a couple hundred dollars to spare, there are books I could buy to decipher his haiku.[1] Meanwhile, I can only guess this poem means that *were it not for the heat and the abundant flies (probably, others who would be a nuisance), he might be in the mood to dally with a beautiful young boy,* as many a man in his position apparently did. I have long thought it amazing that the chrysanthemum could be identified with both the Imperial line (it is their crest) and, even today, with sodomy in general and, in pornographic cartoons, the anus in particular ("censored" as a mum). If you think of the flies as defenders of the flower, you will find wit beyond the allusion, too (In Florida, you must fight fire-ants for okras, but that is another story.).

~~~~~~

1. One of many Kikaku *ku* I could not read: [射ル者ハ中リ奕スル者ハ勝ツ] 蝿打よいづれにあたる点ごころ 五元集（で、其角好きよ、全解注の本をこの貧乏に頂戴！）

~~~~~~

Since flies were not a theme for the linked verse that preceded what came to be haiku – *I assume they first appeared in Japanese poetry as metaphor for trouble in love poems.* Had I the academic association necessary to use a certain data base (a Japanese public research institute that has refused me permission three times to date), or buy expensive CDRoms, I would have checked this theory. I will gladly add a gloss to the second edition if someone with access can do the research on early flies. Meanwhile, another surprising metaphorical use for fly/flies in, or as, a love poem:

待恋　待つ暮や蝿の障子を叩くにも　鷺水　古選
"matsu-koi" matsu kure [koi] ya hae-no shôji o tataku ni mo – keisui? (pre 1763)
("wait-love" waiting evening [love]! fly/flies paper-doors-on beating-to/by-even)

waiting for love

dying for dusk
flies beat on the *shôji*
again and again

longing for love

i wait! my heart
a fly, beating against
a paper door!

The *ni mo* at the end of the poem is very subtle. It means that waiting [for] love – meaning, I think, the visit of a lover – may *even* be compared *to* or described *by* this fly's behavior. Because it describes a state of mind, I made the heart explicit in my second translation. Lovers commute in the dark and flies, no longer longing for the light, stop bashing their brains out against doors and windows. Another version puts love in the poem and dispenses with the preface. Almost surely unaware of this old *ku,* a modern poet writes, with no obvious thoughts of love:

じんじんと蝿じだんだを夜の戸口　振り子
jinjin to hae jidanda o yoru no toguchi – furiko (contemp)
([psychological mimesis for energetic repetition] flies tantrum[obj] night-door)

throwing a tantrum
against the door at night
trapped houseflies

hitting the door
at night, a tantrum of
trapped flies

~~~~~~

CRUELTY TO FLIES

退やらぬ障子の蝿や物ぐるひ　嘯山
nige[noki?]yaranu shôji no hae ya monogurui – shôzan (d.1801)
(escape let-not paper-door's fly/ies!/: riot)

cruelty to animals

not let out
the flies go crazy!
a paper door

Mono-gurui is the sort of frenzied craziness we might associate with hysteria or a breakdown. This poem was right next to the one about the fly praying even as he/she is pinched by Shôzan ("A Supplication of Flies" ch.4) . Talk about a hard-boiled poet! – I'm kidding. He freed the flies for all we know. But side by side, the poems seem a bit sadistic or compassionate, something that can also be said for the next haiku:

羽ネもいだ蝿歩行けり誰か所為　召波
hane moida hae arukikeri dare ga shoi – shôha (d.1771)
(wings-pulled-off-fly walks around[+finality]: whose deed?)

whose deed this?
a fly walks around
bereft of wings

wings pulled off
a fly walks about
who did it?

Shôha, as mentioned once already, is the author of the *ku* about the sad sea cucumber talking to the moon jellyfish (justly famous nonsense which took me pages to make sense of *Rise, Ye Sea Slugs!*). Here are my guesses:

..

1. An *akutarô,* or mischievous boy, for they are always around
2. Shôha's friend Buson, the famous painter-poet, who was no fly-lover.
3. A nimble samurai. Or was *he* that samurai?
4. A mother bird – if cats bring back injured prey to teach kittens to hunt, then is it not possible that birds do the same for their chicks?
5. A person caring for a baby sparrow or, perhaps, another bird.
6. a cat the poet knew
7. fly-paper
8. other

I wish I had found this poem in time for the first edition of TOPSY-TURVY 1585 to add to the commentary about the fly-torturing nobility of Japan; but since Frois specifies that they don't just pull off the wings but "throw out" the flies and it is doubtful the walking fly was noticed outside (I imagine him on the tatami), we may not be talking about the same thing.

..
~~~~~~

長刀でずばときらばや蠅の臑　素柳　国の華
naginata de zuba to kirabaya hae no sune – sôryu (1704)
(halberd-with/by *zuba*[=onomat.]-cut/sliced-if!/:/? fly's shin/lower leg/s)

if with halberd
they could be slashed down
loh, fly shanks

An expression of annoyance against begging bonzes? Gnawing on the shin, or shank of the leg (*sune-kajiri*) is idiomatic for parasitism by humans, so the fly shank makes for fine poetic justice. The only crueler *fly-ku* I know of is this strange poem.
..

首切て蠅は虚空になりにけり　風吟　反故集？(失名ヵと子規分類別)
kubi kitte hae wa kyokû ni narinikeri – fûgin (?)
(head/neck cut fly/ies empty become [final])

its head
cut-off, the fly
is empty

My, my! If Emily Dickinson wrote a *fly-ku* this would have been it (only change the "is empty" to "*proves* empty"). I am not sure how to compare the word *kyokû* (literally empty+air[itself meaning *empty*]) with the far more commonly used Buddhist term *kyomu* (empty+nothingness). But it is fun to wonder whether the fly was thought to share our illusion that this world is this world.

its head
cut-off, the fly loses
its reality

I do know that "air" (*kû*) is used to describe an empty bottle whereas "nothingness" (*mu*) is not, and I have noted that the body cavities of headless little bugs do get eaten clean very quickly. The last translation, a paraverse inspired Keigu to play:

首切て間もなく観るや蠅の夢　敬愚
kubi kitte mamonaku miru ya hae no yume – keigu
(head/neck-cut a while see!/?/: fly's dream)

head cut-off
it plays on for a while
the fly's dream

素っ首を斬られてすぐに蠅の夢　　天気's paraverse

In the early period of haiku, Japanese were crazy about automata (*karakuri*). One senryû in Mutamagawa even attributes dreams to the *automata*, or invisible puppetry of the body's "five-organs!" This popular technology and the budding awareness of life as mechanical that accompanied it was by no means contrary to religion, for Buddhist fatalism (like Calvinism?) saw the whole show as an elaborate *karakuri.* I suspect, that the haiku might be a witticism about an executed bonze: *so there's your emptiness for you!* Another paraverse:

首切て自分がないと仏バエ　敬愚
kubi kitte jibun ga nai to hotoke-bae – keigu
(head cut-off, [it has] no self [says/so/and] corpse=buddha-fly)

no longer so full of itself

its head
cut-off, the fly
is buddha

If the idea is bringing Buddhahood to the bug, then cruelty can be rationalized as kindness.

~~~~~~

FLIES AT THE *INK-STONE* WATERING HOLE

(きれいすき)　硯墨蝿のくふものなかりけり　百里
"kireizuki" suzuri sumi hae no kuumono nakarikeri – hyakuri 1727 (44)
("neatnick" ink-stone fly/ies' food-stuff not-[virtually+emphatic])

living with a neatnick

black ink!
the fly has nothing
else to eat

black ink!
the fly has virtually
nothing to eat

..
The *kari* ending on the *na* = "not" softens, so it is less absolute, while the *keri* makes it emphatic. All this fills out the haiku, but adds nothing in English. We have no verb-endings to simultaneously emphasize and hedge our bets, just bulky adverbs.

古筆や墨嘗めに来る冬の蝿　子規　明治２７
furufude ya sumi name ni kuru fuyu no hae – shiki (d.1902)
(old-brush/es: ink lick-for come winter-flies)

old brushes
coming to lick the ink
winter flies

a winter fly
comes to lick the ink on
an old brush

Shiki puts together two over-the-hill objects, one live and one dead. Here is an older
~~~~~~

ku of an epigram bent:

蝿の手やなづとも尽きぬ硯石　惣今

hae no te ya nazu to mo tsukinu suzuri-ishi – sokon (?)

(fly/ies' hands rub even-if exhaust-not ink-stone)

the flies' hands
rub but never wear out
an ink-stone

a fly's hands
rub but never wear out
the ink-stone

Ink-stone is the most common translation for a rat-trap-sized slab of stone with a slope for rubbing – i.e. finely grating – a bar of solid ink on, and a concavity, which holds the small pond of ink so made. Since one ingredient of the ink is water, the flies use it for a watering hole. I was delighted to succeed in capturing the pivot-line of the original in the translation. Note how the second line seems to refer to the fly's/flies' hands as you read it, then changes to refer to the stone when the last line is read. This is perhaps the most common type of wit found in Japanese poetry. *There may be an allusion to the poet's use of writing to beg for things like a fly.*

雪信の蝿うち払ふ硯哉　蕪村

yukinobu no hae uchi-harau suzuri kana – buson (d.1783)

(yukinobu's fly shooing away inkstone 'tis)

the ink-stone
yukinobu shooed
flies off

yukinobu
shooed off its flies
this ink-stone

a cool scene!

yukinobu
shooing flies off
the inkstone

Yukinobu was the leading female painter of the leading school of Japanese art (the Kano school) about fifty years before Buson was born. In my annotated Buson, the Japanese scholars write: "Yukinobu, still holding her brush/es* is shooing away the flies from the ink-stone, but [the point is] her movements are quite naturally, a woman's, elegant and graceful" (the last two adjectives for the single Japanese word, *yuga.*) Unfortunately, these words do not explain *why* he wrote the poem. Did he, perhaps, see her ink-stone, or a painting of her with it? I also feel the scene is *cool* for three reasons: First , the practice of writing or painting with ink is associated with a meditative state of mind and this calm is cool – the opposite of our frenzied activities such as sports and video games, all of which are *hot*. Second, the poet's name has "snow" (*yuki* = 雪)in it. Third, *suzuri* "inkstone," suggests *suzumi* "coolness." That coolness is a fine foil for the heat of the flies. *I do not know if any Japanese literary critics would agree with a word of this.*

~~~~~~

* **Brushes**. A master painter (Chinese-style landscape) I knew juggled brushes held between each finger!
~~~~~~

FARM FLY

野の家やさ蝿群がる猫の五器　楽散人
no no ie ya sabae muragaru neko no goki – rakusanjin (?)
(field's house: early[planting time] flies gather cat's dishes)

a farm house
planting flies gather by
the cat's bowl

The animals in this poem are treated well, for the name of the early fly, the *sabae* includes a nuance of being rice-planting-related and the usual cat bowl (*neko no wan*) is called "five-dishes" or *goki* – a formal set of dishes for supper – perhaps to imply a water-bowl and separate snack plates, but more probably just to express the poet's idea of non-human animals being an integral part of the farm family.

牧場に生れし蝿とバーベキユウ　後藤比奈夫 (花びら柚子)
bokujô ni umareshi hae to bâbekyû – gotô hinao (mod.)
(pasture-in born flies-with barbecue)

a barbecue
with flies born out
in the pasture

This is a contemporary poem. I imagine the flies born in the dung and growing up on the sweat of the very same animal the poet and his friends are eating.

~~~~~~

FOREIGN FLIES

By *foreign*, I mean what Japanese mean by it. The foreign flies that have found their way into other parts of this book will not be re-introduced here. I have not read much original work in English and for the foreseeable future will not have time to do so; readers are welcome to send *fly-ku* they come across or write for future editions of this book. Anyone with access to a library with plentiful haiku in English is welcome to go even farther and create a top 100 of English language original fly-ku (it could include some already in this book). I did read Cor van den Heuvel's THE HAIKU ANTHOLOGY and found a few including this, possibly the shortest fly-ku:

蝿一つ暑さにきりがなく

one fly everywhere the heat

marlene mountain
~~~~~~

Shortness is no problem for a fine haiku like this (I gave it a short Santôka-style translation, so Japanese readers can enjoy it, too). Slow pronunciation can still find six feet in it, perfect for a fly (笑). The anthologist himself has the shortest haiku of all:

t u n d r a

That's all! Yet, it is enough for me. The tundra fills for us by itself (I put a Japanese font-sized space between each letter, he didn't). Cor van den Heuval's anthology includes a *fly-ku* on the long side, too:

heat before the storm
a fly disturbs the quiet
of the empty store

nicholas virgilio

..

According to the long-standing – and I feel wrong – 5-7-5 syllable idea, this poem is perfect, but 3-3-3 beats sounds 2-beats too long to one who writes haiku in Japanese. Let me paraverse:

heat before the storm
a fly buzzes about
the empty store

I fear I only managed to get rid of one beat (3-3-2), but I think it makes a difference. Do you?

~~~~~~

あかときや蝿打つほかは音もなし エルシー
akatoki ya hae utsu hoka wa oto mo nashi (tenki helped with this trans.)
(dawn light : fly-swat other-as-for, sound-even not)

early light
quiet except for
fly swatter

elsie

..

Googling brought me to Elsie's and two more *fly-ku* in the proliferating haiku megasite called <u>shiki.archive</u> (9906/0025.html, or, re: SHIKI early light). It is a deceptively rich haiku and I could not help translating it for Japanese readers. This next has good enough logic but, as is, it is just tooooo much:

miss meshed swatter
super fly? 69 year old eye?
bug buzzes off

Phil Havey
~~~~~~

Nothing is gained by the "meshed." The buzz adds something, but only if it is tied into the fly's making fun of the poet as Issa does in his "Hit me!" *ku* (pg. 79) The main problem is that this "haiku" is 12-beat – 5 more than the ideal. Two paraverses:

打ち逃がしスーパー蝿の技か老の眼か　ハーヴェ
uchinogashi su-pa-hae no waza ka oi no me ka – havey+keigu
(hitting-escapes, super-fly's skill/technique? old eyes?)

missed him!
69 year old eye?
or, super-fly?

old eyes vs. *super-fly?*

a missed swat
or great escape – is it
the fly or me?

havey+keigu

..

The last of the poems on the web page is stylistically remarkable. 7 words, 7 syllables, 7 beats: your minimal full haiku. I would only add a caption, a dedication to Montaigne, who questioned whether he played with his cat or vice versa:

fly plays
cat and mouse
with me

SUE [Torres]

Sorry, Sue. No Japanese. As with so many witty poems, it will not translate well. There is no "cat and mouse" in Japanese (it's "dog and monkey) much less the expression "*play* cat and mouse." The name of the archive with these *ku*, SHIKI, is not that of the poet we have come to know. It means "four-seasons," shorthand for Nature. The megasite hails from Matsuyama-u.ac.jp. Another finding from the same site (shiki.archive.9707: SHIKI*) called *Fly Orbit* has 5 *fly-ku.*.

..

十分ぞ窓見付かねば助ける、蝿　オメリック
juppun zo, mado mitsukaneba tasukeru, hae

you've got ten minutes
to find the open window,
fly, then i'll help you

omeric

With content this good, I didn't mind the prose. This helpfulness is far more appreciated then utterly facetious maudlinity such as "quietly, i shut / the wardrobe to not disturb / the moths as they eat" (Visnja McMaster (Croatia [k]) in Higgin.:*Haiku World*).

蝿あがく開かない窓に青い空　ノール
hae agaku hirakanai mado ni aoisora – keigu+tenki trans.

struggling fly,
wide blue sky -
my windows don't open

Noor

This, too, is fine! It hurts to see the fly bashing his brains out on the glass. But, it helps to have no way to do something about it.

先生が蝿打上げてサなんだぁと　ユリ
sensei ga hae-uchi agete sa nan da to
(teacher fly-swatter raises, so what[is it]?)

蝿打を上げたまま蝿言うって見な！　ユリ
hae-uchi o ageta mama hae iutte mi na!
(fly-swatter raised-as-is, fly, say what it is!)

蝿叩く教師が蝿に問い質す
hae tataku kyôshi ga hae ni toi-tadasu (a tenki trans.)
(fly swatting teacher fly-to quizzes)

Master raised
a fly-swatter and asked
what is it, fly?

Yuri

To me, "Master" suggests a Zen priest and a *kôan*, i.e., the-fly-as-disciple. Be that as it may, I don't know how Japanese might read this poem. I hazarded a couple translations. One drops the "Master," a word more used by Westerners, whose language is poor at indicating respect in more subtle ways, than by Japanese, and the language is a bit blunter, for the kôan could be asked in a seemingly aggressive way. Tenki's translation makes the Master a "teacher" for the Japanese *sensei,* can be either.
..

夏の暮蝿と分け合う飯の膳　キミ・マーチン
natsu no kure hae to wake-au meshi no zen – trans. tenki
(summer evening: fly-with divide-up[share] meal)

summer evening
sharing my dinner
with a fly

Kimi Martin

I like this *very* much. In Hawaii, I had a cockroach friend who lived in a clump of thin, hairy palms by my desk on the back-porch and always waited patiently on the edge of that desk for me to finish eating so he could clean up for me. After he ate, he would stay around for a few minutes – he never ate and ran – and let me watch as he slowly preened his two long whiskers, one at a time, clasped near the base, then looped outward until the end was reached. I was reminded of a contented cat. (I was so impressed with his intelligence, I wrote NASA trying to find out if the cockroaches that were sent to space got any fitting memorial. Never got a reply.) I have also indulged wasps with drink and observed how the same wasp will come time and time again. You can tell which is which by timing them and observing the angle of their flight path, both of which reflect the location of their hive and their behavior based partly on biology and partly on experience. I have not yet had such intense communion with the common housefly. I like to imagine Kimi Martin offering the fly different things to test its taste. But, I suspect she only means that she was alone with nobody but a fly for companionship that evening.

FRIEND

..

fire flames – your wings
dive
down to the safety net

wlod [wlodzimierz holsztynski]

I don't get this last poem, but it, together with the title of the webpage, did conjure up an image of sputnik-as-fly, and fly-as-atomic-particle. *Even the worst poems (or prose) can prove helpful in one way or another.* I have no flies here, but Wlod reminds me that I did find wings of some insect (probably a termite) on my desk recently:

机上みし小さき羽が君守宮？　敬愚
kijô mishi chiisaki hane ga kimi yamori – keigu
(desk-on see/n small wings, you gecko?)

mystery

on my desk
little wings: gecko
was it you?

and another tiny body part of an even smaller insect.

..

何日もキーボードから縞足一本　敬愚
nan nichi mo ki-bo-do kara shima ashi ippon – keigu
(what[howmany]days-even keyboard[keys]-from striped leg one)

writing with mosquitoes

for five days
between the "u" and "i"
a striped leg!

Actually, the leg stuck up between *three* keys, the "u," the "i" and the "8," but that is close enough. As you notice, mine are far from dramatic poems, but little events like these are all a writer sitting at his computer for 16 hours a day has for "a life."

~~~~~~
~~~~~~

現代＋現在句

New *fl*ies, OR, 1*00* M*ODERN* F*L*Y-KU

拱手して一茶の蠅を見ておりぬ　餡子

kyôshu shite issa no hae o mite orinu – anko

(clasp[reverently]hands-doing, issa's fly[obj] see[+politely])

hands clasped
i take a good look at
issa's fly

kneeling down
i take a good look at
issa's fly

While I had started with the intent to include no flies that outlived Shiki (d.1902), I let my book push me around and ended up allowing a dozen or so later poems to slip by; then, after adding a sample of foreign flies, let in a dozen or so more. When I announced that F*l*y-ku*!* was heading down the final stretch to my Japanese haiku friends, one pointed out something I myself had felt: despite the life/death element noted in the Foreword, fly-ku are, on the whole, *tsukinami*, which is to say not creative as far as haiku go. For some reason, the life and death poems for blowfish (perhaps because *we* are the ones who risk dying!) are more exciting and those for, say, silverfish (*shimi*), though relatively few, more innovative. So, after beginning the final rewrite, I decided to add a chapter of *modern flies* to see if fly-ku could be refreshed. I gathered more modern haiku from Takazawa's on-line haiku data bank and pestered Tenki, host of the on-line haiku pub Ukimidô for help. This result was a collection of modern haiku, 80 representative *fly-ku* (Please bear in mind that this was done quickly and is by no means final. ですから、この句はどうだい？と思われたら、教えて下さい.) with a maximum of 2 *ku* per poet, to which I added another score of *ku* many of which were contributed by Ukimido regulars to a Fy-ku Fest, or *haeku kukai*.

Despite the lead *ku,* above, contributed to the Fly-ku Fest, there is not much direct reference to Issa's poem in modern haiku. In fact, I would not be surprised to learn that the existence of Issa's fly-*ku*, with its supposed anthropomorphic and maudlin sentiment, may have steered people away from flies to less suspect bugs. In the 1997 *Kidaibetsu Gendai Haiku senshû*, the largest printed collection of contemporary haiku (Edited by the Haijin Kyokai, the largest association of haiku poets and published once every 5 years or so), there are only 2 fly *ku* and 1 autumn fly *ku,* as opposed to 137 fireflies, 108 cicada, 48 ants, 33 water striders, 22 spiders, 22 cicada shells, 21 ant-lions, 20 moths, 17 stickbugs, 13 caterpillars, 13 silverfish, 8 mosquitoes, 7 cockroaches – I will skip counting the number of *ku* for the insects of fall, but the result is the same. One might argue that flies have been played out. But that should be equally true for the firefly and cicada, for they, too, were lionized for centuries. And, the firefly today is even more scarce than the housefly. *Flies are just not cool.* That is one reason I am especially grateful to Ukimidô for their cooperation.

damn microsoft word will not let me kill a line of zig-zag (supposedly a border) you probably won't see in pdf – i have successfully killed about 100 of them so far (i had wanted them before finding out they do not pdf) at the cost of wasting 4 hours. I tried marking it (won't mark right) etc. all sorts of things with the borders tab, but the damn thing won't die. I *hate* this cruel invisible bullying that robs me of time better spent editing or translating!

~~~~~~

80 *Gendai* = Modern F*ly-ku*

(*selected for me by Tenki*)

1

一点の蝿亡骸の裾に侍す　石田波郷

itten no hae nakigara no suso ni jisu – ishida hakyô

(one-dot-fly corpse's skirt/hem-on wait/attend)

one fly
attending to the skirt
of a corpse

that dot?
a fly on a cuff of
the corpse

The *suso* (hem) can be the end of a sleeve, the cuff of trousers, on a skirt or a kimono. The "one-dot" in the original is a counter or class noun (such as we might use when we say "a *piece* of paper" or *stick* of gum). It is not a common one for flies and apparently serves here to emphasize the diminutive size of the entourage (if a corpse can be said to have such) or merely indicate that at first glance the fly was taken for an unspecified dot. It is also associated with exceptions – eg. the woman standing out among men is "a red dot in a sea of black." *One life in a larger scene of death?*

2

向日葵の葉にとぶ蝿や南風　　飯田蛇笏

himawari no ha ni tobu hae ya minami kaze – iida dakotsu

(sunflower's leaf/leaves-to fly/flies fly/flies: a south wind)

flies come
to sun flower leaves
a south wind

a fly visits
a sun flower leaf
the south wind

Sunflower in Japanese is "sun-turner." Always facing the sun, their presence makes us more aware of the cardinal directions. Perhaps the poet also thought: *how fitting that the fly comes with a wind from the sunny South!*

3

おっぱいがいっぱい地下鉄に蝿が飛び　笠井亜子

oppai ga ippai chikatetsu ni hae ga tobi – kasai ako (ukimidô fly-fest)

(breasts full-of subway-in fly/ies fly/ies)

flying about
the subway full of boobs
a fly

The psychological mimesis of *oppai* can only be matched by *boob* and the reader is assured that no disrespect is intended for the part of the anatomy that might prompt a biologist fly to exclaim "All those warm sweaty mammals!" In Japanese subways,
~~~~~~

there is generally enough air conditioning to cool the lower but not the upper half of your body, so there are a lot of sweaty breasts. The *ippai* (full of) pegged on to the *oppai* is comical but also brings out the nature of summer. While the *ku* is by a woman and not intentionally erotic, as a man, I cannot help but recall a Fuji Santarô cartoon (*Asahi Shinbun*) where the male alter-ego of the cartoonist just missed jumping onto a train to see a large pair of *oppai* pressed against the train-door window. The caption was *munen* ^{2} (chagrin squared). This *ku* was among the 63 submitted to an Ukimidô fly-ku fest for this book.

4

あきなひや蠅取リボン蠅を待つ　ねじめ正也

akinai ya haetori ribon hae o matsu – nejime masaya

(business/commerce: fly-catching-ribbon fly/ies-for waits)

business
fly-paper waiting
for flies

Is fly-paper, dangling, intended to be a metaphor for *akinai* (commerce, or business, that mostly involves goods), or we are talking about fly-paper on sale at a retail business from the perspective of that paper?

5

蠅ひとつ夜深き薔薇に逡巡す　日野草城

hae hitotsu yo fukaki bara ni shunjun su – hino sôjô

(fly one, night-late rose-at hesitates/pauses)

one fly
late at night pauses
by the rose

An erotic reading is *possible*, but I prefer to imagine a fly curious about the scent of the rose.

6

一点の早蠅清浄白牡丹　阿波野青畝

itten no sabae shôjô shirabotan – awano seiho

(one-dot/speck/mote-early-fly, pure white peony)

an early fly
one mote pristine
the white peony

one mote
an early fly: a pure
white peony

an early fly
the pure white peony
has its foil

an early fly
on the pure face of
the white peony

Again, that *itten* or "dot/point." I am not sure if the idea is that the single early fly on the white peony is as pure=clean-looking as the flower (*here is a fly that has never known shit?*), or that this dot of a fly helps bring out the peony's white by contrast.

The *sabae* or "early-fly" belongs to early summer, true, also, for the peony, which in some old saijiki was considered a flower of late spring. The first reading (two tries) is close to the original. I do not know if the "pure" (*shôjô*) is intended to apply to the fly as well as the peony. The second pair of readings goes for the contrast, possibly intended by the poet. Either way, one might associate the flower with the Pureland Flower Temple (Shôjôke-in) in Kyoto, or more precisely, the *shôjôkôbutsu*, one of the 12 light-emitting Buddhas at the same temple (*shôjô* is a religious word for purity, for one who has been cleansed of sins). This makes the poem similar to the flies-on-the-faces-of-Buddha haiku of Issa. Were the poem by a young contemporary poet, it would be possible to read the characters comprising *shôjô* as *seijô* meaning something like what Usanians call "organic" (which is to say no use of chemical fertilizers and insect repellants) and the translation might have been "an organic / white peony's first visitor / a fly." Tenki thinks the possibility for that reading zero, because the new term is atrocious (and because, I think, flowers are not equated with vegetables: I mean, have you ever come across an *organic rose*?), but I like it.

7

職替へてみても貧しや冬の蝿　安住敦

shoku kaetemite mo mazushi ya fuyu no hae – azumi atsushi

(work changed-tried-even poor/lousy:/! winter-fly)

i even tried
changing jobs but poor's poor
a winter fly

There is a nitty-gritty realism on the human side of this winter fly. Not that it turns the poet into a winter fly rather than vice-versa. But while it may not be a poem about the fly, it does bring out the wretchedness of poor folk in the dark and cold months. They do not get pills, psychiatrists and trips to the tropics to fight seasonal disorders. They do not fly thousands of miles to go snow-boarding. They – or *we*, for I am poor – can more easily identify with the fly, husbanding its dwindling energy, than to the hyperactive life of the average (wealthy) Usanian.

8

蝿生るうつくしき日を浴びながら　依光陽子

hae umaru utsukushiki hi o abinagara -- yorimitsu yôko

(fly born beautiful sun[obj] bathing-as)

flies are born
to bathe in beautiful
sunshine

a fly is born
showered by beautiful
sunlight

flies hatch
soaked in the beautiful
light of the sun

Properly speaking, flies are not born but hatch (*kaeru*) in Japanese, as they do in English. By using a common verb, the flies come into the world sharing the bard's "touch of nature (that makes all men kin)." Flies getting born are found in only two of the old haiku in this book. One, by Baishitsu describes the Autumn fly that is born among us. The other, by Tantan, was the born-to-be-hit poem with its karmic overtones: who can speak of being *"re-hatched?"* There are a surprisingly large number of flies "born" in contemporary haiku. A couple that might be called soundscapes: "how very loud / the sound of the waves / flies are born!" (波の音いと高く蝿生れけり 久保田万太郎) by Kubota Mantarô and "flies are born / to the mooing of poor cows / being milked" (乳牛のひきつる声に蝿生まる 亞子) by Ako in the fly-ku fest. Could this usage result from the unconscious affection for flies in the clean new world? *Are Japanese coming to miss their flies?*

9

はるかぜや玄関番の蝿一つ　永田耕衣

harukaze ya genkanban no hae hitotsu – nagata kôi

(spring-wind: foyer/entrance-guard's fly one)

spring wind
guarding our foyer
one fly

All Japanese houses, though mere shacks, must have a tiny foyer, be it only large enough for one person to stand. That is because shoes, removed upon entering, must have a covered place to wait for their owner. Traditional farm houses need it to store tools and small amounts of produce, and it serves as a liminal space to discuss things with shod members of the family, strangers and others not welcomed in. The spring wind brings living things, visitors. It is refreshing to see the fly as a guard rather than something to be guarded against for once.

10

瓜蝿が瓜蝿を呼ぶ雨催　横山きっこ

uribae ga uribae o yobu amamoyoi – yokoyama kikko (ukimidô fly-fest)

(melon/cucumber-fly/flies melon/cucumber-fly/flies[obj] call rain-sing)

the melon flies
are calling their fellows
looks like rain

..

Another from the Ukimidô fly-ku-fest. Perhaps I can get more information on this apparent weather sign for the second edition.

11

裏の家の樫まで蝿のとびゆける　下村槐太

ura no ie no kashi made hae no tobiyukeru – shimomura kaita

(behind-house's oak-until fly fly-goes/leaves)

the fly flies
to the oak by the house
behind ours

We have seen this poem before. I like it a lot, partly because it reminds me of when my eyes were very, very sharp, though I doubt my mind was calm enough to follow a fly for that long. I apologise for "the fly flies," but what can we do about it?

12

蝿帳を置く場所として拭いてゐる　加倉井秋を

haechô o oku basho to shite fuite-iru – kakurai akio

(fly-cover[fly-guard] put place-as make, wiping)

wiping off
the place reserved for
the fly-guard

This, like the last haiku, is a fine example of the straight realism modern haiku takes pride in. It is *also* funny: the place the fly-guard is put is, to be sure, the place where food is set, so wiping the table is perfectly understandable, but it *seems* to suggest the fly-guard is being treated as something valuable.

••

13

蝿叩鬱々としてわが端坐　加藤秋邨

hae-tataki utsuutsu to shite waga tanza – katô shûson (d.1993)

(fly-swatting gloomy-gloomy-is, my *tanza* (formal-style of sitting)

a fly-swatter
something gloomy about
my formal posture

English has no dignified word for sitting on one's heels, for not only do we not sit on our heels but we have no proper way to sit (women once had, but that had more to do with elegance and chastity). Should we imagine a photo where the fly-swatter is seen to one side? Or, does the poet, probably dressed in fine Japanese dress, pick up a fly-swatter and feel some momentary nausea? The word for melancholy/gloomy *utsu-utsu-to* is a bit humorous for it is homophonic with hit-hit (or, swat-swat).

14

秋の蝿握つてそして放したり　夏目漱石

aki no hae nigitte soshite hanashitari – natsume sôseki (d.1916)

(fall-fly/ies grabbing then release[+indefinite])

fall flies
i grab and then
release them

This poem by the great novelist is dated about the same time as Shiki's haiku included in the body of this book as "old haiku." "Modern" (*gendai*) starts with the 20th century in Japan. the English can not match the indefinite *~tari* suffixed to the verb release (*hanashi*) which works to soften things as the English "some" does in other contexts.

15

梅雨の部屋蠅みな宙をとべりけり　皆吉爽雨

x2 *tsuyu no heya hae mina chû o toberikeri* – minayoshi sôu

monsoon the flies in my room all flying	apricot rain all the flies in the room are airborne

I already put this in *Sundry* (Rain-flies). Folk concerned with tree names call the Japanese plum an apricot, something I usually do not do because of the length of the word, but here I thought it might make for good alliteration.

16

庭土に皐月の蝿の親しさよ　芥川龍之介

niwatsuchi ni satsuki no hae no shitashisa yo – akutagawa ryûnosuke (d.1927)
(garden-earth/dirt-on *satsuki* (old calendar mid-june) fly's closeness/familiarity!)

in my garden

how familiar
the early june flies
upon the dirt

The translation misses this, but I can't help but think the poet, known for his short stories, literary prize bearing his name and interest in the legendary river creature, the *kappa*, chose the old Chinese name for the month because the usual Japanese characters for "fifth-month" has the connection with bothersome flies we have already discussed. It seems a bit late in the year for the flies to suddenly become familiar. Is the heat just enough to warm our hearts toward dirt and flies?

17

蝿飛んで淋しき道のまっすぐに　岸本尚毅

hae tonde sabishiki michi no massugu ni – kishimoto naoki
(fly/flies flies/fly lonely road's straightly)

a fly heads
straight down
the lonely road

A singular fly seems more effective so it is probably what was intended. The protruding eyes of a fly bring out the emptiness of the street better than human eyes, for we see our nose, shoulders and feet. This fly-ku reminds me of a more recent poem read by perhaps ten people. For the *shiritori* (capverse) #3211 at Ukimido (2004/ 8/16), Miyoko wrote "Lose-War Day / down the dry street / flies a fly" (*haisenbi kawaita machi o hae ga tobu* 敗戦日乾いた街を蝿がとぶ　美代子). I am not sure what it means and, if I wrote to inquire, Miyoko would only claim it was a worthless poem, as she earlier claimed with respect to her cap-verse #3205 = "Our ancestors, / all were flies and all / were angels (*sensô mina shôjôbae desu tenshi desu*

先祖みな猩猩蠅です天使です　美代子). Her word for flies, *shôjôbae* means either blood-red flies, an imaginary simian fly or even besotted flies. I find the Chinese character

猩

fascinating as it combines the radical for "wild/ferocious" 犭 and character "star"星.

18

白梅の蘂に光つてゐたる蠅　岩田由美

shiraume no shibe ni hikatteitaru hae – iwata yumi

(white-plum's stamen+pistil-on shining fly/ies)

shining within
a white plum blossom
a fly

on the anthers
of white plum blossoms
gleaming flies

The *shibe* or *zui* (there are two pronunciation possibilities) can refer to either/both stamen and pistil. These stick pretty far out. I imagine the sun shining through and/or reflected from the white petals brings out the gleam of the fly that is half-in and half-out of the blossom, or, perhaps sitting on the anthers (head of the stamen). Readers may contrast the fly with the traditional visitor, the *uguisu* (nightingale/warbler).

19

蠅帳に透けて盃あるはよし　亀井糸游

haechô ni sukete sakazuki aru wa yoshi – kamei shiyû

(fly-guard-in transparently [as a verb] *sake* cup is-as-for, good)

it is good
to see a *sake* cup
through a fly-guard

a *sake* cup
seen through a fly guard:
something good

I associate fly-guards with nostalgic domesticity and blue-collar cafeterias. You do not find them in the New Japan. Either way, the *sake* cup suggests a small but truly appreciated pleasure in a hard-working (60-80 hr/wk) life.

20

蠅叩一日失せてゐたりけり　吉岡禅寺洞

haetataki ichinichi usete-itarikeri – yoshioka zenjidô

(fly-swatting one[the whole]day lost is[+indefinitive+emphatic?finality?])

the fly-swatter
apparently got lost
the whole day

the fly-swatter
tends to stay lost
for whole days

now and then
looking for the swatter
all day long

Fly-swatters are good at getting themselves lost, especially in the home of a writer with papers, magazines and books in constant motion. A fly-ku fest poem: "The fly swatter / one thing that is / always lost" or, "The fly-swatter / one thing i can / never find" (見当たらぬ物の一つに蠅叩き　餡子 = anko). And another last-minute internet find: "Walking around asking / now, where did that / fly-swatter go?" Yocchi (蠅叩どこにいつたと聞きまわり よっち) www004.upp.so-net.ne.jp/ymita/sub426.htm

21

秋の蝿追えばその手にまつわり来　吉田不可止

aki no hae oeba sono te ni matsuwari-ki – yoshida fukashi

(autumn-fly/ies chase-if/when this/that hand-about surround-come)

the flies of fall
approach the same hand
that chased them

autumn flies
attracted to the hand that
would swat them

Issa, as we have seen, has written the same, without specifying the season. Upon this second encounter with the same idea, Keigu's memory has been jolted:

swatting a fly
the hole in the air
quickly fills in

And when it does the flies are sucked back to the same place.

22

一つ追ひをれば二つに夜の蝿　久保田万太郎

hitotsu oi-oreba futatsu ni yoru no hae – kubota mantarô

(one chase if two-into night-fly/flies)

i chased off
one and now have two
night flies

It would be interesting to compile a book of haiku with numbers. Numbers are useful, for despite the fact they may be made up, they always seem authentic and help us to imagine what is described.

23

蝿とんでくるや箪笥の角よけて　京極杞陽

hae tondekuru ya tansu no kado yokete – kyôgoku kiyô

(fly/ies flying-come: dresser's corner/s avoiding)

flies zip in
avoiding the corners
of the dresser

This oft-anthologized poem is, like poem 11, above, a literally *fine* observation. If speed were measured in body-lengths per second, I bet the fly would make even the falcon look slow, yet it manages not to fly into things despite the absence of a sharp bird-eye. We may have gotten to the moon, but will we ever manage to create robots to out-perform flies? (In one of Ed Regis' books, *Nano!* perhaps, a professor pretends to operate an artificial fly; but it was a real one with silvered wings. A fly performance gloss, anyone?)

24

旅を来てこんな元気な秋の蠅と　金子兜太

tabi o kite konna genki na aki no hae to – kaneko tôta

(travel-through coming, so/this well fall-fly/ies-with)

arriving
with so spunky
a fall fly

checking in
with a hyper-active
autumn fly

my spunky
fall fly, are you, too
a traveler?

The original has the simple but sure touch that makes Kaneko the leading late 20th century haijin. I had trouble Englishing the first 5 syllabets, the "travel+coming."

25

秋の蠅にぎり拳の中にいし　熊田ひとし

aki no hae nigiri kobushi no naka ni ishi – kumada hitoshi

(autumn-fly/ies, squeezing fist's inside-of is)

a fall fly
clenched within
my fist

I imagine, and first translated, "A fall fly / quiet inside of / my fist;" but Tenki noticed the additional *quiet* and observed that it was "a *ku* that does not say much." I guess that is true – and interesting if you consider what it is that makes a poem good or bad, old syle or new style, etc. – but I was more upset with the *clenching* (*nigiri*) in the original. If the poet is going minimal, that verb is snake-feet (redundant), for a fist is clenched *by definition*. If Santôka, a haijin who made his poems only as long as he had to (by the same token, some of his came out too long) had written it, he would have cut off those snake-feet and gone with a "too short" *ku.*

26

尾は牛の別の生きもの冬の蠅　後藤青峙

o wa ushi no betsu no ikimono fuyu no hae – gotô seiji

(tail-as-for cow's another living-thing winter-fly)

the cow's tail
is another creature
winter flies

the cow's tail
is not the cow, right?
winter flies

winter flies
the tail of the cow is
not the cow

English makes us feel we must put in a word such as "think the winter flies" or "for winter flies." Maybe we do. Adding an explanation and, in the second poem, paraversing:

the cow's tail
taken for a creature
by winter flies

heavenly cow
winter flies think the tail
is a devil

The use of the word "creature" by itself shows the tail is "another/separate." A less clever contemporary winter fly-cow *ku*: "It found / a bored cow – / the winter fly" – Ôgawa Yôko (退屈な牛を見つけし冬の蠅／大川洋子 屋根 (Thanks AQ))

27

蠅の子の止まりっぷりも物馴れて　高沢良一

hae no ko no tomarippuri mo mono narete – takasawa yoshikazu
(fly-child's *stopping/landing-manner too, thing-used-to*)

its manner
of resting: that fly is
used to me

how it sits
and so forth, that fly
knows me

that fly
acts familiar, even
in the way it stops

Here Takasawa has noted something that is doubtless true. We might fail to observe what a fly does but it is unlikely a fly would not observe us and with time adjust his or her behavior accordingly. People can observe and learn, too. Takasawa also haikus "Chasing a fly / i notice where / it stops next" (*hae no ko no owarete tsugi ni tomaru tokoro* 蠅の子の追はれて次ぎに止まる処　高沢良一). He does not actually say he "notices" in the original, but he surely does. Like sandpipers on the beach, some flies flee far and others but a few inches at a time. I think Issa would have greatly enjoyed Takasawa's eye for bugs. Unfortunately, I fear my translation has not done his familiar fly justice. The verb *tomaru* (stop/alight/stay) includes more than one nuance we are forced to choose from and the *~ppuri* modifying it is a much sweeter (and more economical) way to say "way/manner."

28

一匹の蠅一本の蠅叩　高浜虚子

ippiki no hae ippon no hae tataki – takahama kyoshi (d.1959)

one fly and one fly-swatter

(This is a repeat.) Should we call this minimalism or luxury? In respect to the latter (perhaps the product of my imagination), one might calculate and record the ratio of flies to fly-swatters in various locations. Or, one might do this over time. The use of untranslatable counters (*ippiki* and *ippon*) to fill the syllabets reflects this father of modern haiku's formalist bent and expresses his love for language.

29

金蝿の五重の塔にとまりけり　佐々木六戈

kinbae no gojû no tô ni tomarikeri – sasaki rokuka

(gold-fly's 5-level/story tower-on lands/stops[+finality])

a gold fly
comes to sit
on a five-story pagoda

resting on
the five-story pagoda
a gold fly

If there are dung flies, there are gold flies. Though that is just a name from the gold-green gleam of their bodies, one can imagine them landing on gold and in combination with a pagoda like this, we almost enter the gilt world of the "Chinese Nursery Rhyme" with "little golden sister with a gold whip riding a gold horse, a gold toad (I.T. Headland translates it as a gold *fish!*) in their golden well" and so forth.

30

来て今し冷たかりける蝿の肢　三橋敏雄

kite imashi tsumetakarikeru hae no ashi – mitsuhashi toshio

(coming now chilly[?], fly's limbs)

coming now
the feet of the fly
are chilly

This haiku suggests that *now* is the time that fly legs start to feel chilly on the skin; we do not know *when* that is on the calendar but the old haiku we have seen suggests it is at the start of winter, originally the 10th month. It is hard to say which is better, the "limbs" in this *ku* or the less specific but dated flies in older one.

31

富士山頂吾が手の甲に蝿とまる　山口誓子

fuji-sancho waga te no kô ni hae tomaru – yamaguchi seishi

(fuji peak/top: my hand's back-on fly lands/rests)

on
top of
mt fuji a fly lands
on the back of my hand

Did the fly climb up with them? Or did it fly the hypotenuse from some town near the mountain? Yamaguchi wrote a second, evidently related *ku:* "this fly / came ten leagues to stop / on top of the peak" (*jûri tobikite sanchô ni hae tomaru* 十里飛び来て山頂に蝿とまる). To me, this suggests the flies came by the latter, i.e. direct route. The crater of this 10,000 year-young mountain is 850 meters across and its average temperature at the 12,389 ft summit is 4.9 c in July and 2.7c in August, a bit cold for most flies. There is, however, something besides the sweat of climbers to draw them. A Japanese guidebook recommends that toilet paper rather than kleenex, which does not dissolve in water, be carried up.

32

剃刀に蝿来て止まる情事かな　寺山修司

kamisori ni hae kite tomaru jôji kana – terayama shûji (d. 1983)

(razor-on fly/flies come/came stop/rest love affair / romance 'tis/!/?)

a fly comes
to rest on a razor:
making love

flies come
to rest on a razor:
making love

a fly comes
to rest on the razor:
a love affair

a love affair
how flies came to rest
upon the razor

That Terayama was a playwright and a tanka (5-7-5-7-7) poet, or "kajin," is reflected in this poem that has three problems for translation. First, we might presume that only the fly on the bottom is actually on the blade. In Japanese, one fly may be imagined until the final 5 syllabets where we know there are two. Second, in Japanese, it is unclear whether we are talking about flies copulating or a fly (or flies) on a razor with blood from being used to slash a wrist. Third, this is a Japanese-style poem in the sense that everything modifies the subject (the love affair) at the end. I cannot help mentioning his other *fly-ku* as typical in what way I cannot quite say: "the dust on a piano in a seaside hotel is licked by flies" (海のホテルピアノのほこり蝿がなめる 寺山修司). Note: Tenki says, "*a love affair* is a dangerous enough thing, so you need not think suicide, etc., nor imagine the flies on the edge of a razor."

33

蝿たたき持って立ちたる右翼かな　寺澤一雄

haetataki motte tachitaru uyoku kana – terasawa kazuo

(fly-swatter holding standing right-wing ' tis/!/?)

standing up
fly-swatter in hand
the right-winger

up he stands
fly-swatter cocked:
a real hawk

Unless this was actually seen, it is mighty close to being a senryû. Kyoshi wrote: "Our host / comes and goes / swatter in hand" (蝿打を持つて出て来る主かな 虚子 *hae-uchi o motte dete-kuru aruji kana*). There is something right-wing about all hosts.

34

風ふけば蝿とだゆなり菊の宿　芝不器男

kaze fukeba hae todayunari kiku no yado – shiba fukio

(wind blow-if/when, flies dissappear/die, chrysanthemum lodge/inn/dwelling)

the mum inn
when the wind blows
flies peter out

Chrysanthemum is just too long a word for most haiku. I hope "mum" is acceptable. A "mum inn" is a house in the business of raising this flower (In Japanese, "making" = *zukuri*, for stalks are straightened and supports used). Flies disappearing implies they are usually plentiful. *Why the flies?* Perhaps it is the horse-shit. Issa put mums and manure together more than once. *And the wind?* Do the mum-gardens, unlike most gardens, lack brush for the flies to take refuge from it? Or did the wind bring about a diminishment of flies simultaneous to the start of the mum season? Must we understand to appreciate this haiku?

35

身ほとりに何も叩かぬ蝿叩　手塚美佐

mihotori ni nanimo tatakanu haetataki – tezuka misa

(body-surroundings-in nothing swat fly-swatter)

within reach
a fly-swatter that hits
nothing

near at hand
my flyswat that never
swats a thing

nearby
my swat-nothing
fly-swatter

The last reading is closest to Japanese. I am tempted to write "my fly-swatter / for flies too far away to / look in the eye;" but that would be a different poem.

36

駱駝またたかず瞼の蝿にさへ　宗像夕野火

rakuda matatakazu mabuta no hae ni sae – munakata yûnobi

(camel/s blink-not-eyelid/s' fly-on even)

camels do not blink even for flies on their eyelids

True enough. They have impressive upper eyelids. Can't say why I translated using a single line.

37

蝿生れ早や遁走の翅使ふ　秋元不死男

hae umare haya tonsô no hane tsukau – akimoto fujiô

(fly/ies born quickly flight[fleeing]'s wings use)

born to flee

baby flies
flying flat out
in no time

winging it

baby flies
beating out a fugue
in no time

Of the four F's, *flight* is probably the most important for flies. Looking up *tonsô,* I rediscovered the meaning of a *fugue*.

38

蠅たたく音の大きくのがしけり　小川越人

hae tataku oto no ôkiku nogashikeri – ogawa etsujin
(fly swat sound's largely miss[+finality])

the sound
of swatting that fly
was way off

I do not know whether the poet describes his own or another's swatting. Both possibilities have their charm. Would a single line translation be better here?

swatting a fly: that missed-by-a-mile sound

39

牛の目の蝿をあつめて澄みにけり 小島 健

ushi no me no hae o atsumete suminikeri – kojima ken
(cow's/s/s' eyes' flies[obj] gathering, clear up)

cow eyes
gathering flies
become clear

When you consider that the maggots eating putrified flesh reduce the incidence of serious infection in severe battle wounds, it is possible that flies benefit cow eyes in some herds in some localities, but all I can find on the internet is how flies, eg. "face flies" (*musca autumnalis*), spread pinkeye and other bad things. The bad that bugs do sells chemicals and allows authorities to warn us of this or that; the good things bugs do neither sell things nor justify the existence of the authority.

40

ふとももで呼吸しており秋の蝿　小野田あさみ

futomomo de kokyû shiteori aki no hae – ono asami
(inner thigh-on/at/by/with breath-doing[+honorific] autumn fly/ies)

on my thigh
an autumn fly
breathing

breathing
with its thighs
a fall fly

autumn fly
on my thigh i see
is breathing

Three Japanese poets have given me 3 very different readings of this poem. My last keeps the breather ambiguous. The thigh *should* belong to the woman, for it is erotic (something that is always good) to imagine the poet *staring at a fly on her inner thigh* and because I have read that flies breathe (if that is the proper word for a sort of osmosis of oxygen) through holes in their chests, but do not know anything about the same in their "thighs" (Fly-ologists, glosses are welcome!). Perhaps the poet intended to conflate her breathing and that of the fly. *The slight breathing movement of her thigh (moving slightly up and down) might have given the illusion of the fly breathing.*

41
神馬とて馬の匂ひや秋の蝿　松原安治
shinba tote uma no nioi ya aki no hae – matsubara yasuji
(god/s' horse/s-re., horse's smell/stink:/! autumn-fly)

gods' horses
smell horsey all the same
autumn flies

The flies are the proof. There are many poems about the humanity/animality of men in divine offices, but this is something new again and, I think, refreshing.

42
冬の蝿いきなり飛びて光りけり　深見けん二
fuyu no hae ikinari tobite hikarikeri – fukami kenji
(winter-fly suddenly flies/flying shines[+finality])

a winter fly
suddenly takes off
and gleams!

That is certainly not the "winter fly" we have seen in haiku so far. It seems like a very strong creature.

43
活きた目をつつきに来るか蝿の声　正岡子規
ikita me o tsutsuki ni kuru ka hae no koe – masaoka shiki (d. 1902)

coming to pick at living eyes? – the voice of flies (repeat)

This is an often anthologized poem from a sickbed point of view by the man who summed up old haiku and sparked modern haiku.

..

44
顔の周りを九年飛んでる金蝿よ　西川徹郎
kao no mawari o kyunen tonderu kinbae yo – nishikawa tetsurô
(face's surrounding[obj] nine-years flying gold fly [+emphatic address]

gold fly, yo!
you've circled my head
for nine years!

Here, I carried the Japanese emphatic "yo" right over into English. (I mean, why not? It has been around longer than the Black English *yo* that has spread all the way to my mom's friend Pamela.). If Venus, the "gold-star" (in Japanese) had a 9-year interval . . . but it doesn't. I give up on both the rhyme and the reason.

45

昼寝の国蝿取リボンぶら下り　西東三鬼

hirune no kuni, haetori ribon burasagari – saitô sanki (d. 1962)

(afternoon-sleep's country, fly-capture-ribbon hanging down)

nap country
fly-ribbons
dangling

fly-ribbons
dangling down, this is
nap country

Issa would have loved that "Nap Country." I envision a store or home – or both together, for most tiny shops in Japan are the foyers of homes – in an economically depressed small-town. In Tokyo, only the retired can afford what is considered the luxury of an afternoon nap. When I showed statistics on the benefits of an after-lunch nap to my colleagues and superiors at work in Tokyo, they just laughed. Even science cannot convince people addicted to continuous activity to try the old-fashioned, but as it turns out, more efficient way of life. Napping may reflect a slow economy, but it does not cause it. I cannot say just why the fly-paper is appropriate; it just is. (I'll bet it can be found in Norman Rockwell, too.)

46

地球儀を廻し廻せば蝿生まる　川崎展宏

chikyûgi o mawashi mawaseba hae umaru – kawasaki tenkô

(globe-model[obj] spin, spinning-if/when fly born)

spin a globe
and at each spin
a fly is born

Within flying distance? This representative modern haijin *seems* logical here. Globe and fly are an interesting combination. In the fly-ku fest , AQ quipped "a country / on a globe vanishes / bush flies (地球儀の一国を消す藪の蝿) . Bush-mosquitoes (*yabuka*) are a big thing in Japan/ese, but these were the first bush *flies* I had seen. It is a pun on the name of a certain president. Enough politics. Does anyone make really lifelike fly pin-heads?

47

蝿一つ良夜の硯舐(ね)ぶり居り　川端茅舎

hae hitotsu ryôya no suzuri neburiori – kawabata bôsha (d. 1941)

(fly one good-night's ink-stone licking-is)

one fly
licking my inkstone
on a magical moonlit night

The "good night" is "a beautiful moonlit night" generally but not always in mid-fall.

We have no English term for such a night, so I added a modifier: "magical." The inkstone is, if you recall, a small rectangular stone tray for rubbing one's ink-stick on and holding the ink in its pool. *Imagine a fly narcissus falling in and drowning.*

48

冬の蝿出て来て人にとまりけり　前田普羅

fuyu no hae dete-kite hito ni tomarikeri – maeda fura (d.1954)

(winter-fly/ies out-coming people-on land/stop)

winter flies
they come out and sit
on people

As we have seen, Yamaguchi Seishi has an *Autumn* fly already seeking out his warmth. Maybe he lives further North than Maeda.

49

蝿帳や隅にころげて茹玉子　草間時彦

haechô ya sumi ni korogete yude-tamago – kusama tokihiko

(fly-guard: corner-in rocking/rolling boiled-egg/s) ukimidô fly-fest

the fly-guard
a boiled egg rocking
in one corner

This is one of 63 haiku submitted to an Ukimidô fly-ku fest *kukai* held for this book. Seen through a fly-guard screen, the egg – minus the movement – seems suitable for a mezzotint. Tenki chose it over the more showy: "fly-guard / a transparent view / of cosmology" (蝿帳に透けて見えたる宇宙論　紫野 Shigeno) that garnered 2 votes in the *kukai.*

..

50

文字の上意味の上をば冬の蝿　中村草田男

moji no ue imi no ue o ba fuyu no hae – nakamura kusatao

(letter-on meaning-on[+emphatic], winter fly)

a winter fly
walks on letters *and*
significance

As we have seen already, both flies and fly-shit have been credited with literary activity. The explicit mention of "significance" seems fresh. The italic *and* is my way to signify the untranslatable emphatic particles *o ba,* only found in literature. The closest English would be "on letters, *not to mention* significance." Too long.

51

生まれたる蝿に天井ありにけり　村中とう子（「とう」は女+登）

umaretaru hae ni tenjo ari ni keri – muranaka tôko

(born fly/flies-on/to/for ceiling is[+finality])

a fly
is born with
a ceiling

I wondered if this meant that flies are born to live within fly limits – "a ceiling / built into every / fly born?" – as we have our glass-ceilings (?), while evoking images of actual flies on ceilings. Maybe, I fantasized, they cannot fly high but remain down to earth (Entomologists, a gloss on the relative height at which various bugs fly would be welcome)! Tenki *pooh-poohs* that and writes that he reads it to mean only that *houseflies, like humans, are born indoors.* They, too, live under a fake sky.

52

蝿生れて寺の人出を嘉しけり　大串章

hae arete tera no hitode o yomishikeri – ôgushi akira

(fly born [espec. holy things], temple's crowds approve/good-are[+finality])

flies are born
to celebrate the crowds
at temples

The verb for being *born* used here has sacred overtones and the rarely encountered verb (*yomishi*) used to express that things are good is one used almost exclusively by gods expressing their approval. This gives the poem a supernatural aura hard to reproduce in English.

53

お彼岸の蝿が合掌　無縁墓　大石太

ohigan no hae ga gasshô muenbaka – ôishi futoshi

(pâramita/equinox-fly/flies-the clasp-hand/pray no-relations-grave)

pâramita flies
clasping their hands upon
an untended grave

equinox flies
clasping their hands upon
an untended grave

The seven days in mid-Spring were associated with crossing over to the other bank, or Enlightenment. The middle day is the Spring Equinox. Japanese often visit the graves of their ancestors at this time. Here, the poet sees a grave with no descendents around or any sign of their having visited. Kikko, who found this poem, noted that Ôishi is a homeless old man (her term "*occhan*" means "uncle/gramps" and has an endearing ring to it not found in any English word I know of, though Ronald Regan's self-deprecatory *geezer* sounded good, it would not work for describing another person) and cited a website, *http://www.sohzoh.co.jp/jihi/homeless.htm.*

54
秋の蝿辿る海図の緯度経度　大島民郎
aki no hae tadoru kaizu no keido ido – ôshima tamirô
(fall-fly drift/end-up sea-chart's longitude latitude)

the latitude and the longitude on the marine chart where the autumn fly comes to rest

This *ku,* already introduced, is found in many anthologies and for good reason.

55
補陀落の蠅とディーゼル列車元気　大畑等
fudaraku no hae to deizeru ressha genki – ôhata hitoshi
(potalaka's flies and diesel column-cars/trucks/buses well) ukimidô fly-fest

well as ever
the flies and diesel trucks
of shangri-la

Another poem from the Ukimidô fly-fest. Fudaraku (補陀落/普陀落) from the Sanskrit potalaka, is an eight-sided mountain on the Southern sea-coast of India housing Kannon (Avalokitesvara) an avatar of Buddha associated with great mercy. The feeling here, Tenki believes, is more utopian, i.e., Shangri-la .

56
蝿生れ赤子の涙吸いにくる　中村和弘
hae umare akago no namida sui ni kuru – nakamura kazuhiro
(fly/ies born, baby/ies' tears suck/sip-to come)

flies are born
and come to suck
baby tears

I know babies make great *noise*, but do they cry many *tears*? ("Yes" writes my mother; but Henry Clay's father tells me he thinks he only shed tears about 9 months after birth, when he became conscious of being sad). Regardless, what a sweet poem this is! How different are *these* flies from the disgusting dung-fly! And how similar yet different this *ku* by Issa: "Babe in a basket / butterflies pick away at / his nostrils" (*fugo no ko ya kochô no seseru hana no ana*).

57
蝿来たる神父のどこかに止まらむと　津田清子
hae kitaru shinpu no doko ka ni tomaramu to – tsuda kiyoko
(fly/flies come/s priest's where-on land/sit[+insinuating particle])

a fly comes and
i wonder where it may
sit on the priest

So where will the fly deign to sit. The poet uses pretty fancy grammar, possibly because it is common in haiku, possibly for effect. I guess a fly does not turn a priest into a Beelzebub (a corruption of Ba'al Zebûb, a false god or devil sometimes translated as the Lord of the Flies (and dung), but it is good to find one Christian reference in the largely Buddhist world of the fly-ku. A zero-vote *ku* by Furiko in the Ukimidô fly-fest: "gathering / 'round the candles, flies & / a young priest (らふそくに集ふは蝿と若神父)."

58

一遍踊る我ら句作る蝿たかる　辻桃子

ippen odoru warera ku tsukuru hae takaru – tsuji momoko

(ippen dances, we *ku* make, flies swarm)

ippen dances
we write our *ku* and
flies swarm

Ippen (1239-1289) was an esoteric Buddhist priest who received a revelation to hit the road and spread the Buddhist gospel by dancing chanted sutras, which he did, drawing such great crowds that he got in trouble with the civil authorities (See more in T*O*PSY-TURVY 1585). What is the link between the three parts of the poem? Is it nothing? Or, is it that we all do what we must?

59

晩夏晩年角川文庫蝿叩き　坪内稔典

banka bannen kadokawabunko haetataki – tsubouchi nenten

(late-summer, late years kadokawa pocketbook fly-swatter/swatting)

pocket-book

near summer's end
my end, a kadokawa
for a fly-swatter

kadokawa

my august
using a pocketbook
on a fly

This oft-anthologized poem is hell to translate. For a start, the publisher's name and the English word for a small mass-produced book are both long. Kadokawa publishes many haiku but most of its pocketbooks are fiction, so can we say this is a novel way to use a novel? Keigu can't help a paraverse: *"Musca maledicta / swatted by a pocket-book / Lord of the Flies."* I know, that would be a bit too pat! But who can doubt but the Holy Bible, the Koran and Sutras have been used for such a purpose?

60

人生かがやく空瓶に蝿すみつきて　島津亮

jinsei kagayaku akibin ni hae sumitsukite – shimazu ryô

([human]life shines, empty jar/s-in fly/ies live/settle)

life's splendid
flies feeling at home
in empty jars

In the Sinosphere, "life" in its most significant (emotional and not just scientific) sense, is 人生, a word that includes the human =人. It is not really fair to horses and dogs and for that matter all animals who also have lives, but lacking another term for the same, it has come to be applied to them. Here, the poet feels happy about his life and all life. I cannot recall ever feeling anything quite like this, but I *almost* can.

61

冬蝿やつくづく冬の蝿の顔　松根東洋城

fuyubae ya tsukuzuku fuyu no hae no kao – matsune tôyôjô

(winter-fly/ies: intently winter-fly's face)

a winter fly
i ponder the face of
a winter fly

As long as a winter fly is sitting right there, you might as well look closely at it. The adverb (psychological mimesis) *tsukuzuku* has a reflective quality, suggesting the poet may see something of himself in that fly. The verb that generally accompanies the adverb is absent. We do not know if it is *watch, feel, think*. Hence "ponder." My favorite *tsukuzuku* ku is Issa's "a snipe / watches me intently / this dusk" (*tsukuzuku to shigi ware o miru yûbe kana*). He alludes to the *waka* by Saigyô claiming anyone with a modicum of aesthetic sense feels melancholy at a snipe's flying at dusk. *I don't know about me*, Issa confesses.

62

口論の真ん中にあり蝿叩　藤田湘子

kôron no manaka ni ari hae-tataki – fujita shôshi

(argument's exact-middle-in is: fly-swatter/swatting)

lying between
people arguing
a fly-swatter

in the midst
of an argument
swatting flies

While swatting a fly would make excellent rhetoric in mid-quarrel – I see the movement of the arm standing out more than it would in the USA, for Japanese do not gesticulate with their arms while they speak in the (wild) manner of Occidentals and I can imagine the sound of the swat providing an equally effective exclamation mark whether or not the fly is hit – the first reading is more interesting and therefore (probably) right.

63

蝿叩くには手ごろなる俳誌あり　能村登四郎

hae tataku ni wa tegoro naru haishi ari – nomura toshirô (d. 2002)

(fly-swat-for-as, handy is/become haiku-magazine is)

a magazine of
haiku just the right size
to swat flies

a magazine
of haiku, perfect
to swat a fly

there is this
haiku journal handy for
swatting flies

Another publication? Actually, a haiku magazine, unlike the pocket-book mentioned in the earlier(?) haiku, is perfect and it makes a statement about the nature of *haijin.*

64

手まくらにラヂオ快調蠅うまる　飯田蛇笏

temakura ni rajio kaichô hae umaru – iida dakotsu

(hand/arm-pillow-to, radio pleasant-pitch[working well], flies born)

the radio crisp
as i nap on the tatami
and flies hatch

while i nap
the radio blares away
flies hatch

Old-fashioned radios and flies go together, why I do not know. And something about the rawness of both goes with the texture of the tatami mat we imagine the man naps on because a bed would have a real pillow. I dropped the "arm-pillow," for English has no such word. Japanese has many kinds of pillows not found in English; Issa even invents a *shiri-makura,* or buttocks-as-pillow. I dropped the "born" for "hatch" because it fits my feeling for the grainy blare of the scene.

65

鑁阿寺(ばんなじ)の鑁の字に付く冬の蠅　飯島晴子

bannaji no ban no ji ni tsuku fuyu no hae – iijima haruko

(bannaji[banna-temple]'s "ban" letter-on attach/cling/ winter-fly)

鑁

a winter fly
clinging to the ban
of bannaji

I thought the abnormally speckled appearance of this character *ban* ↑ (enlarged to font-size 24) might draw flies or seem appropriate for some other reason, but Tenki thinks the extraordinary character caught the poet's attention and the fly was spotted while gazing at it. The character is so dense that if it was written in black paint on a white sign, we may hypothesize that its literal warmth attracted and kept the fly.

66

山川に流す蠅捕リボンかな　富安風生

yamakawa ni nagasu haetori ribon kana – tomiyasu fûsei

(mountain stream-in flow fly-capture ribbon [fly-paper])

flowing down
a mountain stream
fly-ribbon

Here, I have used the Japanese "ribbon," as is, rather than "correcting" it to "paper," for it seems to go better with the river. Sometimes *teipu,* or "tape" is used, but not in any *ku* in this book.

67

暖かき地べたを蝿の歩きけり　富田木歩

atatakaki jibeta o hae no arukikeri – tomita moppo

(hot earth fly walks[+finally])

a fly walks
on the warm surface
of the earth

68

冬の蝿　牛にかなしきまつげあり　富澤赤黄男

fuyu no hae ushi ni kanashiki matsuge ari – tomisawa kakio

(winter-fly/ies, cow/s-on sad eyelashes are/have)

winter flies
cows have sad
eyelashes

a winter fly
our cow has these
sad eyelashes

Compare this to the camel's eyelids (#36 above). What a difference in character!

69

身に余る羽を重ねて蝿生る　平畑静塔

mi ni amaru hane o kasanete hae umaru – hirahata seitô

(body/ies-on/to exceeding wing/s doubled fly/ies born)

with folded wings
too big for their trunks
flies are born

born with wings
longer than their bodies
folded: flies

All growth in life involves not only expansion but unfolding as we see in this haiku. Incidentally, insect wing storage is incredible. Adult ladybugs, whose wings do far more than simply double to fit under their tiny shells, amaze me.

70

金蝿やあら銀蝿や老夫婦　鳴戸奈菜

kinbae ya ara ginbae ya rôfûfu – naruto nana

(gold fly and, my!, silver-fly!/: old couple)

a gold fly
and, oh my! silver fly!
an old couple

It is heart-warming to think of an old couple identifying types of flies. We have bird-watchers but no "fly-watchers," and butterfly collectors but no "fly collectors," unless we include scientific research . . . Or, are *they,* the old couple, the flies?

71

冬蝿の住みゐる魔法のランプ買ふ　有馬朗人

fuyubae no sumiiru mahô no ranpu kau – arima akito

(winter fly's living in magic lamp buy)

my buying
a magic lamp with
a winter fly

magic!
within the lamp i buy
a winter fly

i had to buy
a magical lamp and
its winter fly

I like to imagine the old lamp was bought at a used-thing-store (*furumonoya*) , an old house in a long thing lot (called *an eel's bed = unagi no nedoko*) with junk piled up all over – I describe the one where I bought something – which is, to me, in itself a magical place.

72

冬の蝿病めばかろ〜抱かれもし　鈴木真砂女

fuyu no hae yameba karogaro dakare mo shi – suzuki masajo

(winter fly/ies sick/weaken-if/when lightly/gently hugged/made-love-to also am)

winter flies
sick, he embraces me
very gently

winter flies
sick, we still have
gentle sex

a winter fly
sick, i am gently
screwed

When it comes to sex, English is a real problem. It lacks a decent verb. Forgive the last reading, but it reads nicely, I think.

73

致し方なく冬蝿の歩きけり　痾窮

itashikata naku fuyu hae no arukikeri – akyû

(doing-way-not[it can't be helped], winter fly's walking [+finality])

for lack of
anything else, winter fly
walks on

nothing better
to do, a winter fly
totters on

There is a *ku* not used describing a fall fly as a "disoriented deserter." This is much better. It describes hopelessness or beyond hopelessness. The fly no longer makes much of an effort to seek sunlight, it just crawls on, perhaps in response to a dream of warmth.

74

無人機の裏はくらやみ冬の蠅　佐山哲郎

mujinki no ura wa kurayami fuyu no hae – sayama tetsurô (ukimidô fly-fest)
(drone [un-manned machine]'s back/underbody-as-for pitch-black winter-fly)

winter flies
behind the ATMs
utter darkness

I first thought the "unmanned machine/s" was a drone (on the dark / belly of the drone / winter flies). Tenki says they are automated teller machines, but not at a bank. They are at a money-lenders, one of those sorry stores where blue-collar workers cash their checks and send money home, etc. I had to put the flies first rather than last, for otherwise it would seem that the flies were behind rather than in front of the ATMs. The flies might be men and the darkness, well . . .

75

蠅打ちしあとの窪みや革布団　島村元

hae uchishi ato no kubomi ya kawabuton – shimamura hajime
(fly- swatted mark's depression: leather cushion)

a dent left
in a leather cushion by
a fly-swatter

swatting a fly
leaves an impression
the leather cushion

Excuse me for making light of a serious matter. If the fly bought the farm, we might title the poem "memento mori" or "he sure left an impression!" (笑)

76

ぶしつけな蠅取紙のねぢれやう　村田紫野

bushitsukena haetorikami no nejireyô – murata shigeno
(ill-mannered fly-capture-paper's twisting) ukimidô fly-fest

the fly-paper
hung without thought
twists slightly

In the same Fly-fest, Tenki garnered 5 votes for his *ku* "the fly-paper / hangs right in the center / of our family (蠅取紙ぶらり家族の中心に), but later confided that he thought Takasawa's simpler "back home / in a house with / fly-paper" (帰省せり蠅取リボン吊る家に　高沢良一) better. And, he chose to introduce Shigeno's *ku* which was chosen by only 2 people. As Tenki explains to new-comers, the ones that are most popular by the vote of the participants are not necessarily the best poems. This is partly because poems that grab you quickly are not necessarily the ones that still hold your interest a week or two later. Santôka had a good fly-paper *ku* (蠅があるいてゐる蠅取紙のふちを　山頭火) that deserves to be squeezed in:

a fly is walking on the edge of the fly-paper – santôka (d.1940)

77

体毛の少し斜めや蠅止まる　水星人

taimô no sukoshi naname ya hae tomaru – miyamoto kayono

(body-hair's slightly tilted/diagonal:/!/? fly/ies stop/s/land/s) ukimidô fly-fest

on arm hair
with a slight slant
the fly stops

This *ku* from the Ukimidô fly-fest gained 7 votes, the most of any poem. I first imagined flies singling-out hairs particularly angled with respect to the skin and, thinking of that hair, translated another poem in the fly-ku fest by Furiko as "landing on people / flies incline as they / come to a stop" (にんげんに蠅は傾斜をして止る (*ningen ni hae wa keisha o shite tomaru* = 振り子), *imagining the flies as fighter-planes and the hair serving as trip-wires on an carrier.* Actually, it is a simple observation of how flies tend not to be perfectly horizontal to the ground after they land and it gained 5 votes including one "best poem" vote.

78

昼餉の蠅ゼロ戦の角度ではないか　山口振り子

hiruge no hae zerosen no kakudo de wa nai ka – yamaguchi furiko

(lunch's fly/flies zero fighter's/s/s' angle is it not?) ukimidô fly-fest

lunchtime flies
that angle, is it not
a zero's?

flies drop in
for lunch at the angle of
zero fighters

at the angle of
a squadron of zeros?
lunchtime flies

Ditto, from the fly-kukai. This is good light-verse that, heaven forbid, reminds one of spam-ku (Note: you will find several of my sea slug (cucumber) *ku* at the spam-ku site). It represents but one of Furiko's diverse styles of haiku, many of which are *much* harder to translate.

79

十七階に会議はつづく夜の蠅　山口東人

jûnana kai ni kaigi wa tsuzuku yoru no hae – yamaguchi tôjin

(seventeenth-floor-on meeting-as-for continues/ing night-flies) ukimidô fly-fest

trapped in a meeting
on the 17th floor
night-flies

This, too, from the Fly-fest. None of my translations worked until "trapped" came to mind. If you don't believe me, try for yourself. Speaking of *stories*, I like this:

二階から家に出入りの蝿である　桑原三郎
nikai kara ie ni deiri no hae de aru – kuwahara saburô
(second-floor-from leave-enter fly is)

that fly
enters and leaves from
the 2nd floor

that is a fly
who enters and leaves from
the 2nd floor

80
人間に毛深き蝿の生れけり　島谷征良
ningen ni kebukaki hae no umarekeri – shimatani seirô
(people/human-on/from/in hirsute fly/ies born [emphatic?+finality?])

those born
of man are very
hairy flies

hirsute flies
are of mankind
born

Is this about flies that hatch from maggots that clean human wounds or eat dead men or both? Francesco Redi (d.1697) wrote of "black eggs" that "laboured fourteen days to produce certain large black flies striped with white, having a hairy abdomen, of the kind that we see daily buzzing about the butchers' stalls." (M. A. B. Bigelow trans.) Or is it genetic engineering? The "born" suggests to me the latter though it seems ridiculous. (Entomologists: What *is* the hairiest fly?) **Add:** *Is it possible, asks my mom, that this is about reincarnation? Good question. See the next edition!*

~~~~~~

＋２０→１００ f *l* y－k u !

(*chosen by the author for strange reasons*)

In Japanese, where 8 means *plenty*, 80 is a fine number to stop at, but I will add 20 more, chosen not for their excellence but for their wit and/or translatability. The inclusion of such *ku* in a same-language collection might be hard to justify, but those who cannot read Japanese will benefit from the fuller picture such translation provides. Most of the *ku* are from the Ukimidô Fly-ku Fest, the serving of instant flies I was treated to, and I leave the names as they are (haigô=pen-name=only).

81
食台の蝿の誓いを見届けり　ざんくろー
shokudai no hae no chikai o mitodokeri – zankuro (ukimidô fly-fest)
(dining-table's flies' vows[obj] see-reach[through until the end])

after the meal
flies making love
on my table

I think my added "after the meal" saves the poem, though the compound verb ending the original is witty enough, especially in combination with "vows."
~~~~~~

82

蠅の羽の震わす夢に醒める午後　ざんくろー

hae no ha no furuwasu yume ni sameru gogo – zankuro (ukimidô fly-fest)
(fly's wings shake dream-from awake afternoon)

one afternoon
i wake from a dream knowing
the wings of a fly

The poet writes that he wishes he had wings but is not particularly attracted to *fly wings*. The original is: "waking from / a dream shaking [my] fly wings / one afternoon." He added that it was too ambitious, i.e. expected the reader to read his mind. Does my "knowing" save the *ku?* (We have now seen two Zankuro *ku* though not 1 of his 4 entries to the Fly-ku Fest was selected by anyone.)

83

飛び立つ時少し泣いたり冬の蠅　亞子

tobitatsu toki sukoshi naitari fuyu no hae – ako (ukimidô fly-fest)
(fly/take-off time slightly cry[+indefinitive] winter-fly)

a winter fly
each take-off brings
wet eyes

I surprised the poet by wondering if this was a description of geriatric sex. She took it in good humor and replied that "in the winter, people and (other) animals are not well and lack confidence, and I put it in a hyperbolic way . . ." (3 of Ako's 6 *ku* entered were selected by someone, but not this seemingly maudlin one.)

84

半身に痒さ渦巻く夜の蠅　亞子

hanshin ni kayusa uzumaku yoru no hae – ako (ukimidô fly-fest)
(half-body-in/on itchiness/ticklishness whirlpool[=verb] night-flies)

half my body
in a maelström
night flies

Ditto for this one, here only because I could not leave behind the word *maelström*. I do not know that I have ever experienced flies so dramatically, day or night. The tickles failed to make it into the translation. The side of the body facing up is *flied.*
..

85

銀蠅にたかられてゐる擬態かな　萩月

ginbae ni takarareteiru gitai kana – hagizuki (ukimidô fly-fest)
(silver-flies-by swarmed-am mimicry 'tis/!/?)

mobbed by
silver flies: is it
mimicry?

A self-portrait? If so, Hagizuki-san does not dye her hair and follows the tradition of amusing self-depreciation of which Issa was the master. In Japan, silver is not connotative of shiny beauty. Rather, as Tenki pointed out to me, it generally *contrasts* with gold luster, evoking a soft if not dark quality. It is also associated with senior citizens who sit on the *shiruba-*, or "silver" seats on the train, etc.. This *ku* was not selected by anyone, but students of biology will appreciate it.

86

バス停の時間 蝿らの群るる空　萩月

basutei no jikan haera no mururu sora – hagizuki (ukimidô fly-fest)

(bus-stop's time/s flies' gather sky)

time for the bus: flies appear in the sky

The poet did not think much of her own poem (my apologies for using it!) – again, not selected – but I think the idea of flies smart enough to tell time – and who knows but that they do! – splendid. (Again, a comment from an entomologist would be welcome.)

..

87

叩かれて原風景の蝿である　萩月

tatakarete genfûkei no hae de aru – hagizuki (ukimidô fly-fest)

(swatted original/primal-scene's fly/flies is/are)

swatted
it turns out to be
a classic fly

After 6 unpopular poems, finally a winner. Two people selected this and one made it his top choice. I tried all different things (*swatted / it turns into a fly / of my childhood & swatted / it turns out to be / a fly of old & swatted / the fly releases / the 1950's*), but none succeeded in recreating the original for, owing to an accident of psychiatry, "the fly of *the primal scene*," a term that ought to mean a "coordinate origin within oneself"(Hagizuki) means something else in English. My translation, thus, had to part from the original and re-create what may be a different poem.

88

貝殻のあたりにボッティチェリの蝿　天気

kaigara no atari ni bottecheri no hae – tenki (ukimidô fly-fest)

(shells-empty area-in/by botticelli's fly/ies)

over there
by the empty shells
botticelli's flies

This was not meant to be a stand-alone *ku*. It is a cap-verse linking not to the usual one *ku* but to *two* of them (an emergency service Tenki performs as the host of Ukimidô), one of which is a taciturn seashell in the surf on the "Lose-War-Day" (敗戦日浪に無口な貝の殻　痾窮) – a common Japanese expression for the end of World War II – and the other inadvertently written simultaneously and posted slightly later (Miyoko's *ku* about a fly on a dry street noted in the explanation for poem 17 of the 80 above). Tenki took the *shell* from one *ku* and *fly* from the other.

89

富士塚につひにおちつく蠅叩　振り子

fujizuka ni tsui ni ochitsuku haetataki – furiko (ukimidô fly-fest)

(fuji-mound[mock-up]-on/by finally rests fly-swatter)

leaning against
a sacred mount fuji
an old fly-swat

leaning against
a sacred mount fuji
the old fly-swat

Mount Fuji became an object of worship and pilgrimage in the 18th century and there are quite a number of mock Fuji-sans (usually about 10-feet high) to be found within Shinto shrines or in more secular settings such as streets with many merchants (main streets). This is one. Centers of social activity in Japanese cities are warm (*pleasant*). Neither cold (*sterile*) modern business districts, hot (*dangerous*) inner cities, nor cool (*wealthy*?) museums of period architecture, they *live.* Local folk still put together traditional street-fairs and bon-dances. This spirit, like Mount Fuji is relatively dormant but far from dead. Please note that the original does not article the swatter shortened to "swat" to save the beat. "An" is probably right, but I also did a "the" reading because I dislike two "a/an"-prefaced nouns in a row. It warms up the swatter a bit, doesn't it? This neither meaningful nor meaningless Fly-ku Fest *ku* was a zero vote *ku* by a poet who got many votes for her other poems.

..

90

銀蠅がピカソの青に止まりけり　東人

ginbae ga pikaso no ao ni tomarikeri – tôjin (ukimidô fly-fest)

(silver-fly-the/a picasso's blue-on lands/rests)

a silver fly
rests on a picasso
blue period

This got 3 votes. The silver fly has a silver sheen with a tint of bluish green.

91

蠅じっとベリーダンスを見てをりぬ　天気

hae jitto beridansu o mite-orinu – tenki (ukimidô fly-fest)

(fly still[unmoving] belly-dance[obj] seeing-is)

a bar-fly just
sits there watching
the belly-dance

This, but 1 vote. There is no such thing as a "bar-fly" in Japanese, but real flies can be mesmerized *for I have done it.* You circle your finger-tip around starting big, spiraling smaller and smaller until you rest it right on the head of the fly.

92

大仏の胎内を飛ぶ秋の蝿　秋山未踏

daibutsu no tainai o tobu aki no hae – akiyama mitô?
(large-buddha[statue]'s body-inside[obj] fly autumn-fly)

the great buddha
in the fall an aerodrome
for some flies

flies zip about
in the autumn body
of the daibutsu

one fly fills
the autumn body of
the great buddha

Note the way people are free to walk around *inside* monumental statues of the Buddha. This is no idol. It is empty. Emptiness is vanity, something bad; but becoming empty is exposing that vanity for what it is: the fly, too, is a *hotoke.* (Buddha). Why an autumn fly? Fall is the season when awareness of the full and the empty hit at the same time. *Moreover, the fly might find it warmer inside.*

93

暗がりを蝿飛ぶ音のがらんどう　紫野

kurogari o hae tobu oto no garandô – shigeno (ukimidô fly-fest)
(darkness[obj] fly flies sound's emptiness)

the empty sound
of a fly zipping about
in darkness

I was fascinated by the word *garandô,* meaning empty but containing a hint of vastness (perhaps because the sound approximates "grand?") and, like everyone, have experienced this.

94

春の蝿リビング狭く往き惑ふ　初期痾窮句

haru no hae ribingu semaku iki-mayou – akyû (early haiku)
(spring-fly living-room narrow go-troubled)

spring flies
find my living room
too narrow

spring flies
is my room too small
for decent laps?

Two hundred years earlier, Issa apologized to his fleas for cramping their space to jump. That was facetious (fleas do not jump *that* far), but this "early period Akyû" haiku (not in the Fly-ku Fest which he was part of) is completely credible.

95

蝿叩き難ければ肘折り曲げて　　高沢良一

hae tataki muzukashikereba hiza-ori-magete – takasawa yoshikazu

(fly-swatting difficult-if, elbow-bend)

if swatting a fly
is hard for you, try
bending that elbow

In other words, swatting flies is more like *karate* than *golf.* This is the only haiku-as-advice I can recall reading!

96

春の蠅町内会の薄きお茶　東人

haru no hae chonaikai no usuki ocha – tôjin (ukimidô fly-fest)

(spring-fly/ies town-within-meeting[place]'s thin [green] tea)

thin green tea
at the local clubhouse
spring flies

Tenki and I alone chose this poem. My "clubhouse" is not quite right. It is the place where local events are planned. The tea was hot but the little left in the cups has cooled off and this haiku seems right to me for I feel sure I have seen it. Five people (including Tenki) preferred a different setting: "by a basin / a worn hand-towel and / a night fly." (手水場に手ぬぐひ痩せて夜の蠅　紫野 = shigeno).

..

97

猫飯に蟻蟻蟻蟻蟻蟻蝿　横山きっこ

nekohan ni ari ari ari ari ari ari hae – yokoyama kikko

(cat-food-on ant ant ant ant ant ant fly)

on the cat-food
ant, ant, ant, ant, ant,
ant, ant, fly

This predates the Fly-ku Fest. What is the ant:fly ratio on *your* cat or dog's food?

98

蝿つけて売られし苗は八つ頭　依光陽子

hae tsukete urareshi nae wa yatsugashira – yorimitsu yôko

(fly/ies added sold, seed-eighthead[yam])

sold to me with
all its flies, a budding
eight-head yam

The *yatsugashira*, literally "eight-heads" is a large lumpy purplish yam. Call me a nominalist, but I like the fly+head combination. Another of her *ku* is in the 80-*ku* list.

99

金蝿の贅を尽くして来たりけり　かげお

kinbae no zei o tsukushite kitarikeri – kageo (ukimidô fly-fest)
(gold-fly's luxury[obj] exhausting[go all the way] coming[+finality])

a gold-fly
flies in dressed
to kill

a gold fly
the picture of luxury
flies in

a gold-fly
flies in decked out
like a pimp

5 people voted for this fly-ku which, as is, does not English well because we have no good way to express pulling out all the stops, or exhausting luxury other than idiom that stinks of slang. I was thinking of metaphor, but "a gold fly / as shiny as a new car / just waxed" or "freshly polished / and just off the lathe / the gold fly" seem ridiculous. Because I have been impressed with the shinyness of some flies, I belatedly came to like the poem I first overlooked. I apologize for my last version, but how else can a very shiny outfit be described at the start of the 21st century?

100

蝿が擦る手足吾をば軽んずる　未定

hae ga suru teashi ware o ba karunzuru – not given
(fly/ies rub hands-feet, me[obj+emphatic] make-light-of)

a fly wrings
its hands and feet, making
light of me!

This *ku* was submitted to the huge *Gendai Haiku Kukai.* I found it at http://www.gendaihaiku.gr.jp/haikukai/result/28_itiran.htm (#164). Wanting the poet's name, I searched using parts of the poem, but found no other hits, which suggest no one voted for it, because people only reveal their names after the selection=judgment has ended. It seems to me the *ku* is as facetious as the old *ku* it plays against when it pretends to say, *"Fly, if you think I am such a sucker as to fall for your supplication, think again!"* Since the very complaint is premised on an anthropomorphic reading of the fly's hand-rubbing behavior (not really "wrings" but rub=prays to), it contradicts itself. Several hundred years ago, this *ku* would have been highly appreciated. I am afraid that such logical play, however deftly handled, is anathema today.

蝿蝿蝿

The M*an* Who B*ore* Flies

The theorist of "Politiques and Democraticall Government" James Harrington (1611-77) who was big on rotation and ballot, ended up, as might be expected for anyone who took sides in an age of fierce power-struggle, doing time in the Tower and Portsey Castle. John Aubrey (1626-97) describes the result:

His durance in these Prisons (he being a Gentleman of a high spirit and a hot head) was the procatractique [*originating*] cause of his deliration or madnesse; which was not outragious, for he would discourse rationally enough and be very facetious company, but he grew to have a phancy that his Perspiration turned to Flies, and sometimes to Bees; and he had a versatile timber house built in Mr Hart's garden (opposite to St JAme's parke) to try the experiment. He would turne it to the sun and sitt towards it; then he had his fox-tayles there to chase away and massacre all the Flies and Bees that were to be found there, and then shut his *Chassses* [window]. Now this experiment was only to be tried in Warme weather, and some flies would lye so close in the cranies and cloath (with which it was hung) that they would not presently shew themselves. A quarter of an hower after perhaps, a fly or two, or more, night be drawen out of the lurking holes by the warmeth; and then he would crye out, Doe not you see it apparently that these come from me? 'Twas the strangest sort of madnes that ever I found in any one: talke of anything els, his discourse would be very ingeniose and pleasant. From *Aubrey's Lives.*

蝿蝿蝿

The M*an* Who K*new* Flies

The first person to demonstrate that maggots were not the result of the putrefaction of flesh but were produced by flies – thereby demolishing the favorite "proof" of spontaneous generation" – was a physician to the Duke of Tuscany, Francesco Redi. His use of controls in biological experiments is generally considered a first, 200 years ahead of its time. Equally amazing, in the context of this book, alone: he was born in 1626 and died in 1697 (Look at Aubrey, above!) Here are snippets from his charming record of his fly experiments as translated by M.A.B Bigelow and reproduced in THE ORIGINS AND GROWTH OF BIOLOGY (1958), an excellent anthology edited by Arthur Rook.

. . . although it is a matter of daily observation that infinite numbers of worms are produced in dead bodies and decayed plants, I feel, I say, inclined to believe that these worms are all generated by insemination and that the putrified matter in which they are found has no other office than that of serving as a place, or suitable nest . . . in which they also find nourishment . . . At the beginning of June I ordered to be killed three snakes, the kind called Eels of Aesculapius. As soon as they were dead, I placed them in an empty box to decay. Not long afterwards I saw they were covered with worms [pupae] of a conical shape and apparently without legs. [*They ate the meat down to the bones and escaped from a small hole in the box, so he did the experiment over and closed every hole with the result that he was able to see the worms shrink into eggs (how that happens I do not know) and 8 days later these hatched tiny flies "torpid and dull, misshapen as if half-finished, with closed wings; but after a few minutes they commenced to unfold . . . then the whole creature, as if made anew, having lost its grey colour, took on a most brilliant and vivid green; and the whole body had expanded and grown so it seemed incredible that it could ever have been contained in the small shell." Redi describes ontogeny beautifully, but to return to the subject* –] ". . . I began to believe that all worms found in meat were derived directly from the droppings of flies . . . having observed that before the meat grew wormy, flies had hovered over it, of the same kind as those that later bred in it. Belief would be vain without the confirmation of experiment, hence in the middle of July, I put a snake, aome fish, some eels of Arno, and a slice of milk-fed veal in four large, wide-mouthed flasks; having well closed and sealed them, I then filled the same number of flasks in the same way, only leaving those open. [*The reader needs not to be told what happened. Let me add that Redi even tried burying meat far underground (no worms/flies) and he tried experiments with dead pupae and dead flies. Why?*] ". . . Father Kircher, though a man worthy of esteem, was lead into erroneous statements in the twelfth book of the *Subterranean World*, where he describes the experiment of breeding flies in the dead bodies of the same. 'The dead flies', says the good man, ' should be besprinkled and soaked with honey-water, and then placed on a copper plate exposed to the tepid heat of ashes; afterwords very minute worms, only visible through the microscope, will appear, which little by little grow wings on the back and assume the shape of very small flies that slowly attain perfect size.' I believe, however, that the aforesaid honey-water only serves to attract the living flies to breed in the corpses of their comrades and to drop their eggs therein . . . [*After this, realizing that suffocation might invalidate his closed vessel experiment, he redid it*] . . . in a large vase covered only with a fine Naples veil, that allowed air to enter. For further protection against flies, I placed the vessel in a frame covered with the same net. I never saw any worms in the meat, though many were seen moving about on the net-covered frame. These attracted by the odour of the meat, succeeeded at last in penetrating the fine meshes and would have entered the vase had I not speedily removed them. [*He then notices something I never have: namely, some flies do not even alight on the mesh but drop their worms from the air. He concludes* –] ". . . It is true that some kinds of flies bring forth live worms and some others eggs, as I have proved by experiment."

We tend to think of a wormy-thing as post-egg, but if pupae are always pre-egg, then oviparous flies are the more "advanced" ones, halfway to us mammals.

蝿蝿蝿

THE FLY IS DEAD! LONG LIVE THE FLY!

(*or, why we have nothing to worry about*)

敲かれに生るるを蝿の千とせ哉　淡々
tatakare ni umaruru o hae no chitose kana – tantan (d. 1761 at age 88!)
(beaten/struck-for, born yet, fly's thousand-years 'tis)

born to be hit
the housefly lives on
a 1000 years

born to be hit
houseflies still live
on and on

born for hate
musca maledicta
lives forever

born
to be killed
fly has
a thousand
lives

I am reminded on Shiki's poem about the sea cucumber thriving for eons because it did nothing (Actually, they work all night and we see them in the daytime when they are sleeping). The creatures could not be more contrary, yet both, the sluggish easy mark and the annoying speedster of the air, do all right, thank you.

仏生（性）や叩きし蝿の生きかへり　虚子
busshô ya tatakishi hae no iki-k[g]aeri – kyoshi 1955-7
(buddha-nature: the swatted fly, alive-returns)

buddhahood

swatted
my fly returns
to life!

miracle?

holy ghost!
the swatted fly
revives

swat!

apotheosis?
a fly not missed
reviving!

testament

a fly i hit
rises up from
the dead!

蝿蝿蝿

afterword

FLIES & I: A CONFESSION

I have *never* felt the least disgust or antagonism toward flies. Perhaps this was because I grew up barefoot, with salt water, dirt and, when I pole-vaulted – which was all day all summer year after year – sawdust sticking to my skin. The tingling of little fly feet was nothing to me. The idea of flies as being particularly "dirty" didn't wash either. I, or rather we, lived with a zoo of pets, including dogs and cats who licked what all of their kind lick, a raccoon that washed food in its toilet bowl, played in ours and woke me up by prying open my mouth, jamming its snout in and breathing, a parakeet that pooped on my head, garter snakes that pissed on my arms, and cockroaches with the disconcerting habit of flying smack into your face at night. And I forgot to mention the muck-filled swamp that began less than thirty yards from the cottage. Sure, I washed my hands before eating and racked up a high score with a fly-swatter when my grandparents visited. I also killed many tiny creatures for the four or five years I suffered (before finally catching up from being a premature baby with a late birthday in high-school) in the cruel boy's world portrayed so knowingly by Golding in THE LORD OF THE FLIES. I confess I found perverse relief experimenting on – i.e. torturing – not only bugs but an occasional lizard and frog; but all of this was done in cold blood, which is to say unconsciously. My *hate* was reserved for things that hurt me or could hurt me: mosquitoes, horseflies, scorpions, rattlesnakes and mean classmates (I had a bow and must admit to dreaming of using it on the worst of them). I was amazed and mystified by my grandmother's evident *hate* for houseflies.
..

蚊の声に蝿の憎さは忘れけり　沾峨(山は上ですが) 吐屑庵句集
ka no koe ni hae no nikusa wa wasurekeri – senga (1776)
(mosquitoes' voice-by flies' hatefulness-as-for, forget[+finality])

hearing mosquitoes
hate for flies
forgotten

As an adult, I came to actually *like* flies. They are fun to watch, fun to try to catch, and fun to show-off when you succeed. They also provided me with one of my greatest little mysteries, *the case of the chicken-skin eating bamboo..*

~~~~~~

In Japan, I was in the habit of throwing food out my window for the *tanuki,* a fat little fox with the face of a raccoon, and according to folklore – but not in reality – enormous balls. Now, it happened that a piece of chicken fat wrapped part way around a big bamboo and stuck too high for the *tanuki* to get to it. Over the next few days, I observed almost two whole foot-long segments of the bamboo became shiny as if they had been shellacked. Before long, I had concocted an amazing theory about how bamboo absorbed oil. This was significant for everyone with any sense whatsoever wants to have shiny bamboo. *It reflects the moonshine better. Japanese traditionally splashed the bamboo with water on the night of the full-moon. Or, at least an old haiku I read suggests one poet did.* I could go on for pages about my
~~~~~~

theories and tests made to get to the bottom of the mystery, but the long and the short of it is that it turned out that *flies and flies alone* were responsible for polishing the bamboo. They would sit on the fat then move over to the bamboo nearby and clean/eat off their little hands and feet. This they repeat thousands of times, and the oil spreads up, down and, with some help from the flared joints, around the bamboo. From this, I noted, it follows that if one so desired, flies could be put to work spreading good rather than bad things. An oil with a pleasant fragrance, for example.

~~~~~~

Again, I *like* flies. But I also like people who *dislike* flies, for I respect honesty. Wondering how normal or abnormal my lack of disgust for flies and my enjoyment of observing flies are, I questioned people in Coconut Grove, Florida, while I wrote F*L*Y-KU*!*, about their feelings toward flies. Samantha, a young woman working at an outdoor organic vegetable market, who I thought likely to give me an ecological reply about how we share the biosphere with them, or how the most valiant of them protect land from human exploitation by spreading disease, etc. fooled me completely when she readily confessed that *they gave her the creeps*, for she hated the way they walked all over and seemed to *lick* her. Now *that* is an answer to kill for. After I got it, I stopped my survey.

A Victorian novelist might say, the flies took undo advantage of her. In Japanese, it just so happens that, even today, to take advantage of someone is to "lick" (*nameru*) them. The closest Japanese can come to "don't mess [f___] with me!" is *nameru na* (lick[me]-not! (the "not" being a rough "not"). Strangely enough, this idiom has not been taken advantage of by haiku poets. I haven't read any haiku about pushy flies licking people in Japanese – that is to say, lapping up their sweat. Too bad the diva Sei Shônagon didn't live six or seven hundred years later and write haiku, for that, as we have seen, was just her complaint!

Now for the real confession. Despite the good logical reasons for examining fly haiku given in the *Foreword*, I am not certain I am the right person to have done this book, for my feelings about flies are just not strong enough. Sure, I watch them sometimes; but, lacking passion, it was all too easy for me to get *bored with the flies* as I worked and reworked my translations. I really can't wait to start work on insects I *am* passionate about, fleas, mosquitoes, fireflies, cicadas and crickets, because these creatures have either tortured or delighted me. Indeed, I have written hundreds of haiku about them and only a few about one fly, the tiny one with perfectly clear wings, a shiny green metallic body, long thin legs and a cool presence that was probably not a *musca maledicta.*

So why flies first?

My discovery of the senryû behind Issa's famous poem gave me a legitimate reason to write about fly-ku, and I could not resist exercising my newly found authority (I joke. I wanted to get the news published before someone else discovered the same). I did, however, find every minute spent working on *anthropomorphism in haiku* absolutely delightful, and feel my extended treatment of rubbing=praying hands is an important contribution toward understanding why it is not so much the *art* of translation, as the *nature* of translation that is imperfect. And it delights me to know that no one who reads the first three chapters of this book will take translated haiku for granted.
~~~~~~

In Japan, it is standard practice for a postcard to be included in the book for readers to contact the author and the publisher. I was happy to receive delightful observations, intense testimonials (One translator felt my book on mistranslation in Japan was a knife to her throat and I had to assure her that since she realized the problem existed, she, of all people, had better stick with it. Since then we have become friends and she has translated some very good books) and, most useful of all, *corrections*. I would have included a postcard in this book, but thought I would save the trees. So, please visit me at paraverse.org and give me your impressions in the more ecological fashion!

..

～～～～～～～～～～～～～～～～～～～～～～～～～～～～～～～～～～～～～～

お詫び！　句+人索引きは、第二版まで。

～～～～～～～～～～～～～～～～～～～～～～～～～～～～～～～～～～～～～～

APOLOGIA FOR THE *LACK* OF A PROPER *BIBLIOGRAPHY* & *INDEX*

Unlike *Rise, Ye Sea Slugs!* which was an encyclopedic presentation of a small theme, Fly-ku, for better or worse, is sketchy. While there are a number of haiku the sources of which I wanted but could no longer find (this book was mostly written before I could afford a bilingual pc), I did not feel further effort to peg down names and dates was worth it, for I hope eventually to be blessed with help from others to do this (*I am in debt and falling more in debt every day, so I cannot afford to hire anyone*), and choose to use my limited time=money to prepare other books for publication. These include the first of my IPOOH (*In Praise of Olde Haiku*) saijiki=poem-almanac series, *The Fifth Season,* Vol. I of the New Year, and a large spin-off on (cherry) blossom-viewing, *Cherry Blossom Epiphany.*)

Suffice it to say that most of the traditional fly-ku came from two sources, Shiki's *Categorical* anthology of old haiku (分類俳句全集) and/or an on-line haiku-search resource created by Takazawa Yoshikazu (same as Takasawa Yoshikazu, whose haiku are included in this book). The other main sources are *Haiku-daizen* and the Kaizôsha *Haikai-saijiki,* both about 80 years old (See the Annotated Bibliography in *Rise, Ye Sea Slugs!* for more) and Issa's *Zenshû.* While I did not feel obliged to date the poems (this is not an academic book), I was able to pin down many thanks to Katô Ikuya. Shiki's *Categorical* is great for giving the source anthology for most poems (this is, regretably, rare in haiku), but only Katô's anthology 滑稽俳句大全 provides dates for many of those old anthologies.

With regret and apologies, I am doing without a *poem* and *author index* this time. I love indices and ideally would have a half-dozen (poet names, other names, poems by alphabet, poems by date & ideas) but, as Japanese say, *binbô ni hima nashi,* "the poor have no time to spare." Living in a garage apartment lacking hurricane shutters, I even had to spend=lose over a 100 hours packing (wrapping stuff in plastic bags and boxes, squeezing them into closets and barricading them) and later unpacking for two hurricanes (unlike most people, who lose only a few hours on their shutters, or the wealthy who have someone else do that) – not to mention spending days off the island. So much for the trimmings on this book! Speaking of which, the failure of zig-zag wave patterns to pdf robbed the interior design of the *fly-like quality* intended. Microsoft Word and Adobe Acrobat have got to get their act together if we writers who have no time to learn complex programs (nor to use them) are to produce better books.

Thank you for reading. With hope for improvements in my life and computer software which will permit a second edition with no apologies, I am your grateful author, editor and publisher. – rdg

..

envoi

a fly's death:
the only news to speak of
this whole day

蝿の死のほか語る事なき一日(ひとひ) 痾窮
hae no shi no hoka kataru kotonaki hitohi – AQ
(fly's death's otherwise talk thing not, one [whole] day)

a fly died
today that is all i
have to say

蝿蝿

appendix

for readers of japanese

一茶名句＜やれ打つな＞の背後に川柳あり

七、八年前に武玉川や柳多留の川柳を全部読もうとした。中で一茶の一番有名な蝿句の創作にかかわる川柳もみつけた。半年前 (約２０００年？)に、そのことを矢羽勝幸氏に打ち明けて、それがまだ知られていないかどうかを尋ねたところ、「「やれうつな」と「やれたつな」の関連は、私もはじめて知りました。おもしろい解釈です。大いに宣伝して下さい。」と言われた。その宣伝をはたすには十分用意しているとは言い難いが、一茶研究の一人者の氏のアドバイスに甘んじて、俳句先輩の諸助言も取り入れて、次の論を敢えて書いてみました。

~~~~~~..

１．数珠する弁慶

・やれたつな／＼て[で]武蔵数珠をすり　芳蝶（柳多留２４、追善玉柳：寛政３？）
・やれ打つな蝿が手をする足をする　　一茶（梅塵八番：文政４）[1－1]

ずばり言う。川柳の方が約３０年も先にできた。一茶の名句は、この川柳に大いに借りがあることは明白で、このことが今までに指摘されなかったのを不思議に思っております。後で、背後にある、現代俳句研究界における川柳音痴の話に言及する[1－2]　が、先ず、川柳の意味を説明しておかなければならぬ。手元の川柳集を隅から隅まで読んでいた１９９０年代の半ばに、たまたま＜やれたつな＞に出くわした時、目がまるくなり、「やれやれ！一茶の名句の「本歌」は、なあんとバレ句だった！」と自分に言い聞かせて独り興奮した。一生涯女子を一度しか知らなかった弁慶が、立ちたがるのは無理もない。一休曰く「八寸推根尚勝人」の一物に困っていることを想像していたという訳。

だが、間もなく、すでに読んでいた下記の川柳を思い出し、川柳の罠――バレ句の見せかけ――に嵌まってしまったことに気付きました。濡れ場は濡れ場でも、《船弁慶》という劇［能］で、立ったものは、アレではなく、荒海の波の方であった！

・へどをふみ／＼弁慶ハ祈る也　無名　(柳多留：１１・２５）

１ー１　名句の変種。名句には、＜やれ打　つな蝿が手をする足をする＞の他に、三
~~~~~~

通の変種もある。<やヨ打つな>と<ソれ打つな>というのが川柳と外れる一方、二種にある<蝿ハ>、又、一種にある<手するモ足するモ>と<手をすリ>は逆に川柳に近付くか、その連想を強める。［わがソフトで強点を打つ方法ないから、変ったところを片仮名にした］。

１－２　俳界の川柳音痴。確かに、一茶の名大根句の川柳上がりは、１９９０年代より、よく知られている。しかし、それがとく前に気付かれていないのが、おかしい。<ひんぬいた大根で道を教えられ>という川柳は、柳多留初編だから、見逃すのは、そう簡単ではない！（因みに、私は、武玉川四編の七七調<抜た大根で道をおしへる>を“本句”とする。何故かと言えば、一茶は句を換骨奪胎する時 (See 注７－５)。それを必ず改造するが、<ひんぬいた>の方がむしろ一茶の句より一茶調だから）。一方、<やれたつな>は、柳多留２４編だから、川柳趣味でない俳句研究者の目を引かなかったはずです。ところで、日本の中にも川柳に気づく俳句研究者もふえているという気がします。わが悪趣味を知った友人から『（蕪村の師）巴人の全句を読む』を送ってくれたが、丸山晴彦とその夜半亭の皆さんの輪読には、川柳そのものがあまり出なかったが、その意識 — 川柳も考えないと解き難い俳句ある — が、常に感じられて良かった。

~~~~~~

２＝<やれ打つな>既解

<やれたつな>の発見が<やれ打つな>の読みに対し、どんな変化をもたらすかを論じる前に、後者が今までどのように理解されてきたかということについて少々触れなければならない。

敢えて一般化すれば、それが弱者・小生物に同情心の強い一茶ならではの細かい観察として素直に読まれるのが多数派で、それとは逆に、蝿が打たれてしまう一茶の別な句を、鬼の首でも取ったかのように取り上げる者も少なくない。

・蝿一つ打てはなむあみ[だ]仏哉
・縁の蝿手をする所を打たれけり [2－1]

だが、それで名句の価値（あるいは無価値）が変るわけではない。一茶の大ファンの一人の金子兜太氏は、

蝿が手足するのを「嘆願と見るのは読者の独断であり」、句意を「<打つなよ打つなよ、まあ御覧よ、手を擦たり足を擦たりして、気持ちよさそうにしているじあ【＝わがマイコンで打たないちっぽけな「あ」です】ねえか。」とする(『一茶句集』）。「可哀相だ、打つのを止め給え -- という受け取り方を［略］一茶に合わないと見」る金子氏の気持ちは、よくわかるが、嬉しげに手をする仕種が、当時代に知られていたかどうか疑問です。英語でも rub one’s hands in glee と言うが、日本の古句などには、どうでしょう？
~~~~~~

＜やれ打つな＞のたった二年前に、一茶が妻と子の前の、男の哀れなる立場を見事に描いた：

・手をすりて蚊帳の小すみを借りにけり

そして、この夏の句の直ぐ後に、手も足もそろって出た狂歌もある：＜世に住ば手をすり足をすりこ木にしてかけ廻る年の暮哉＞（風間本八番日記）。「足をすりこ木に」、とは、走り回って痩せこけることになるが、手のそれは、商人がお客さん向きの「お愛想」「へつらい」仕種よりも、年末の借金返済の猶予依頼をめぐる、激しくお詫びしたりする様相で、やはり、一茶にとって、手を擦るイメージは「気持ちよさそう」とは程遠い。[2−2]

２－１　蠅を打ってしまう句。上記二句は一番はっきりと蠅の死に至るためか、例に挙がりがち。他にも、＜蠅一つ打ては山を見たりけり＞＜蠅打や友となりぬる峰の松＞＜蠅打に敲かれ玉ふ仏哉＞＜蠅打の四五寸先の小てふ哉＞＜群蠅の逃た迹打皺手哉＞＜打て／＼と逃（のがれ）て笑ふ蠅の声＞等、元気で蠅を打っている一茶の句もある。

２－２　「する」感覚。足ずりは、手ずりと違って人間の動作は蠅のと全く違うが、比喩上の意味が間違っても単語に付くから、人間の足ずりの意味も考えなければならない。Rodrigues の信頼できる『日葡辞書』（１６０３－４年）によれば、axizuri（あしずり）は「許しを乞う」意味もあった。 しかも、何百年間を見渡しても、厳かな場面にて「すり足」でこすりながら進むのも、偉人が入る瞬間、口から「シーッ」という音を発するのも、擦って（摩擦による）緊張間をかもすという、落ち着きと正反対、日本的堅苦しさの特徴になります。つまり、足ずりも気持ち良さそうな「いい気分」からほど遠い。次章に見るが、時代によって足ずりの意味がまた変る。

---

3 手をする蠅句

蠅が手を擦るところを一度も見ていない者は一人もいないでしょう。中華文明圏においては、その身振りは祈願・命乞いを意味するとすれば、命乞い蠅も必然的に生まれて来る。中国の詩はよく判らないが[3−1]、俳諧にはやはり、一茶の名句以前にも祈願・命乞い蠅句がよく詠まれていた。５句ばかり見れば十分。

・つままれて手をする蠅の命かな　葎亭嘯山[3−2]（『松島眺望集』）

この句は、殊に好き。「命かな」とか「命なる」という英語にない日本語の表現に惹かれるし、この句では命が辞典上の意味「蠅の天命」と「蠅の唯一の頼み」に加えて、その「命の価値」とまで考えさせる曖昧さを活かす。これらの点において、一茶名句と合せて考えるといい。

・手を摺て拝むやのりにたかり蠅 貞房 （『崑山集』）
・蠅が手をするはぼさつのおだい哉 正次 （『崑山集』）
・こっちから蠅に手をする昼寝哉＞ 文右衛門（古選）
・蠅にならびて君に手をする＞ 正友 （『談林十百韻』）

それぞれの句の解説と評価は、控えますが、私にとって、おかしいとしか思えないのは、今まで読んできた一茶名句の解説や説明の中で一度も、これらの先例が紹介されていないということです。何故でしょうか？句作は、観察と即興によるものである、いや、でなければならないという建前のために、先例類句を紹介しなくともいいと思っているからではあるまいか」[3−3]

3-1 中国の蠅詩。蚊も命がはかないで喰わせてあげろ、という漢詩をどこかで読んだが、手をする蠅の詩はまだ。見つけたら、紹介して下さい！英語でＦＬＹ－ＫＵ！（蠅句！）という本もほぼ出来ているが、その中に入れたい。
3-2 嘯山の句。嘯山の句をもっと読みたい。日本俳書体系にある『葎亭句集』は読了しましたがが、万が一活字になった版あれば、後年の『葎亭画賛集』を、何よりも読みたい。その集には、古句風の字義通り滑稽も可笑味が多くて「頗る不感服」と批評家いうが、老俳人ならでの自由もあるかもしれない。
３－３。先例類句の紹介。《コメントあれば、どうぞ！》

~~~~~~

4 類縁の蕨句

初期俳諧の中で蠅の手すりに似ているものものをみつけました。蠅句そっくりの命乞いあるいは志願でもないが、蕨の手の描写にはそれに近い可愛いさがある。手にまじわる多くの蕨句の中で、『崑山集』（1651）[4−1]より、やはり一手ほどの例を見ればわかる。

・おられじと手をつくねたる蕨哉＞ 貞徳？[か、重便？『崑山集』）
・やせたるは折[る]もかいなし蕨の手＞ 同？（同）
・手占[うら]せよ遅き桜の下[石]わらび＞ 同？（同）[4−2]
・百足より蕨手多しくらま山＞ 同？（同）
・雪消[え]て手に汗にぎる蕨哉＞ 政辰 （同）

上の句の中で、最初の＜折られじ＞だけは、他の幾つかの句集に見たことがある。同じ擬人主義といわれても、読者のこころに訴える動物なる蠅と植物なる蕨は異なる―― そのため、蕨が滑稽に成りがち[4−3] ―― が、一茶はこの句、少なくとも、＜おられじ＞と＜やせたる＞の蕨の命にかかる二句を再読して泣いた可能性があると思います。何故かといえば、『おらが春』に次の言葉があるから：
~~~~~~

「此おさな[稚児]、仏の守りし給いけん、逮夜の夕暮れに、持仏堂に蝋燭てらして鈴[金＋輪の右側]打ちならせば、どこに居てもいそがはしく這よりて、さわらびのちいさき手を合わせて、「なんむ／＼」と唱ふ声、しほらしく、ゆかしく、なつかしく、殊勝也。」（全集６）「夕になれば いざ寝よと 手を携はり 父母も上は勿放り 三枝の 中にを寝むと 愛しく」描かれた山上憶良の子の死で、わが目も潤んだ。そのお父様のＭａｒｋＴｗａｉｎ について、可愛い可愛い伝記も書いた愛嬢 Ｓｕｓｉの夭折にもそうだが、一茶のさと女は、格別だ。私は『おらが春』を何回読んでも、泣きます。その「さわらびの」は、当座の適切な修飾語句として使ったか、＜折られじ＞ と＜やせたる＞蕨の句を念において、死の前兆として当の文章に入れたか、今になっては知る由もないが、私が名蝿句を読むと、蕨もさと女も見えてしまう。

4-1 『崑山集』。当の集にいける蕨句が一番多いと思うが、『ゆめみ草』のより多い凡句の中でも、この楽しい二句がある：＜手鏡と見るや蕨の露の玉＞＝玄「」雹、＜猿猴が露の月とる蕨の手＞＝成利。（多分『崑山集』は岩波大系にあるが、国語言語研究所のその On-line 捜索 DB の利用申し込みを三回も断っているから、調べる方法ない。無所属貧乏はどんなに勉強しても、どんなに日本の文化のため尽くしても、所詮犬の糞に過ぎない。お金持ちせ大学所属なら岩波を買うか、図書館でよんでもいいが、吾が輩みたいな者にとって研究に不可なこのサービスを、断られてばかりは、いたい何の神経？しかも、20 年間わが税金も受けたお前たち！

4-2 「下」か「石」。 前者は、多分、『俳書文学体系』かどこかより、後者は、『分類俳句全集』より。

4-3 滑稽の蕨。 例えば、『毛吹草』に＜うでたてをしてや折らるゝ蕨の手＞（重方）や乙由の＜仙人の碁にも指さす（指さして）蕨哉＞。

5 蝿の足をすること

何万もの川柳を読んだが、蝿の足に殆ど出くわさなかった。[5−1] 一茶の句より古い蝿の足と言うと皆無だ。川柳は、black humor でグロテスク風もあり、それにミニアチユアは欠かせない要素だから、蝿の足がざらとあっても不思議はないのに。一茶より早い例としては、蝿に一番細かい川柳と言えば足すらない、欠雄の川柳があるのみ。[＝川柳の date が見当らない。見つけなければ、「より早い」を抜くしかない＝御免！]

・飛んで来た蝿拝んでは首を撫で　(Blyth：*Japanese Life and Character in Senryû*)

Blyth は、一茶の素晴らしき名句と違って、この川柳が人間の世界に対するつまらないパロデイに過ぎないと、きつい評価を下した[5−2] が、蝿の首撫で仕種までピックアップできたのも川柳の功だ、と私は思う。首を撫でて「どうもどうも」というのも、ごく和風なる仕種で、日本人ならではの観測だ。他にも、一茶名句後の川柳に、＜飴の蠅足一本を置いてにげ＞（Ｙ９３）も細かいが、足をする観測はない。

俳諧にも蠅の足が珍しい。それも、ほとんど踏む足である。そのねばねばした足で人の顔も踏むからこそ、「蠅を＜憎らしいもの＞（＃１４）に入れたかった」と清少納言は、＜虫＞の項目（＃３０）《和文はここにない》に述べたが、その辺の嫌みを言う句には、「足」そのものをクローズ・アップするより、踏まれる行為を描くものが多い。その句の中での傑作は、手も足も効果的に持ち込んだという点で一茶の蠅句に近いと思う：

・頬を蹴手をもむ蠅のにくさ哉　　蘭秀（題発句集）

だが、「足すり」その言葉という点で一茶の句に一番近い俳句は、『俳諧江戸蛇之鮓』という風変わりな句集の中にある。その前には＜蚤虱いかではてなんはだか嶋＞（幸順）、後には＜数かくや来ぬ夜の暁蚤の跡＞とある次の句。

・足摺や蠅も流罪の鉢の海　　調加

この句を初めて読んだとき、鬼界島に流罪された俊寛僧都が独りで岬の上で足をずりずりしながらくやしがるという謡曲「俊寛」の場面を知らなかったので、わが無鉄砲なる想像が蠅を、椀縁に立ちながらその寂しい後ろ姿の足でフラストレーションを示したか、鉢の中の汁に、仰向いて浮かんでいては、六つ足も天に摺る滑稽をばかり瞼の劇場に登場させたが、正解（有難う KS！）は、祈る足ではなかった。汁の真中に盛る具の山の上にとまった蠅が、取り残された俊寛に見立てたものでありました。

この俊寛蠅[5－3]の足ずりが『日葡辞書』（１６０３－４）のいう、「許しを乞う」手ずりの足版か不安でもじもじしているよりも、古典的意味での無念を示す地団駄として私は見ているが、祈願と考えたほうが正しかもしれない。[5－4] どちみち、見立ての句なので、蠅の動作及びその意味に凝る必要もない。

5-1　蠅足の川柳。小生の見逃されたものあれば、送ってくれませんか、誰か。

5-2　Blyth とは。Reginald H. Blyth（1898-1964）は、誰よりも、俳句、川柳、そして禅を英語圏に紹介した。間違って（その俳句観は禅に凝る）も、怒らせて（その女観は Schopenhauer 並み）も、いつも面白く読めるのは、いい選句と英文学の知識とその堪えないユーモアーのおかげである。原文もともに掲載されているので、ブライスで俳句を初めて発見した日本人もおられる。（そのことを書いた記事を、二つほど見た）。上記の本は、Hokuseido：1960。

5-3　俊寛蠅。一度、句の見立てが解ったら、虚子の次の句も思い出した<蓬莱に徐福と申す鼠かな>。他にいいものご存知なら、人見立て集でも組みましょう！

5-4　足ずりの意義史。「足ずり」という言葉は古典文学には、今でいう「じだんだを踏む」という意味に使われていたが、『日葡辞書』（１６０３－４）には、Axizuri（アシズリ）の意味として「両足をすり合わせる」となりますから、江戸時代に入ると、すでに別な意味をもつ。今日と同じように、決まった意味がないから、一茶名句にみえるように、手すりの「志願」を足も仮装してもいい。しかし、俊寛蠅句は、昔の人物の見立てだから、蠅に地団駄を踏むという時代遅れの「足ずり」を認めたい。この動作は蠅にとって否現実的であろうが、言葉上に存在しうると思います。

~~~~~~

6 手と足で倍なるぞ！

すると、一茶の蠅の足すりは、いったいどういう意味をもつでしょう？

原稿を直す過程を経て、［足ずり］の意味論でどたばたしたと言っても過言ではない。初稿では、足すれば、手ずりの「命乞」に加えて、祈願力が２倍になるはずだ、とごく簡単に読んでいた。[6－1] それを読んでくれた友人ＣＺ（日本人）が、足にかかわる仕種（たとえば、足を相手に向かう）は、大抵無礼なことで、日本人にとって、２倍説は受け入れ難い。むしろ、手で祈るが「＋」とすれば、足で祈るが「－」で、２倍どころか、総合効果「０」になるわい、と。[6－2]

それで、私は、なにより頼りなる『日本国語大辞典』（小学館）を引いてみたが、「足ずり」にも「足ずる」にも、２倍説に合う定義は、皆無。あるのは、１）怒りまた無念で足ずる、そして、２）つまずくのみ。すると、前者を子供っぽい仕種として（源氏・蜻蛉＝あしずりという事をして泣くさま、若き子どものやうなり）捉えれば、可愛いさはないでもないから、蠅が手で「お願いだから！」と祈り、足で、「いやいやあん！」というだだをこねる身体合唱でアピールする読みしか残らないか。あるいは、ＣＺが考えたように、足ずりがもじもじすることであっても、可愛さ効果が多少あるだろう、と。[6－3]

..

第二稿でそう述べながらも、祈願する足は、捨て難くて、困っておりました。嬉しいことに、Ｋ氏は、既に述べた日葡辞書』（１６０３－４）の定義を紹介してくれた上、江戸時代では足ずりが「無念・怒り」という古典的（限られている）含味が失せて、現代の感覚とそう変らず、ただ「こすり合っている」になってきたので、「祈り」と見立てもさしつかえないし、「蠅が人に向かって手をするのであれば、足をすっても、その足は人には向いていないのだから、失礼にはならない」と（私も思ったが、外人としてＣＺに敢えて言えなかった）ことを、はっきりと書いて、安心させてくれました。
~~~~~~

さて、足ずりも手ずりのごとく命乞いの仕種に読みうるとすれば、経蔵やら祈り車やら百度参りの仏教の中で祈りの数が効くと言うわけで、２倍説には、ある種の logic がないわけでもない。[6-4] しかも、英語と違って、砂の数（万葉集＃５９６）とか波の数（同＃__）で恋ごころを表現した昔の日本だからこそ、２倍説は国民性にお似合いの発想だと私は思う。

二倍説が許されるなら、名句のこころは、蠅のみせかけ擬人化[6-5]にだけではなく、蠅と人間との比較にもあるということを、「船弁慶」の川柳と併せて読んで、初めて考えついた。 つまり、手に足を加えたら、「やれやれ、蠅が人様の倍も祈るんじゃ！」という捉えかたが、比較を仄めかす川柳のおかげで、その説得力こそ高まるかと思います。

~~~~~~

6-1 二倍説。 私とは別に、William Ｊ. Higginson も「蠅は多くの人間の二倍も祈る」と述べた（The Haiku Handbook : Kodansha １９８５・８９）。やはり、「足ずり」の普通の使い方にひっかからない外人にとって、ごく自然に思い付くことだ。

6-2 ＣＺ「わい」。 他のところで大変いい指摘したＣＺを馬鹿にするつもりではない。本人は、２０代のくせに「わい調」使うおもしろい雑学者です。その website は http://homepage2.nifty.com/CHARLIE-ZHANG/MAIN.html です。

6-3 ２倍説の現代版。 ＣＺの足ずり＝はにかみ解釈を可能の限りに認めるＫ氏は、子供の頃に手洗い足洗いイメージを抱いたと述べた。そうだとすれば、２倍も清潔じゃ！現代の蠅＝不潔だから絶滅すべきという発想（占領軍が日本に普及してしまったらしい＊）からして、微笑ましい。（＊「天声人語」昭和 21/7/15、22/6/11、25/5/19 を参考）

6-4 数で効く祈り。 仏教の祈り拡大機械の類は、日本にもある。「「一粒万倍日」といって、その日にお参りすると、通常の何倍ものご利益があるという信仰も盛ん」（K）と言えるが、日本よりネパールとかブータンのような宗教国家（？）でよく伺える。それを祈りのフアースト・フードと呼べば、失礼でしょうか。

6-5 みせかけ擬人化。 「擬人化」とは、人でない生き物を間違って人らしく理解する、という批判になりがち。一茶は、蠅が祈っているとは、無論、思ってもいなかった。あったかもそうだと詠んでいる茶番だ。英語でいえば farcical あるいは facetious anthropomorphism（見せかけ擬人化）と呼んでもいいと思う。

~~~~~~

7 川柳との結びつき

その構造、また内容上の共通点の他にも、名句と川柳を結ぶものは、三つある。

まず、第一に、文脈的（contextual）証拠である。名句が現れた（＜やよ＞変種は、「風間本八番日記：文政４年６月[7-1]）一ヶ月以内に、一茶は次の句も詠んでいる。

・堂の蠅珠数する人の手をまねる　（風間本八番日記　文政４年７月）

これが「蠅」と「数珠」を結び付ける一茶の唯一の句であるということは、名句も「数珠をす」る弁慶の川柳の恩恵を受けている可能性をそれだけ高くしてくれる。確実とまで言えなくとも、highly probable（高確実[7−2]）の範囲にあると思います。

第二は、空想的結びつきである。名句と川柳を結びつけるために、句作の過程をたどる plausible story（説得力ある筋？）である。

私が想像するのは、一茶が＜やれたつな／＼て[で]武蔵数珠をすり＞を読み、あるいはどこかで聞いたら、他の川柳もいうへどを踏み踏み英雄の嘆願する場面を情けなく思われて、武蔵坊の苦境を俳諧の伝統ある命乞い蠅のイメージと重なって瞼に浮かべ、何回もすでに見た蠅の足ずりの意議を、やっと悟った：「蠅だって、手ずりに止まず、足も使うぞ！」と大声で言って、笑いながら、川柳の構造をもって、答句を詠んだ。
..
あるいは、逆に、一茶がある日、蠅の手ずりを見たとき、はたしてどれだけの効き目があるだろうかと、たまたまそのあいだ聞いた川柳を覚えて、人間の祈願もひょっとすれば蠅のとそれほど変わらない、と沈想にふけながら、あの時までべつに意義あるものと見なかった蠅の足ずりに懲りて、「なんんじゃ！おらが人間の倍にすってる！」と悟り、頭にあった川柳の力強いノリを頂戴した。ただし、最初は、「やよ」で少しは、その借りをごまかした。

上記のいずれのストリーにも、自信ない。説得力ある筋さえ書ければ、私はとっくに小説家になりました。が、一応、トライせざるを得なかった。

第三には、より広い情況的証拠　（circumstantial evidence）、つまり一茶の川柳への関心とか、蠅句以外の川柳からの借りの程。残念ながら、そうした精密な研究はしていないし、何万ものの川柳も私も使える data base に入っていなければ、しようと思っていない。[7−3]　ここで言えるのは、ただ「信濃者」を馬鹿にした川柳が多かっただけに、一茶が川柳を強く意識せざる得なかった。やつら何を書いとるか、と気になって、ときどき読んでみたに違いなかろう。蠅句の他にも怪しい大根句も、小家の大桜句[7−4]　もある。２万句の中でそれだけあるとは偶然発生の範囲に入るかもしれないが、読解力不足の私でさえこれだけ見つけたのだから、きっともっとあると思われる。その表現やテマの中で（たとえば、「慰みに」とか「小便」）も、川柳っぽいと思ったものもあるが、それがどれだけ川柳の恩恵か、共通のセンスか、素人には判るすべがない。

また、川柳の借り事を考えたとき、俳句のそれも一緒に考えたいが、一茶が恩師成美に対して一語の借りまでも気付かっていたと言われても、他の俳家に対しては、そうでもなかったかようです。[7－5]

7-1 作句 date。 名句の＜やれ打つな＞また、＜やよ＞以外の変種（注 1-1）を精密に日付けるのが、私には無理。

7-2 Possibility／Possible と Probability／Probable。日本語では、前者に近い「可能性・的」はあるが、後者に近い一般単語はないから、「確実」という用語っぽい言葉を使わなければならない。

7-3 俳句・川柳 data bank。 古句俳句のそれが、確実に増えているが、川柳のそれが、どうも見当らない。双方とも、はやく出来上がれば、研究者には、情報収集に追われずじっくりとものを考えることも出きていいと思いませんか。ただし、これらの data bank は、open でなければならない（公のはずである日本の一番大きな data bank は、ケチで小生みたいな無所属者の利用は、お断りがち）。

7-4 小家の大桜句。一茶の句は、＜にくい程桜咲たる小家哉＞。川柳が紙切れに書き移して５、６年前に机の左側の鏡に tape で貼っていたことをはっきりと覚えているが、川柳そのものを覚えていない。たしかに一茶のそれより古かったが、構造が「にくいこと 大物もちの小男」と近いか「小男のくせに大物は憎い」かという詳細も覚えていない。7-3 でいう川柳の d b すらあったら、直ぐに解るのに。

7-5 俳家からの借り。その判断が難しい。例えば、一茶の　＜男といはれて涙ほろほろたうがらし＞　は、几董の　＜賭にして唐からし喰ふ泪哉＞ と内容的にそっくりであっても、一茶が酒場で直観したものと思わせる他の句も同じ時に出来たから、偶然の可能性はある。あるいは、一茶の　＜おりよ雁一もくさんに我前へ＞は、士郎の　＜西湖］いま一度堅田に落よかへる雁＞　の焼き直しと見えるが、士郎が若き一茶の（書き残っていない）発想を借りて詠んだ（あるいは師として取った？）ことがあった、二、三十年後に老一茶がそれを取り戻しても不思議はない。などで、確信して何にも言えない。

---

８ 締めくくり：証拠より論

結局、以上の状況証拠よりも、自分の古句観から、川柳を名句と結び付けたくなる。金子氏の無理な解釈に対して、私がその「気持ちがよくわかる」と述べたのがレトリックではなかった。この句の従来の見解をめぐっては各論ありと私も思っている。一茶に対する評価にもかかると、私も疑わない。ただし、＜やれ打つな＞　を情緒的、偽善的、女々しい、子供向き、うさん臭い駄作で俳家大師として見っともないと感じる日本人、とりわけ男性の批評家によく見られる危惧は、私のとは、ちょっと異なる。[8－1]

名句を読んで、一茶をずっとうさん臭く思ったら、ついに蠅が打たれてしまう

「さっぱりした」という別な一茶句を発見して、[8-2] 一茶を考え直した（好きになった）という文章を何回か拝見した記憶あるが、いずれも、それで名句そのものを見直そうとはしなかった。それが残念。一茶には打つ心もあったら、名句に、一つではなく、二つの調子で読めるはず。一つは、例の、可愛い仕種をする蠅を温かく読む声。　もう一つは、にゃにゃと笑う反語的＝皮肉さった＝声。説明し難いですが、 要するに、読み方（tone of voice）次第で、一茶の両面も映る。ご自分の声で名句をコミカルに読んでみたら、お判りになるとおもいます。機智さえあれば、演歌顔負けの感傷的でおげさな情緒も許せる。むしろ、持ち味に転じる。

俳句の機智は、多くの場合、複層的意味の擦り合う所に生まれる。一茶の名句は、見立てや古典的隠喩もなく、上記のいう二面読みで活かされても、上等の機智が要る深層は　。。。　それは、人とその神の関係までも考えさせてくれる時、初めて認められる。蠅も人も上（かみ）さまの手から、運命から救われないかもしれないが、句は、確かに救われる。そして、その意識は、名句を『船弁慶』の川柳と合併せて読めばこそ解るから、たとえその川柳が名句の「本歌」だと皆さまも納得できるまで証明しかねても、世にご紹介する価値はあると思う。

川柳からの借り、知的要素など、「素直」でないものを、句の敵とばかり見る俳諧純粋主義者に言わせれば、わが主張[3] はトンデモナイと言うか、邪道に他ならないでしょうが、古句を読めば読むほど、そう言った　– 俳句と川柳 (俳諧と雑俳？）が道別れした以前の、一茶より古い時代の – 不純の要素にも注目を置きたい理由は、それで俳句が面白くなると確信しているからである。

8-1 男の批評家： 主に、名前も覚えていない雑誌の記事や『一茶全集』の投げ込みの記事から、この印象を受けた。又、情緒的一茶象の反発としてでも、逆に粗野までも荒い？一茶像もある。金子の蠅句の読みを受け入れなかったが、氏の『一茶句集』は、両派に忘れがち一茶の知的面と広い読書を紹介した、初心者に読みやすい好著だ。

8-2 　確かに、蠅に甘く、恋しくなる時もある。名句の翌年の句＝＜とく逃よにげよ打たれなそこの蠅＞。誰にもそう時もあるかどうかわからないが、私には、ある。名句の３年後に、一茶が、新しい共感的見せかけ擬人化を考え付いた＝　＜蠅の身も希（ねがい）ありてや灰浴る＞か、と同時に、同じ行為について、蠅を叱った＝　＜しこつ蠅火入の灰を又浴る＞。　嫌いも好きの内か？

8-3 　わが主張。大切なのは、ある句に素直な読みの他の読みモ見つけたら、それで素直な読みデハナク、ということではない。あるいは、それよりも大切なのは、複数意味の共存です。

~~~~~~

おまけ

Ｋ氏は,下記のコメントも私に紹介した。

ちなみに、加藤楸邨（かとうしゅうそん）の『一茶秀句』（春秋社。１９６４年）に、次のような記述がありました。これが普通一般の解釈でしょう。作品（４）は、虐げられた弱者一茶の弱小な動物への愛憐のあらわれということができる。「蠅が手を摺り足を摺る」から「やれ打つな」というところ、音調も軽快だし、そのしぐさも人間の命乞いそっくりで軽妙だ。そこが世人の共感を呼ぶ所以なのである。蠅のしぐさを巧みにとらえて、人間と同じような解釈を施した発想である。一茶には常套的な手法だが、口語的な呼びかけの表現が人のよろこぶところとなって、きわめてひろく人の口にもてはやされている。人の口にもてはやされた一つの理由に、「蠅は手を摺る足を摺る」と伝えられ、その繰りかえしの調子がよいという点がある。しかしこれは真蹟にもあるように、「手を摺り足を摺る」のほうが正しいし、そのほうが句も安定する。蠅のしぐさを人間くさくとらえたところはなかなかおもしろいが、句としてはそれだけのものである。

~~~~~~

名句の音について、もう少し触れるべきだったかもしれない、と思わせる内容。「虐げられた弱者一茶の弱小な動物への愛憐」という語句も、結構ですが、本文で述べたように、蠅の手すり伝統にも触れるべきだ。一茶が蠅の仕草の発見家などではないから。

蠅蠅蠅蠅蠅蠅蠅蠅蠅蠅蠅蠅蠅蠅蠅蠅蠅蠅蠅蠅蠅蠅蠅蠅蠅蠅蠅蠅蠅蠅蠅蠅蠅蠅蠅蠅蠅蠅蠅

while writing this book

fly after fly
while i am eaten alive
by mosquitoes

~~~~~~

F*ly*-P*ower,* A*nyone*?

Can anything beat solar power for responsible living? How about flies? Are they not out more often than the sun? I found the following in Chuck Shepherd's *Weird News*.

> *New Scientist Magazine* reported in September (2004) that Chris Melhuish (University of the West of England, at Bristol) was readying his EcoBot II, a self-powered robot that runs on energy produced by catching and digesting houseflies (and breaking down their sugars to release electrons). The major downside: The most efficient way to attract flies is with sewage, which makes EcoBot II unfriendly to humans. (*www.NewsoftheWeird.com*)

I would guess the stink is created from the energy gained from the flies, for that would make it perpetual.

~~~~~~

a fly
his introduction
to Zen

. . . .

on the mirror
a dung fly
radiant

beauty happens

the buzz
of flies
sweet wine

burgundy

on the wall
who is annoying who
a few flies

god knows

early
in the morning
a fly on his willie

untitled

flies breed
in carcasses
Sinai desert

oasis

fish market
doubts of freshness
all those flies

prejudice

metamorphosis
from egg to fly
unnoticed

little things

worship
the flies mate
on the pulpit

incarnation

TITLES & DESIGN **MY IR/RESPONSIBILITY**

These are some of many fly-ku by Geert Verbeke, who combines memory (*grandfather sleeps / a fly on his moustache / my childhood*) with experience (*a fly / on a cucumber / a greenhorn* [an experienced fly would go elsewhere]) and humor (*under his hood / a shaved head / and a fire-fly* [enlightenment?]). I think of clustering poems as a new sort of editing, and titling them as a game. One need not combine them as I, unwisely, have here.

excited
by a fly
the old cat

lucky

chasing
the flies on the sink
our tomcat purrs

blessed

eating flies
how old are you?
stupid cat

affection

the flies
on the bonsai
swaggering

perspective

downpour
a swarm of flies
finds a shelter

relief

the contrary wind
sweeps the flies away
from the screen

see-saw

The best of Geert's diverse haiku are indeed haiku in the classic sense of being literally fine observations (*On the bell / a sunbeam / and one fly.*) I do not know how many he jots down on the spot, how many he fishes out of his memory and how many he invents. I will not ask him because that is the type of thing even i don't care to know.

---

with a cold
in her hot milk
a drowned fly

still-life

Geert sent me hundreds of fly-ku under the title *Bzz* within weeks of receiving a reading copy of my book and I would guess from the content that he had been collecting fly-ku for longer than I have collected haiku. But Geert writes as freely as a fly flies, so it is hard to say and, again, it is fun not to know what is what. More:

The green fly
A troika of flies
on her wings
on the milking machine
a rainbow.
Maybe a pilgrim
In the chapel
rural residents.

the fly strolling around
a fly on the crucifix
on his bible.
By moonlight
ecce homo.
Bleached bone
two nipples
under the ferns
and a fly.
Your grandson
the flies are gone.
is chewing on a fly

GEERT VERBEKE'S ***BZZ***

grinning.

EXPERIMENTALLY ARRANGED (with apologies!)

I invented *poem clusters* for multi-translations in *Rise, Ye Sea Slugs!* A page ago, I took advantage of Geert's fly-ku to try it for the first time with *different* poems. Here, I try something different↑. Since a single *horizontal* line does not look as good as the single *vertical* line most common with haiku printed in Japan, I played with a compromise. Should we call it *steps* or *terracing*? Japanese usually make all the haiku on a page of equal length by regulating the space between letters↓. Still, they cannot match the perfectly square Chinese poems.

Masked ball
flies floating
in the punch

Crushed between
The *Song of Songs*
梅 a 桃 葡 fly 萄

On her letter
lies a dead fly
lit by the moon

Geert Verbeke's books of haiku AND musical bowls are found at http://users.skynet.be/geert.verbeke.bowls/

*Philosophic*al & *Physic*al F*lies*

Geert Verbeke's *Bzz* includes the following *ku:* "His god / is omnipresent / like a fly." It is true that a fly seems to have the ability to be in more than one place (or time) at once. Not being much into things of the spirit, I might put it like this: "The fly / makes time go / bananas" or, "Houseflies: / here and there time / goes crazy" or, "The housefly / now and then time / changes place" or, "Some flies / laugh at the present / past and future" or, "fellow fly / once time jumped around / for me, too." *You can see why I am no poet.* But it is a fact that whenever I hear of quantum physics' experiments about time and the observation/manifestation of reality, I think of *flies* (not cats, even if they do have nine lives). If any physicist got into flies, I hope someone will send me a paragraph or, if really good, a page about it for the next edition (The one about the fly flying back and forth between closing trains does not count, for that fly might as well have been a bird!)

When it comes to philosophy, we have Wittgenstein, who stated his aim in philosophy as follows: *"To shew the fly the way out of the bottle."* According to a paragraph about a play called The Fly-bottle, the bars in Vienna used empty beer bottles for fly traps (we used beer or coke bottles for cockroaches, but who would want to help *them* out?) This was an allegory for invisible (i.e., glass) linguistic traps which made philosophers argue about nothing and hence go nowhere fast. *There is something to this.* But it is not only traditional Western philosophy that is trapped. A famous Indian philosopher in England wrote knowingly about how desire came first and the object – the details silly Western philosophy argued about – only becomes problematic later, giving for his proof (?), sentences starting "I want . . ." or "I wish . . ." *– Oh, yeah?* In Japanese, it is normal for the object to come *first* and the "I" is not even stated. I don't know if Wittgenstein (or Saussure), or anyone for that matter, ever escaped their Indo-European languages but, where was I?

I remember. The same young mathematician I met on the train on Xmas 2004 who told me about Wittgenstein's fly also introduced Kierkegaard's. "Of all ridiculous things," he wrote, "the most ridiculous seems to me, to be busy – to be a man who is brisk about his food and his work. Therefore, whenever I see a fly settling, in the decisive moment, on the nose of such a person of affairs; or if he is spattered with mud from a carriage which drives past him in still greater haste; or the drawbridge opens up before him; or a tile falls down and knocks him dead, then I laugh heartily. And who, indeed, could help laughing? What, I wonder, do these busy folks get done?" (Does anyone know the name of the translator?)

But these great philosophers only *use* flies. Neither managed to capture the real fly as well as a Mexican agronomist I knew in Hawaii. Once, driving along a rocky coastal road, Eduardo explained his common hands-off-the-wheel-head-turned-to-talk-to-you-in-the-back-seat practice as follows:

As a person of faith, a Catholic, he claimed it was safest to live like a fly. *What did that mean?* Well, he was always having to free *bees* from collection bottles whereas *flies* usually managed to free themselves. Was it because the bees were not so bright as the flies? *No.* If anything the opposite was true. Everyone knows about bees with their languages and good memories for places and so forth. The problem was rather that the bees thought. "Like you gringos," he could not resist adding, "they think too much." They saw the light and strove to follow it out. As it happened, there was no exit on the brightest side, so that only ensured the bees remained trapped. They butted their rational heads into the glass time and time again until they knocked themselves out. The flies didn't reason about it, they just flew randomly about. That looks crazy, but before long hit upon the way out. "The flies leave it up to God, so they are saved!" As he told me this he opened his arms so widely that I who don't believe, prayed that the car wouldn't go off the road.

This was 25 years ago. Eduardo, are you still alive?

..

~~~~~~

In the cloud-boiling sky a baby grabs a fly - Akaishi Norihiko
雲湧く空で赤ン坊蠅ひと握み／赤石憲彦 norihiko（俳句未来同人）

Does the reader recall the haiku by Seibi about the overwhelming desire to swat all flies? I cannot refrain from collecting all fly-ku, especially when they are sent my way. AQ , who posted the above in time for this revision, wrote another *ku* I cannot do justice to without at least five paraverses: 人はいさ壁の模様の冬の蠅 痾窮. Here are the bare bones: person/people-as-for eventually/worst-case, wall's figure/pattern's/s' winter-fly/flies. *You try!*
~~~~~~

Reviews of Previous Work by the Author

re: *Rise, Ye Sea Slugs!* 1000 holothurian haiku (2003)

"Gill appeals to readers who revel in ideas and expansive footnotes. . . . Some of the most engaging commentary on haiku (and senryu and the occasional tanka or kyôka) ever to see print. . . . one of the most original minds to take up the related subjects of haiku and cross-cultural communication. . . . may be our best English-language window yet into the labyrinth of Japanese haikai culture . . . As a translator, I find Gill's approach stimulating and challenging. **He has raised the bar very high in terms of a translator's responsibility** (. . .) to the text. . . . **If you have read Yasuda, Blyth, Henderson, Ueda, and Shirane, then read Gill. He will expand your mind. If you have not read those guys yet, then read Gill first. He's more fun.** – William J. Higginson, dean of haiku editors in the USA and author of the international classic *Haiku World,* in *Modern Haiku* (a 5-page review in vol. 35.1 winter-spring 2004)

"You may think you need a system of bookmarks to keep on the subject, but it is easiest to just give your mind over to Gill and follow his incredible journey on printed pages. . . . If you ever thought haiku were not erotic, this book alone could change your mind forever. **If you read it, I can guarantee you will not be the same when you finish it! . . .** Incredible work." – Jane Reichhold (host of the marvelous Aha! poetry web-ring) in her *Lynx* (February, 2004)

"Gill's tone is relaxed and informal and he doesn't take himself too seriously or struggle for academic respectability, but he is still **precise in his own way, and insanely erudite**. . . . All told, it's **an original undertaking carried out with style**. . . . [An example haiku in the review]: *a few drinks / and i am a sea slug / out of water* Gijô (1741) – Danny Yee in Dannyreviews.com (solid reviews of eclectic books Down-under)

"This book gets **my vote for the most original literary theme of the decade**." – Jim Nollman, author of *Dolphin Dreamtime*, in Interspecies (his fine ecological newsletter Spring 2004).

"Already a classic . . . like the work of Blyth." "The *ante y después* of critical studies of haiku" (The Sino-japanese phrase *kuzenzetsugo* would work, but what can English do with *antes y despues*?) – Vincente Haya, author of *Corazon de Haiku* from 2 postings at *El Rincon de Haiku* (an online haiku forum in Spanish).

re: anti-stereotype books published in Japanese only.

"I bow my head to the author's linguistic prowess." – Inoue Hisashi (on a reader's card) – a top Japanese novelist and playwright. [re. *Omoshiro hikaku bunkakô*, later republished as *Eigo wa konna ni nippongo* = English is This Japanese! (Chikuma bunko)]

"What felt good about reading it [Han=nihonjinron = anti-Japanology, (Kousakusha: 1984) was that the book **doesn't get bogged down in Japan, but develops into a theory of culture** [bunkaron] . . . it is **remarkable for not being prejudiced either for or against the past**." – Itasaka Gen (review in *"Honyaku no Sekai"*), a Japanese literature scholar who formerly taught at Harvard and later became the president of Tenri University.

"The author's Thoreauvian naturalism is splendid . . . and the book [*Han=nihonjinron*] leaves you feeling better than reading ten of those popular Japan-as-Number-One type books." – Matsuoka Seigow (review in an NTT book) – one of Japan's top editors and well-known avant-garde thinker.

"A splendid deconstruction [on Ibid] **of longstanding stereotypes of Japanese national/ cultural character** (nihonjinron) that, wearing the academic guise of cultural anthropology and topographic/climatic reductionism, (fudoron), have titillated our pride." – Kyodo News Service (review carried nationally).

"Whether due to the flexibility and uniqueness of the perspective or the continual dissimulation of the author's Japanese writing, this book [*Nihonjinron Tanken* TBS-Britannica (1984)] is simply thrilling. Introducing example after example of things from other cultures that have been held to be unique to Japan, **the author's point is that we must not allow our obsession with "Japaneseness" to stop us from facing up to the human agenda in this Age where we are capable of spoiling the earth."** – TSUMURA Takashi (also Kyodo), a well known practitioner and advocate of Eastern medicine and meditation.

(The reason I did not try to get these or my other books translated is because I tailor my books to the understanding of my imagined audience. Books that would make sense to everyone tend to be trite – or, stylistically speaking, overly plain – for they must be both redundant and general.)

More reviews & links at http://www.paraverse.org

Paraverse Press: Books Full of Ideas

Rise, Ye Sea Slugs! 1,000 holothurian haiku compiled and translated by robin d. gill (480 pgs $25)
ISBN# 0974261807

Our instant classic. *See reviews on the previous page.* Actually, it has only 900 haiku about sea cucumbers, but the next expanded edition will complete the bill. This is not just a book of translated haiku, but of natural history, literary criticism, metaphor, food and ambiguity. Two quotes from scientists. One concerns *Rise!* itself; the other evokes the metaphysical bent of the subject:

> "It's amazing; I absolutely love it. I've spent many years studying my little friends and have always felt that they have been unkindly maligned or forgotten. The contrast between Japanese and European literature on cukes [sea cucumbers] couldn't be greater . . . Alas, the divide between science and literature, even in terminology much less in theory, is quite vast at points and I admire your blending of the two in a deep and satisfying way." – Dr. Alexander Kerr, evolutionary biologist, James Cook University.

> "Surviving by eating the sand one lives upon is like realizing the dream of living in a gingerbread house. The sea cucumber by staying still and learning to live on so little, has turned this world into its paradise." – Dr. Motokawa Tatsuo (Tokyo Institute of Technology, Echinoderm+material-science research & author of best-selling books on basic biology.)

Topsy-turvy 1585 – a translation and explication of Luis Frois SJ's TRATADO listing 611 ways Europeans & Japanese are contrary by robin d. gill ISBN#0974261815 (740 pgs $33.33)

Herodotus made *dozens* of black and white contrasts (between Eygpt and the Greco-Roman civilization he called "the rest of the world"); but no one has made *hundreds* as did Frois, who was also *the* most prolific writer on Japan in the 16th century. Gill translates Frois' skeletal distiches – two lines that might be called *heroic contrast!* originally written in Portuguese – explains and plays with them (95% of the book) in a manner reminiscent of Barthes' *Empire of Signs*. The contrasts are often amusing in themselves (we pick our noses with different fingers and sniff the opposite ends of melons to ascertain if they are ripe, etc.), but they are also significant for their relationship to the Jesuits' attempt to accommodate themselves to Japan, something that preceeded and paved the way for the more famous effort of Ricci in China described by Jonathon Spence and others. One might even call the TRATADO an apology for "going Japanese."

Orientalism & Occidentalism: Is the Mistranslation of Culture Inevitable? (180 pgs. $12)
ISBN# 0974261823

While the argument has broad implications for translation, sociolinguistics and cross-cultural comparison, this essay that should interest all who love words and ideas has been slow to take off. If you enjoy it, please spread the word! Summary:

> When two different languages cross, they inevitably create misunderstanding. Japanese and English are exceptionally far removed, i.e., exotic, to each other. In "direct" translation they not only fail to convey the feeling of the original, but create prejudicial feelings with respect to the original language and those who speak it.

> Orientalism is not vital to the self-identity of most Westerners. That may be one reason why our scholars are able to discuss it so matter-of-factly. But, it is not so easy for the Japanese, whose very identity is the antithetical stereotype of the Westerner, to reappraise their Occidentalism. Neither is the prejudice (for Occidentalism is as biased as any Orientalism) held by Japanese a matter of pathology or plot, as some Western writers would have it. Given the translations that Japanese constantly encounter, and their understandably mistaken ideas of what it means to speak English, it is perfectly normal for Japanese to feel as they do. Rather, it would be strange if they did not feel so.

> Polemics cannot banish prejudice. Polite explanation backed up by convincing proof is needed. As the author notes in the text: A bit of knowledge makes the East East and the West West. A bit more can put them back together again.

This is the old character for
“ fly.”

This is the new character for
“ fly.”

Doesn’t the old character seem the more organic of the two? With poor copies, it was often impossible to tell which was which and, as Japanese editors often use whatever character they feel most suitable, even if I tried to get them right, it would have been impossible, so I didn’t.

..

~~~~~~

To learn more, please visit our website, http://www.paraverse.org, or send a stamped, self-addressed envelope to: Paraverse Press / pmb #399 / 260 Crandon blvd, suite 32 / Key Biscayne, FL 33149-154. First try E-mail if you can because it saves trees (I print out little) and fuel for transportation: info@paraverse.org, or uncoolwabin@hotmail.com.
~~~~~~

Coming Soon or Already Out
depending upon when you read this.

new books by robin d. gill

Cherry Blossom Epiphany: The Poetry and Philosophy of a Flowering Tree.

700+ pages, 1000's of haiku on cherry blossoms and blossom-viewing. Be prepared for plenty of thinking and plenty of drinking.

Probably out in the Spring of 2005. Followed sometime within the year by the first volume of:

The Fifth Season, The Haiku of the Japanese New Year.

Or, the first core book of my *In Praise of Olde Haiku* (IPOOH) saijiki project.

The New Year is a fifth season that once boasted as many haiku as any other season,

yet no one has introduced more than a token sampling to date.

www.ingramcontent.com/pod-product-compliance
Lightning Source LLC
Chambersburg PA
CBHW080514090426
42734CB00015B/3050

* 9 7 8 0 9 7 4 2 6 1 8 4 3 *